Marketing Schools, Marketing Cities

Marketing Schools, Marketing Cities

Who Wins and Who Loses When Schools Become Urban Amenities

MAIA BLOOMFIELD CUCCHIARA

THE UNIVERSITY OF CHICAGO PRESS   CHICAGO AND LONDON

Maia Bloomfield Cucchiara is assistant professor of urban education in the College of Education at Temple University.

The University of Chicago Press, Chicago 60637
The University of Chicago Press, Ltd., London
© 2013 by The University of Chicago
All rights reserved. Published 2013.
Printed in the United States of America

22 21 20 19 18 17 16 15 14 13   1 2 3 4 5

ISBN-13: 978-0-226-01665-8 (cloth)
ISBN-13: 978-0-226-01682-5 (paper)
ISBN-13: 978-0-226-01696-2 (e-book)

An earlier draft of some material in this book appeared as "Re-branding Urban Schools: Urban Revitalization, Social Status, and Marketing Public Schools to the Upper Middle Class," *Journal of Education Policy* 23 (2): 165–79. I am grateful to Taylor and Francis Ltd., for permission to use the material in revised form.

Library of Congress Cataloging-in-Publication Data
Cucchiara, Maia Bloomfield.
    Marketing schools, marketing cities : who wins and who loses when schools become urban amenities / Maia Bloomfield Cucchiara.
        pages   cm
    Includes bibliographical references and index.
    ISBN 978-0-226-01665-8 (cloth : alk. paper)
    ISBN 978-0-226-01682-5 (pbk : alk. paper)
    ISBN 978-0-226-01696-2 (e-book)
        1. Education, Urban—Pennsylvania—Philadelphia. 2. Educational equalization—Pennsylvania—Philadelphia. 3. Public schools—Pennsylvania—Philadelphia. 4. School integration—Pennsylvania—Philadelphia. 5. Grant Elementary School (Philadelphia, Pa.) 6. Urban renewal—Pennsylvania—Philadelphia. I. Title.
LC5133.P5C84 2013
307.9173'2074811—dc23   2012045002

Contents

Illustrations

Maps

Tables

Figures

Acknowledgments

This book has been a long time in the making. In the years from its early stages as an idea for a dissertation to its final incarnation, I have been blessed by many teachers, colleagues and friends, all of whom contributed to my growth as a scholar and helped keep me sane. My dissertation committee at the University of Pennsylvania—Kathleen Hall, Michael Katz, Frank Furstenberg, and David Grazian—stuck with me even when I hit some rocky periods and never failed to encourage me to keep going. Michael Katz's support was especially important, as was Kathy Hall's mentorship, scholarly feedback, and friendship. At the University of Pennsylvania, Ruth Curran Neild, Jennifer Riggan, and Aiden Downey were all instrumental in shaping my thinking on this project. Jennifer Riggan in particular read numerous drafts of these chapters and always insisted that I was "on to something important." I am also grateful to the Spencer Foundation for its support of my graduate studies through the Spencer Urban Research Fellowship.

Annette Lareau and Erin Horvat read multiple drafts of the entire manuscript, providing invaluable feedback. It was Annette who encouraged me to write a book, at a time when I had decided to give up on the project, and her interventions at certain junctures were critical. Her input, especially the great care she took in reading the manuscript when it was nearly finished, greatly improved the book. I am touched by her attention to my work and thankful for her support and friendship. Erin has been the best of mentors, colleagues and friends—supportive, smart, kind, and a pleasure to work with. I feel very fortunate that our paths crossed nearly ten years ago. Josh Klugman also read the entire manuscript shortly before it was completed; his helpful feedback and on-going enthusiasm for the project were invaluable.

I am grateful to M. Katherine Mooney for the role she played in the long process of moving from dissertation to book. Her assistance with my prose was enormously valuable, but the feedback she gave me on the strengths and weaknesses of my arguments, the structure of the chapters, and the kinds of evidence I needed to provide was instrumental. Without her help, this project would likely have taken much longer and would certainly have been less rewarding.

At Research for Action, I was lucky to work with a wonderful group of scholars studying school reform in Philadelphia. Not only did I learn a great deal about the craft of research from my experiences at RFA, but I also benefited from the researchers' deep knowledge of Philadelphia's education scene. The study of civic engagement in Philadelphia school reform was led by Eva Gold and Elaine Simon, both of whom have a remarkable ability to combine rigorous scholarship with a commitment to public engagement and social justice.

I have also been fortunate in my colleagues at Temple University, including Julie Booth, James Byrnes, Corrinne Caldwell, Jennifer Cromley, Steven Gross, Annemarie Hindman, Will Jordan, Novella Keith, Kent McGuire, Michelle Partlow, Joan Shapiro, Marcia Whitaker, and Celestine Williams. I am especially thankful for James Earl Davis's unfailing support of my scholarship and career. Temple University supported my work on this project with two Summer Research Fellowships and a Pre-Tenure Study Leave. I am also grateful to Temple students Harvey Chism, Erin Rooney, and Jessica Speakes. This project further benefitted from conversations with many other scholars, including Suzanne Blanc, Kim Goyette, Shelley Kimelberg, Judith Levine, Kristine Lewis, Pauline Lipman, Ruth Lupton, Linn Posey-Maddox, Jeffrey Raffel, Karolyn Tyson, and David Varady.

Michelle Schmitt of Temple's Metropolitan Philadelphia Indicators Project and David Ford of Temple's Social Science Data Laboratory assisted with the quantitative data analysis for this project. David Ford's map-making skills, and his patience with my many requests for modifications and alterations, were particularly helpful. David Van Riper and the staff at the Minnesota Population Center provided last-minute help with U.S. Census data, for which I am especially thankful. My research in Boston would not have been possible without Melina O'Grady's organizational skills, large network of contacts, and thoughtfulness.

I am especially indebted to the parents and educators at "Grant Elementary" for welcoming me into their school and sharing their experiences and perspectives with me. While they may not always agree with the analysis I put forth in this book, I hope they realize how much I valued my time with them and respected their commitment to the school. I am also grateful to the School District of Philadelphia and Center City District administrators involved with the Center City Schools Initiative and to the many civic, business, educational, and political leaders who participated in this study. In particular, I would like to thank Heather Frattone, both for her interest in this project and for her important insights into the inner workings of the school district.

It was a pleasure to work with the University of Chicago Press on this project. Elizabeth Branch Dyson has been a wonderful editor, furnishing feedback, support, and enthusiasm in exactly the right amounts and at exactly the right times. Two anonymous reviewers gave my manuscript careful attention, providing feedback and insights of which I am very appreciative.

In addition to my professional colleagues, I have been supported throughout this time by a host of good friends, who fed me, made me laugh, and shared the experience of raising children and balancing work and family. These include, Philip Glahn, Nell McClister, Evelyn Polesny, Kevin Rasmussen, Jennifer Simon-Thomas, Vivian Su, Sonya and Pierre Terjanian, James Unkefer, and Mitchell Young. I have been particularly thankful for Michele Belliveau's friendship and for the ability to share so many aspects of my life—school, work, and family—with her. Her insights into this project have been invaluable, and I will forever appreciate her continued engagement with me on this project, especially when we disagreed. Anna Forrester read the manuscript when it was nearly finished. Her enthusiasm about the project and interest in the issues it raises were very encouraging, and her friendship has sustained me through the long writing process. I will be forever indebted to Abigail Hanson for her love, friendship and support.

I would also like to thank my neighbors in Philadelphia. Not only do my family and I enjoy the time we spend with the wonderful friends and neighbors on our block, but I have also profited greatly from my relationship with such kind and talented people. Alison Buttenheim gave me excellent feedback on several chapters of this book and helped with the tables and figures. Her husband, Paul Saint-Amour, is an inspiration and a joy to know. Mey-Yen and Takashi Moriuchi have been the sources of unending support and interesting conversations. Peter Siskind provided important assistance with Philadelphia's history, and Judi Cassel helped me understand key aspects of Philadelphia politics.

I have also been lucky in family, namely my parents—Timothy Bloomfield and Mignonne LaChapelle—my stepmother, Susan Bloomfield, my half-sister, Grace Bloomfield, and Patricia and Roy Cucchiara, in-laws and grandparents extraordinaire. My father proofread the entire final manuscript, catching many errors and improving my prose (although I still maintain that "contestation" is a word). His attention to my work and praise of the book meant more to me than he will ever know. Many thanks to all of you for your love and generosity.

When I began this project, I was the mother of a baby girl. I now have two beautiful children, Amelia and Eliza. I am so grateful for their presence in my life, their spirits, and their love. My husband, Brett Cucchiara, read multiple drafts of the manuscript, helped me with any number of book-related tasks, and never wavered in his enthusiasm for this project. His love, humor, and insight were indispensable as I wrote this book and, more important, have enriched my life beyond measure.

Abbreviations and Terms

CCD	Center City District—a business improvement district promoting revitalization in Center City Philadelphia
CCSI	Center City Schools Initiative—an initiative designed to attract "knowledge workers" living in Center City to the area public schools
Center City	Philadelphia's downtown
Center City Academic Region	The administrative unit created within the School District of Philadelphia to consolidate all schools in the extended Center City area
Extended Center City	Philadelphia's downtown plus gentrifying neighborhoods to the north and south
SRC	School Reform Commission—the governing body for the School District of Philadelphia installed by the state in 2001

A Strategic Opportunity

If people want white and affluent parents to send their kids to public schools and have a greater stake in the system, some accommodation has to be made. —Editorial, *Philadelphia Daily News* (2006)

Philadelphia is a divided city. The downtown, which has been the target of sustained public and private investment, is bustling and affluent. Other parts of the city, where streets are dotted with long-vacant factories and crumbling rowhouses, are very poor. As in cities across the country, revitalization strategies over the past decades have focused on attracting and retaining professionals or "knowledge workers," with the assumption that this group—with its skills, motivation, and expendable income—would help revive the city's economy and build prosperity. In the early twenty-first century, Philadelphia's civic, educational, and business leaders applied a similar strategy to the schools, hoping to convince young middle- and upper-middle-class families in the downtown to use their local public schools rather than fleeing to the suburbs when their children reach school age. City leaders marketed a handful of downtown public schools to professional-class families, using a set of policies and practices that treated them as highly valued customers. In other words, as the editorial suggested, "some accommodation" to the special demands and expectations of this group was made.

Philadelphia is not alone in hoping to bring middle- and upper-middle-class families back to the city and city schools. Urban areas have experimented with voluntary choice programs, magnet schools, charter schools, and, in some cases, city-suburban integration—all designed, at least in part, to slow suburban flight and increase race and class integration in schools.[1] Yet in contrast to these other strategies, Philadelphia's school campaign drew heavily on market strategies of urban development that identify "knowledge workers" as critical to the city's future and seek to use key amenities to attract and retain this group. This book examines Philadelphia's effort to market public schools to professional-class families and the questions it raises about equity and the nature of citizenship in an era of market-oriented solutions to social problems.

In the late twentieth- and early twenty-first-century context of ideological shifts to the right and government retrenchment, a set of solutions to chronic social problems—such as persistent poverty, urban decline, and ongoing school failure—has emerged. These include the creation of mixed-income housing, the "revitalization" of downtowns as centers of the information economy, and policies (and informal practices) that strive to increase economic integration in urban schools.[2] Though they address a diverse set of problems, such efforts share key assumptions and a core logic that attempts to use various incentives to bring the resources (social, cultural, and financial) of the middle and upper-middle classes to bear on major social problems. While there is no doubt they produce some positive outcomes, the costs and limitations of such policies have not been adequately explored. In this book, I use a study of an education initiative in Philadelphia to examine the consequences of policies and policy discourses that position the middle and upper-middle classes as inherently more worthy and important than other sectors of the population.

Perceiving families as unequally valuable is at the heart of the school-reform policy I discuss in this book. The Center City Schools Initiative (CCSI) was a Philadelphia effort to use market strategies to lure middle- and upper-middle-class families into the city and the city schools as a way to reverse urban decline and improve public schools. The initiative aimed to further the revitalization of Philadelphia's downtown (already home to a sizable white, highly educated, and relatively affluent population), increase the city's tax base, generate political support for the public school system, and catalyze improvement efforts at targeted schools. It has been widely touted as a pioneering solution to chronic urban challenges.[3]

In Philadelphia and around the country, the renewed interest in city living among middle- and upper-middle-class families and the efforts of business, civic, and political leaders to attract and retain such families is reshaping urban educational policy and practice. In cities such as Baltimore, Boston, Chicago, Richmond, Milwaukee, and San Francisco, public schools have reached out to these families, trying to convince them to enroll their children in urban schools.[4] And in some areas, groups of middleclass parents have started their own campaigns to transform and market their neighborhood schools. These parents hope that by attracting other middle-class families, they will be able to improve local schools enough to avoid the need to move to the suburbs or use private school.[5] Philadelphia's CCSI bears some resemblance to these other efforts, but it is unique in two important ways. From the beginning, the initiative drew an explicit and public connection between attracting professional-class families and the future of the city, and it was created as a public-private venture—a partnership between the public schools and the Center City District (CCD), a local business improvement district (BID).[6] Thus, a study of the CCSI is uniquely suited to shed light on the consequences of marketing public schools to the middle and upper-middle classes and on the degree to which an infusion of market principles creates new mechanisms and spaces of privilege within a public institution.

The particulars of this initiative are unique to Philadelphia. The story I tell, however—of discourse about middle-class virtue and value, of urban decline and "revitalization," of the dominance of market-oriented ideas and practices, of growing spatial inequality, and of dynamics of privilege and marginalization at a local elementary school—is shared across many cities nationwide. Focusing on Philadelphia's experiences offers a revealing look at efforts to enlist schools in the pursuit of a particular vision of urban prosperity.

In 2004, just after the CCSI was unveiled, I began conducting research: asking questions; reading documents; following media coverage; and interviewing business and civic leaders, school district officials, policymakers, parents, and other stakeholders. My goal was to understand the initiative's origins, evolution, and consequences. To examine the "on-the-ground" effects, I conducted a two-year ethnography of one of the targeted schools (see appendix A for more details).

In my research, I encountered a range of assumptions and tensions around issues of urban growth and education and around the benefits of an increased middle-class presence in cities and schools. Many of my informants struggled to balance ideals of equity with more "pragmatic" goals.

The CCSI brought to the forefront the clash between market principles and strategies and ideals of justice, fairness, and equality. In doing so, the initiative posed questions that usually go unasked. What does it mean to sacrifice equity in the pursuit of a greater "common good"? How do strategies for reversing urban decline or improving public schools that rely on the resources of the middle class reshape the relationship between citizens and the state? The answers draw attention to the complicated outcomes of market mechanisms when they are applied to public institutions.

While sympathetic to the goals of the CCSI and the problems it was trying to address, I argue here the benefits of this project came at some cost to important sectors of the population. Low-income and minority students in particular found their access to resources and opportunities constrained by the initiative. The CCSI was successful in bringing more middle- and upper-middle-class families into five Center City schools, but it also exacerbated the ongoing stratification of Philadelphia and its schools. It brought additional resources to a few relatively high-performing schools and helped an already advantaged population secure access to them, while marginalizing other families and making it more difficult for them to share in the benefits of the best of Philadelphia's schools.

The Genesis of the Center City Schools Initiative: "You Have to Deal with the Fact that People with Six-Year-Olds Keep Moving to the Suburbs"

When he was interviewed for a 2007 *Wall Street Journal* article, CCD president Paul Levy explained his organization's focus on encouraging more families to live downtown by noting that "empty nesters and singles are not enough." If Philadelphia was "to sustain the revival" that had been drawing highly educated young professionals to the region, the city needed to convince the "people with six-year-olds" not to head for the suburbs.[7]

The CCD, whose 120-block span (roughly one square mile) makes it one of the largest BIDs in the nation, has worked for the past two decades to promote the revitalization of Philadelphia's downtown, locally known as Center City.[8] In 2004 the CCD, led by Mr. Levy, approached the School District of Philadelphia with a proposal aimed at retaining the downtown's young, affluent residents as they married and began families. Given an abundance of evidence that "the percent of the downtown population ages 25–34 has steadily grown," an early CCD report identified "a strategic opportunity for Center City to become a premier neighborhood of choice in the region for young families with children—*if we can improve the quality and customer focus of public schools.*" In partnering with the downtown business community, the school district would, among other things, embrace "an entrepreneurial model in which principals are encouraged to see their primary role as attracting and retaining Center City families by delivering a high-quality educational experience."[9] The CCD hoped that as more Center City families entered the public schools, suburban flight would be stemmed, the city would be more affordable for middle- and upper-middle-class parents (because they would not have to pay for private schools), and Philadelphia's appeal as a place to work and live would be enhanced.

With the school district's collaboration and support, the CCSI evolved into a multipronged effort to rebrand downtown elementary schools.[10] The initiative was comprised of a marketing campaign, an increase in resources for certain Center City elementary schools, and a change to the district's administrative structure to create a new academic region. In addition, it gave students who lived in the downtown area priority over students from other parts of the city in admission to some of the district's most desirable elementary schools, which were located within the newly formed academic region. The initiative re-envisioned public schools as a potentially alluring amenity of urban life. Like museums, boutiques, sidewalk cafés, and attractive housing within walking distance of work, these newly marketed public schools were cast as a perk of life in the city and another way for families to participate in an affluent urban lifestyle.

Meanwhile, the explicit emphasis on the downtown area and professional families led one school district insider to exclaim in an interview, "They don't even pretend it's for the whole city. It is for Center City to try to draw whites back into Center City, to appease Center City businesses. . . . It is elitist. A lot of people are very upset!" Educational policy and practice traditionally have been heavily informed by ideals about equality of opportunity. These ideals combined uneasily with the CCSI's goals and strategies.

American Cities in the Twenty-first Century: Splendor, Decay, and the "Creative Class"

In 2009 Kristian Buschmann and Carol Coletta, from a national organization of business, civic, and political leaders called CEOs for Cities, praised

Levy as a "particularly bold urban pioneer" for his work on the CCSI, proclaiming him "the first of what will likely become a steady stream of urban leaders who realize that this market [of professionals] is ready to return to cities that will solve their problems."[11] Why would a public-private partnership that markets public schools as an urban amenity generate so much enthusiasm? The answer lies in the scope, severity, and longevity of the problems the CCSI and other revitalization strategies seek to solve.

Over the past half-century, a series of social, political, and economic developments crippled once-vibrant industrial centers in the Northeast and Midwest, leaving cities like Philadelphia, Baltimore, Newark, Chicago, and Detroit facing unprecedented social and economic decline.[12] In response, late twentieth-century urban policy sought to transform cities to better compete for mobile capital and labor and slow middle-class flight to the suburbs. Former manufacturing centers compensated for the loss of industrial jobs by recreating themselves as centers of the new service and information economy, assuming their economic future was dependent upon the ability to compete in these arenas. Thus, revitalization efforts in the closing decades of the twentieth century generally involved such projects as the construction of downtown shopping malls, the creation of gentrified areas within distressed cities, and the formulation of downtowns as business-friendly centers for corporate offices, hotels, convention centers, and entertainment complexes.[13]

Many of these projects were designed to bring middle- and upper-middle-class residents, workers, and visitors back to the city, in large part because these groups are seen as vital to a city's economic health. Not only are these people essential to the businesses—such as law, insurance, architecture, and banking—that cluster in revitalized downtowns, but they are also the "knowledge workers" or "creative people" whose skills move the new information economy along.[14] Perhaps no one has done more to popularize the connection between urban economies and the highly educated than Richard Florida. In *The Rise of the Creative Class*, Florida argues that "scientists, engineers, artists, musicians, designers and knowledge-based professionals," or people who are "paid principally to do creative work for a living," are essential to urban prosperity, and that they find some cities more appealing than others.[15] He dubs these cities "Creative Centers," noting that they are characterized less by shopping malls and entertainment districts and more by "abundant high-quality amenities and experiences, an openness to diversity of all kinds, and above all else [provide residents] the opportunity to validate their identities as creative people."[16]

It follows, then, that if cities are to compete in this new economic order, they need to provide these sorts of amenities and opportunities. In struggling cities, the task is larger still: urban leaders must not only create such amenities but also market the new urban lifestyle to potential middle- and upper-middle-class residents and workers.[17]

But such efforts sometimes require pushing others out. As part of the overall strategy to "attract mobile capital and labor," in places like Newark, Chicago, Detroit, and elsewhere, low-income neighborhoods were razed to make room for mixed-income developments. The ongoing gentrification of neighborhoods in Philadelphia, New York, San Francisco, and other cities, which often drives out low-income residents who can no longer afford to live in areas "reclaimed" by the middle class, is another example of the price some groups pay for urban redevelopment.[18]

Another outcome of these processes is the emergence of an increasingly bifurcated urban workplace, with highly paid knowledge workers on one side and unskilled, poorly paid service workers on the other. In 1991 John Mollenkopf and Manuel Castells coined the term "dual city" to describe new patterns of urban inequality. Although *Dual City*, their study of New York City, was published twenty years ago, the dynamics it identifies appear to have only intensified over time.[19] Indeed, large cities have become increasingly populated by the affluent and the very poor, with middle-income households representing an ever-smaller portion of the populace.[20] "Dual cities" is by no means a perfect metaphor (as Mollenkopf and Castells were careful to acknowledge).[21] However, the term usefully highlights patterns of inequality and reminds us that shiny new downtowns tell only one part of the urban story.

One assumption underlying efforts to attract middle- and upper-middle-class residents to the city is that their presence will lead to improved conditions for all, as the often-used phrase "a rising tide lifts all boats" implies. However, the persistence of urban poverty even in "revitalized" neighborhoods and cities suggests that this assumption may be unfounded. Indeed, it is not at all clear that, in the absence of broader policy changes, an influx of middle-class residents can overcome the structural causes of urban poverty.[22]

Debates about urban policy often embody tensions between two goals: growth and equity. Should cities promote economic development and the competition for mobile capital and labor (growth), even at the expense of low-income communities? Or should cities advance the interests of their least advantaged (equity), even at the risk of becoming less attractive to capital investment and middle- and upper-income families? In the end, urban leaders in the United States have most often embraced growth-oriented policies, believing (not unreasonably, given the larger context of "fend-for-yourself federalism") that cities that did not compete effectively for capital investment would not survive.[23]

What we sometimes lose sight of is that neither these sorts of choices nor the larger context of which they are a part is inevitable. Urban scholars Peter Dreier, John Mollenkopf, and Todd Swanstrom argue that each of the federal and state policies that contributed to urban decline in the latter half of the twentieth century "began with serious debates about substantially different options." They continue: "Had national policymakers been prompted to make different choices—for example, to support public transportation, to provide subsidies for mixed-income housing, to invest defense dollars and other public facilities in cities—our current metropolitan landscape would look substantially different."[24] By the same token, there are alternatives to the focus among urban leaders on short-term economic growth at the expense of other goals. In the urban-planning field, there is an ongoing conversation about strategies for the creation of more equitable cities and regions, including the identification of policies that would further the goals of democracy, equity, and diversity while still promoting overall economic development.[25] In fact, as political scientist and urban scholar Clarence Stone reminds us, there is more than one way to understand a city's best interests. Even given the "high-stakes game of economic competition" cities must play, longer-term investments (e.g., in education and youth programs) can contribute to future economic growth.[26]

While this book does not engage these conversations directly, it is clear that the CCSI was informed by the same assumptions about economic competition that shaped late twentieth-century urban policy. The designers and supporters of the initiative firmly believed that without special incentives, middle- and upper-middle-class families would leave the city, neighborhoods would stagnate, and revitalization would cease. Such assumptions loomed large in the politics around the initiative, serving simultaneously to constrain notions of what was possible and to justify inequitable policies and practices. Yet just as there are alternatives in urban development, there is more than one way for a district to engage middle-income families while also fostering improvement for students in low-income areas. Some examples of alternative strategies are discussed in chapter 8.

Can the Middle Class Save Urban Schools?

Similar issues are at play around schools. Some scholars, and certainly the media, portray efforts to attract and retain middle-class families to urban public schools as beneficial to both cities and schools. In *Selling Cities*, for example, a book about the potential for education and housing programs to reverse middle-class flight to the suburbs, David Varady and Jeffrey Raffel argue that when middle-class families choose public education, they help improve the schools. With their political savvy and investment in education, middle-class parents hold school officials to higher standards and facilitate class and race integration, potentially raising achievement among low-income students. Other scholars similarly maintain that urban education policy should be informed by concerns about middle-class flight.[27]

This focus on attracting middle-class families to urban schools is understandable given the literature on the benefits of economically integrated schools. Beginning with the 1966 Coleman Report, decades of research have documented the impact of school composition on student achievement. Low-income students do significantly better in low-poverty schools, whereas all students who attend schools with high concentrations of poverty have a greater chance of adult poverty.[28] In a city like Philadelphia, where so many ambitious reforms have foundered and student achievement remains low, creating economically integrated schools is an appealing reform strategy.

There are many reasons schools with predominantly middle-class populations tend to promote high student achievement. Middle-class parents are more likely to be involved in parent-teacher organizations, are more informed about their children's schooling, have higher expectations for their children, and are more likely to use their knowledge, skills, and social connections to advocate effectively for their children.[29] Richard Kahlenberg, a researcher at The Century Foundation and prominent advocate of economic integration, identifies several additional factors. According to Kahlenberg, middle-class students have higher educational aspirations and tend to more motivated academically, which positively affects other students. In addition, low-income students often have greater educational needs and are more likely to demonstrate challenging behaviors (such as disrupting class or being absent or tardy), so large concentrations of these students negatively impact the classroom environment. In general, teachers in high-poverty schools are also less qualified, are more likely to be teaching outside of their field, and have lower expectations for their students.[30]

A Troubling Side

Whereas research on economic integration provides support for initiatives like the CCSI, other literature raises questions about social processes within economically integrated schools. Middle-class families, for example, often pursue exclusionary agendas, such as tracking, and their involvement can negatively affect other students, particularly those who are not from middle-class backgrounds. This research suggests that a rise in the number of middle-class parents in urban public schools could actually lead to increased stratification, within and across schools.[31]

Some scholars, most notably Pauline Lipman, offer a critical analysis of efforts to attract middle- and upper-income families to urban public schools. Connecting Chicago's post-1995 reforms with the broader goal of positioning it as a "global city," Lipman argues that the reforms provide new educational opportunities for some students (largely those from middle-class families) but relegate the majority of Chicago's students to "schools organized around basic literacies that are likely to prepare them primarily for low-wage jobs." Also focusing on Chicago, Janet Smith and David Stovall contend that reforms designed to attract middle-class families "allow the interests of [the] middle class to trump educational opportunities for students classified as low income."[32]

Policies and practices aimed at creating more economically integrated schools can also embody the same class bias that sociologist Mary Pattillo described in her study of gentrification in Chicago. According to Pattillo, city officials and the new residents assumed that the presence of middle-class residents would be good for low-income communities, both because they would bring improved services and resources and because they would "model" appropriate behaviors.[33] Thus, as Janet Smith and Ruth Lupton observe, efforts to increase economic integration in schools and neighborhoods can position low-income students, families, and communities as deeply flawed and in need of the "up-lifting" that contact with the middle class could provide. Smith and Lupton further distinguish between "social mix" (or economic integration) and "social mixing." Whereas diversity generally has multiple benefits for participants, policies designed to *create* diversity, particularly those that use market strategies and incentives to attract the middle class, can result in the marginalization of low-income families.[34] This is an important warning. It reminds us that, while the image of urban schools serving racially and economically integrated student populations is greatly appealing, *how* we get to that place demands far greater consideration than it is typically given.

One Strategy: Reinvent the "Neighborhood School"

This is not the first time middle-class families have gone against the norm in their neighborhoods and sent their children to public schools serving mostly poor children. There have been waves of this in the past. But it is a trend that is receiving enthusiastic attention, including portrayal as a positive outcome of the economic recession that began in 2008.[35]

In *How to Walk to School*, parent Jacqueline Edelberg and principal Susan Kurland describe the transformation of Nettelhorst Elementary. The school, located in a gentrified Chicago neighborhood, had long been overlooked by parents who were intent on private or magnet schools for their children. The book tells a compelling tale of a group of middle-class mothers whose casual conversations at the local playground grew into a movement to market Nettelhorst to other middle-class parents and, in the process, dramatically improve the school's physical appearance, social climate, and academic programs. In subtitling the book, "A Blueprint for a Neighborhood School Renaissance," Edelberg and Kurland signal their belief that the transformation of Nettelhorst can be replicated in urban schools across the country. This blueprint—by which a private, relatively affluent group uses largely private resources to improve an underfunded public institution—offers a solution to the challenges of urban education that is particularly appealing in the current context of government retrenchment. Both the school and the book have received extensive local and national attention.[36]

The Nettelhorst parents accomplished through grassroots means the same changes the CCD aimed to catalyze in Philadelphia, and many parts of the story are powerful. But there is a troubling side as well, one that is missed in all the celebratory language. The low-income and minority families whose children attended Nettelhorst before the "reformers" (i.e., the middle-class parents) became involved in the school are entirely silent in *How to Walk to School*. They are portrayed either as satisfied beneficiaries of middle-class largesse or as parents who simply did not care where their children attended school. Indeed, the book, as well as media coverage of similar developments in other cities, is replete with assumptions about the superiority of middle-class parents and the straightforward benefits of their involvement in a neighborhood school. *Marketing Schools, Marketing Cities* offers a different perspective. In addition to representing the ideas and attitudes of middle- and upper-middle-class parents whose children attended a Center City neighborhood school, I delve deeply into the views of working-class parents at the same school, showing how they experienced both the CCSI and the involvement of their more affluent peers. I argue that these parents had their own notions of parental involvement and their own hopes for the school that did not always match those of the middle-class families.

Social Problems, Market Solutions, and the Challenge to Citizenship

Much of the discussion to this point has been designed to position the CCSI as a market-driven response to early twenty-first-century urban and educational dilemmas. Market assumptions about the battle for scarce resources and the use of amenities and incentives to attract mobile capital and labor have powerfully impacted late twentieth- and early twenty-first-century urban policy. Increasingly, education too has been subject to market forces, manifest in (among other things) expanded school choice (e.g., vouchers and charter schools), privatization of school management, and an emphasis on the economic purposes of education, including training workers and promoting growth.[37]

Many scholars and activists have written about the tension between markets and the public sector, maintaining that the infusion of market principles into public institutions is inherently problematic.[38] It is important to note, however, that market strategies can also bring about positive outcomes in education. For example, large school systems that can seem inured to the needs of the families they serve could certainly benefit from improved customer service, and choice can be a powerful vehicle for school improvement and family involvement.[39] While treatments of market influences on public education are often abstract, removed from the actual policies and practices of schools and school districts, this book takes a different approach. It aims to contribute to the conversation about the interplay between market forces and public institutions by showing how it manifests at the local level, in a particular city, school district, and school.

"Market" is a term that is widely used but seldom defined. At the most basic level, a market is a set of social relations organized around exchange. A person's ability to participate is determined by his or her possession of something of value to exchange. Markets do not operate in isolation. Nor do markets unilaterally "take over" functions previously reserved for governments. Instead, it is the interrelations between markets, states (or governments), and society that shape a host of outcomes, including policies, exchange values, and social practices.[40] The story of Philadelphia's CCSI exemplifies these interrelations, showing how an infusion of market principles into the city's education policy arena influenced district rules and practices, as well as relations between individuals and schools. This story also shows that local politics and culture intersected with market-driven policies, sometimes resulting in "pushback" and sometimes in an embrace of the changes the policies sought.

Americans generally view markets as fair and powerful engines for growth, innovation, and prosperity. As Calvin Coolidge famously said in 1925, "The chief business of America is business."[41] Beginning in the 1980s, however, the values and mechanisms of the market have become more dominant, reshaping social policy and political discourse in profound ways. Indeed, the past three decades have been marked by what sociologist Margaret Somers calls the growth of "market fundamentalism," or "the drive to subject all of social life and the public sphere to market mechanisms."[42] Market fundamentalism conceives of the market as an efficient, self-regulating mechanism. Material incentives are the animating feature, with people pursuing those incentives as a way of advancing their individual interests. A key assumption is that the social and natural worlds alike are characterized by scarcity and a struggle to survive. Thus, markets—the site of this struggle and the mechanism through which scarce goods are distributed—also are understood as natural and inevitable.

Somers goes on to argue that with respect to the state and its responsibility to its citizens, the rise of market fundamentalism has led to "the transformation of the rights and obligations of citizenship from an ethic (if not always the reality) of noncontractual reciprocities based on the rights and responsibilities of equal inclusion, into one in which the right of social inclusion is conditional on being party to a market exchange of equivalent value." She calls this the "contractualization of citizenship." In his analysis of the evolution of the welfare state and its deterioration in the late twentieth century, historian Michael Katz makes a similar point. He argues that rather than being accorded by virtue of birth or nationalization, a person's right to full benefits has become contingent on his or her willingness or ability to do some form of paid labor. In this new context, "only those Americans with real jobs are real citizens."[43] Thus, with the marketization of so many aspects of public life has come a replacement of basic notions of entitlement with an emphasis on exchange. People are entitled to full civic participation only if they have something of value to offer.

But what does "citizenship" really mean? What exactly are the rights and entitlements the term suggests? In his classic treatise on citizenship, sociologist T. H. Marshall argues that the institution has evolved over hundreds of years, coming, by the twentieth century, to incorporate three elements: civil rights, political rights, and social rights. His conception of social citizenship is particularly useful here: it refers to an individual's right to a variety of goods from "a modicum of economic welfare and security to the right to share to the full in the social heritage and to live the life of a civilized being according to the standards prevailing in the society." Marshall sees education as among the institutions most closely related to social citizenship: "The right to education is a genuine social right of citizenship, because the aim of education during childhood is to shape the future adult."[44] In other words, in the twentieth century, citizenship as commonly understood in the West came to include much more than the right to vote or own property; it included, among other things, the right to an education and to various basic securities.

In this conception, citizenship and equality are intertwined. Despite myriad differences in social rank and class status, all who have the status of citizen are "equal with respect to the rights and duties with which that status is endowed," meaning that the government has an obligation to treat all citizens equally.[45] Because education is both compulsory and a right due all citizens, the *expectation* that children be treated equally by educational institutions is also central to American ideology. Thus, in the 1954 Supreme Court case *Brown v. Board of Education*, the U.S. Supreme Court invoked the Equal Protection clause of the U.S. Constitution to declare that "separate educational facilities are inherently unequal." In fact, America's conception of itself as the "land of opportunity" rests in part upon the assumption that schools should provide all children with the chance to advance in the social structure. While American schools, like other public institutions, often fall short of this ideal, the ideal itself remains powerful and continues to shape education policy and politics.[46]

The relationship between education and citizenship is important here because the dynamics around the CCSI resonate with Somers's and Katz's descriptions of the changing nature of citizenship in the contemporary United States. The initiative, and its attendant discourses and policies, subtly recast families' entitlement to public education. A family's entitlement to the public schools became linked not simply to its residence in Philadelphia but to its social status and ability to help improve the schools. At the same time, the CCSI's use of market mechanisms to attract such families to the schools positioned them as the city's "true" citizens and its most valuable customers. Other scholars have examined the renewed engagement of middle-class families in urban schools. They have documented how this engagement affects school resources, status and power within the school, and student enrollment patterns—findings that are similar to mine in many ways.[47] What has gone unexamined thus far, however, is the relationship between such processes and conceptions of citizenship and entitlement to public goods.

The CCSI was heavily rooted in market-driven approaches to urban and education policy. In addition to assuming the city needed to compete for mobile capital and professional-class residents in order to survive, the policy used school choice and improved customer service to attract middle- and upper-middle-class families to downtown public schools and positioned schools as vehicles for economic growth—all hallmarks of the marketization of education. It is not the case, of course, that the school system before the initiative was immune to market influence. There were always market elements at work, including, as I show in chapter 3, a process for choosing schools and, after the 2001 state takeover, the outsourcing of district functions and a top-down commitment to running schools "like a business." However, the CCSI brought market-oriented principles of urban and education policy to bear on Philadelphia's schools in new and powerful ways.

A Note on Class

Most Americans shy away from talking about social class.[48] When asked directly, they overwhelmingly describe themselves as "middle class," despite significant differences in their income, education, occupation, and wealth. Much like the general public, academics who write about class in the United States tend to define the middle class very broadly.[49] This is more than a matter of imprecision. "Middle class" indexes virtues Americans hold dear, including hard work, responsibility, and social stability.

For this reason, politicians jockey to be the voice of the middle class, and programs said to benefit the middle class hold wide appeal.[50] Yet "middle class" can be used to describe everyone from a postman to a corporate lawyer, obscuring crucial differences in wealth and status. I argue that discourse about the need to retain the middle class in Philadelphia is at once a response to a set of real challenges and a way of justifying policies that actually benefit an already advantaged subset of residents. And I strive to make distinctions between the much-vaunted middle class and many of the people targeted by the CCSI.

My analysis follows from French sociologist Pierre Bourdieu's conception of class as a power relationship that is shaped by social and cultural as well as economic factors. Bourdieu sees the struggle for power as central to all social practices, but he broadens the terrain of this struggle beyond material considerations. He identifies a variety of resources—cultural, social, symbolic, *and* financial capital—upon which people draw in their efforts to achieve social distinction for themselves and their children.[51] For example, members of the middle class will work hard to distinguish their choices (such as the books they read, the art they enjoy, or the way they raise their children) from practices they associate with the working class. Ultimately, people's status, power, and ability to move within the class structure are contingent upon not just how much money they have but also upon whom they know and whether or not they possess the cultural capital (or various kinds of skills, habits, and knowledge) that allows them to advance within schools and other institutions.[52] This approach to class analysis makes distinguishing between classes difficult. In fact, Bourdieu argues that clear interclass distinctions are artificial, a tool for social scientists rather than a reflection of people's lived experiences. However, as Bourdieu shows in *Distinction*, his analysis of French society, it is possible to identify social groups (or classes) by virtue of the conditions and practices they have in common.

In making distinctions between groups that are often indiscriminately merged into the single category of middle class, I am drawing on research that describes upper-middle-class professional and managerial workers as somewhat different from white-collar municipal employees, teachers, small business owners, and other members of the middle class.[53] For example, educational researcher Ellen Brantlinger refers to the "educated middle class" as a group whose "educational credentials raise them to the status of a cultural bourgeoisie with the specialized expertise to shape institutions, establish official knowledge, set standards, define social space, and generate cultural distinctions."[54] While this literature generally describes "upper-middle-class" status as a function of employment and education, it also addresses practices that reach beyond individuals' occupations to encompass what Bourdieu would describe as their *habitus*.[55] Thus, I use the terms "upper-middle class," "professionals," or "professional class" to describe a group whose levels of economic, cultural, and social capital place them in a more elevated position than the bulk of the "middle class" in the United States.[56] I include doctors, lawyers, architects, academics, and those working at high levels in finance, real estate, and the arts in this category. It is this group, those the CCD refers to as "knowledge workers," that urban leaders across the country are trying to woo to their cities.

In this book, when I discuss abstract assertions or assumptions about the benefits of a middle-class presence (i.e., for cities and schools), I use "middle class." In discussions of Center City and its immediate environs, I use "middle and upper-middle class" (and sometimes, for variety's sake, "professionals"), as many Center City residents would more accurately be labeled "upper-middle class" or "professional class." In referring to a particular individual or groups of individuals, I draw from my data to identify class status as precisely as possible. While this is not a perfect solution, it best suits my purposes of distinguishing, whenever possible, between the mythic "middle class" and the class statuses of those targeted by the CCSI.

Book Overview

In the chapters that follow, I tell the story of the CCSI and explore its implications in Philadelphia and for other cities. Chapter 2, "From 'Philthadelphia' to the 'Next Great City,'" sets the stage by describing Philadelphia's journey of the past half century from industrial powerhouse through decades of postindustrial struggles to the revitalizing—yet deeply divided—city of today. Because this book is also the story of urban and education policy in an era of local, state, and federal government retrenchment, chapter 2 describes the financial challenges facing cities like Philadelphia, the growing reliance on market-driven solutions to entrenched social problems, and how this reliance has reshaped local policies and politics.

The effort to market a subset of schools in Philadelphia also occurred within a particular educational context: the School District of Philadelphia, a system plagued by chronic fiscal shortfalls, low student achievement, bad publicity, and turmoil. This is the focus of chapter 3, "Institutions of Last Resort," which describes a highly stratified district, home to a relatively small number of high-achieving schools, including several in Center City. Chapter 4, "Revitalizing Schools," provides more information about the CCSI. It describes the initiative's origins and the assumptions about urban growth and school change that informed it. This chapter further explores the politics of the CCSI, particularly the tensions it raised for local actors between ideals of equity and the benefits of retaining the middle class.

Chapters 1–4 set the stage for the next two chapters, which explore the marketing of Center City schools from the perspective of a targeted elementary school. Chapter 5, "This Is Not an Inner-City School!," introduces Grant Elementary (a pseudonym), a school located in an affluent part of Philadelphia's downtown.[57] Drawing from over two years of ethnographic research I conducted with Grant's parents organization, chapter 5 describes how a group of middle- and upper-middle-class parents marketed the school to other professional families and the correspondence between their efforts and the CCSI. It picks up on an earlier theme—a consensus within the city about the virtues of middle-class families and their role in sustaining the city—and shows how that same consensus was manifested at the school level. Chapter 6, "This School Can Be Way Better!," continues the story by examining how parents' different positions in the educational marketplace affected their status and power within the school. In addition to documenting the improvements middle- and upper-middle-class parents made to Grant, this chapter also delves into the perspectives and experiences of another group: the African American working-class parents whose children transferred to Grant from other parts of the city.

Chapter 7 is titled "The Segregated Schools Initiative?," the name by which many district staffers referred to the CCSI. This chapter examines the evolution of the initiative—particularly in response to criticism within the district around equity issues—and its longer-term consequences. The chapter argues that while the partnership between the School District of Philadelphia and the CCD was relatively short-lived, its impact has been profound.

"Citizens, Customers, and City Schools," the conclusion, returns to the larger questions raised in this book about equity and entitlement, market solutions to social problems, the valorizing of the middle class, and the tensions between notions of public benefit and private costs. It also outlines key considerations emerging from this research that could be used in devising more equitable policy solutions and draws from the cases of Boston and Wake County, North Carolina, to suggest policy alternatives.

In many ways, the CCSI is an overt attempt at what other urban districts do in far less obvious ways: make the public schools appealing to the middle class in order to prevent these families' flight to the suburbs.[58] The dynamics set into motion by this policy thus have implications not just for Philadelphia but also for other "revitalizing" American cities. As such, the overall mission of this book is to raise awareness of critically important social justice issues embedded in contemporary urban policy and school-reform decisions. Not all city residents fit into the dominant narrative of the "revitalized" city. To avoid exacerbating existing inequalities, it is important to know which groups are helped and which hurt by efforts to transform cities and schools.

This is an inevitably complicated undertaking. When I presented some preliminary findings at an academic conference, an audience member objected to my critique by describing the failure of high-poverty urban schools as a "knotty problem" that has seemed impervious to solution without significant demographic changes in cities and schools. Indeed, the fact that they serve overwhelmingly disadvantaged constituencies is one reason urban schools are so difficult to reform. Without the intervention of concerted community organizing efforts, low-income and minority families can have great difficulty raising expectations for schools and ensuring that students receive the instruction and services they need.[59] The ongoing fiscal challenges that plague urban systems can also be traced to demographics: middle-class flight has resulted in a shrinking urban tax base, which in turn means less money for schools.

The budget deficit confronting Philadelphia's schools in spring 2011 (a shortage of hundreds of millions of dollars that emerged when federal stimulus funds dried up) exemplifies this dynamic. As city officials debated whether to fund such basic services as busing and full-day kindergarten, and the mayor argued that to do so without raising taxes would force the city to cut other essential services, the need for a broader, more stable tax base in the city could not have been more apparent. Periodic budget crises are a reality in Philadelphia, as is the fact that the city is home to thousands of families desperate for high-quality schools. Middle-class and low-income families alike are justified in demanding more for their children—in Philadelphia and nationwide. Given these realities, should we not greet an effort to create more economically and racially diverse schools with enthusiasm rather than criticism? In many large cities across the country, this important question is being answered in the affirmative. This book aims to clarify the costs and benefits of doing so.

There are good reasons to believe that creating greater economic diversity within American neighborhoods and institutions could be beneficial. However, this study of the CCSI raises questions about *how* such diversity is created and what is lost by adopting strategies that place great weight on the resources of the middle class. In the context of dwindling government resources devoted to addressing poverty and urban decline, policies that give special treatment to the middle class and upper-middle class are frequently legitimized as a means of bringing about some larger social good (e.g., saving the city or fixing the schools). This book chronicles Philadelphia's mixed experiences combining urban revitalization with school reform. But it also tells a bigger and more troubling story about the systematic movement away from the core democratic ideals of seeing each citizen as equally valuable and worthy of full participation in public institutions.

CHAPTER TWO

From "Philthadelphia" to the "Next Great City"

Revitalization in a Postindustrial City

We are in a moment in the life of the city when much is possible. It's time to catch the wind that has propelled other cities on a course of growth. —Center City District, Summer 2008

Sharon is an attractive, outgoing blonde woman who lives in Cobble Square, an affluent part of Philadelphia's downtown area.[1] In 2002 she enrolled her son in kindergarten at Grant Elementary School, the public school in her neighborhood. In doing so, she bucked the trend in her community—far more people used one of the local private schools—and took on a mission that would occupy much of her life for the next several years. In addition to volunteering in the classroom at Grant, Sharon became involved in the school's newly revived Parent Teacher Organization (PTO), hoping to help improve the school and convince more parents from Cobble Square to consider Grant. In the fall of 2003, she represented Grant at a citywide meeting of PTO representatives. In an interview, she described her experience listening to parents from other city schools:

This guy got up and starts talking about how he just got out of jail and they really need to work with keeping the kids out of jail, and I'm like, this isn't for me. Like this is not, I have nothing to do with this. I came, I signed in, but I can't contribute anything. Like, I was raising my hand to ask if we could get a yoga class [rueful chuckle]. I mean, literally, this guy is up there practically crying that he just got out of jail. So I'm like, yoga's probably not up for discussion.

Sharon left the meeting early, frustrated that her goals for, and concerns about, her child's elementary school were too different from those of the rest of the parents at the meeting for it to be worth her time. As Sharon was leaving, she ran into an education reporter from a local daily paper who asked her what had happened at the meeting. Sharon explains:

> And I'm like, "Sure, I'll tell you about the meeting, but are you aware of the Grant School Initiative?" And she says, "No, I'm really not." And I said, "Well, there's actually a lot going on at Grant. It's a Center City school and there are a lot of new parents . . . it's sort of a whole trend now." And [I mentioned] the Center City Schools thing. And she's like, "This is fascinating! I'm going to pitch this to my editor, and I'd really like to talk to you some more about this." And I'm like, "Great! Here's my number." So I don't know if she ever even wrote the article about the [PTO] meeting.

Several weeks later, a story about Grant appeared in the paper, lauding the involvement of Sharon and her peers.[2]

Sharon's experience is telling for two reasons. First, it is a small but real example of the vast divisions in Philadelphia, where neighborhoods wracked by persistent poverty encircle a vibrant, affluent downtown. Second, Sharon's ability to use this experience to generate media interest in the involvement of Center City parents in Grant exemplifies the social and cultural capital middle- and upper-middle class parents possess and their skill at activating this capital to advance their agendas, a topic that will be taken up in chapters 5 and 6.[3] The Center City Schools Initiative (CCSI), an effort to market downtown public schools to parents like Sharon, was a product of just these sorts of dynamics. To understand why a parent like Sharon would feel so disconnected from the majority of public school parents in Philadelphia, and why a local reporter would find the activities of a group of middle- and upper-middle-class parents who send their children to public school "fascinating," we must first explore the context in which the initiative emerged.

A Divided City

In August of 2005 I spoke with an administrator at the Center City District (CCD), the business organization behind the CCSI. This administrator, a tireless champion of Philadelphia's downtown, characterized his decision to bring the interests and energies of the CCD to bear on local public schools as a "light-bulb" moment. But the initiative's origin had as much to do with a particular set of social, political, economic, and ideological conditions as with a single flash of inspiration. This chapter and the next explore these conditions, focusing on the city of Philadelphia and its schools. Here, I begin with the city. The CCD's close involvement in Philadelphia's public schools was made possible by the cumulative and intertwining effects of national and local history, global markets, large demographic shifts, and trends in redevelopment policy. These factors shaped the definition of the major problems challenging Philadelphia in the late twentieth and early twenty-first centuries and also helped determine which solutions would gain traction. In examining Philadelphia's recent history, I focus on three key themes: a sense of crisis about the city's future, a growing faith in market solutions, and increasing economic and geographic stratification.

Philadelphia's trajectory from "Philthadelphia" (a city known for its rubbish-strewn streets) to "the next Brooklyn" (an inexpensive haven for artists and other escapees from Manhattan) is in many ways representative of decline and resurgence among older, postindustrial cities in the United States.[4] At times during the later decades of the twentieth century, many Philadelphians considered their city's long-term survival uncertain. As newspaper headlines such as "City Waits for Rescue Amid Cries of Chaos," and "Failed Deal Worsens Philadelphia Crisis" suggest, this perception of impending doom was based upon real—and severe—problems. Defining Philadelphia as a city on the edge of dissolution paved the way for dramatic "solutions," including the rise of public-private partnerships and an embrace of market models of social policy and urban development. The economic outlook has improved in recent years, but like other major postindustrial cities, Philadelphia has become a "dual city," increasingly polarized between affluent and poor.

Much of the resurgence of Philadelphia's downtown is credited to the efforts of the CCD, its pioneering business improvement district (BID). In the closing decades of the twentieth century, BIDs emerged nationwide as a way to address the challenges—political and ideological as well as structural—that many large cities faced. The CCD's approach to Philadelphia's redevelopment is heavily rooted in the market logic discussed in chapter 1. While the CCD has been an effective agent of change in the city, its successes have been accompanied by continued—and growing—stratification, between affluent and poor citizens and between the thriving downtown and the deteriorating neighborhoods that spread across most of the rest of the city.

One reason the reporter was so interested in Sharon's story of Cobble Square families sending their children to Grant is that much of the popular and political discourse in the city has been shaped by widespread fear of suburban flight. Images of white and middle-class families fleeing for the suburbs have both symbolized and encapsulated the city's problems in a particularly dramatic way, depicting Philadelphia as a city left behind by anyone with the resources to go elsewhere. Thus, I conclude this chapter with a discussion of flight to the suburbs and how this flight was understood by Philadelphians anxious about their city's future.

Philadelphia: Exemplar of Decline and Resurgence

In 1989, a year before the City Council authorized the establishment of the Center City District, a newspaper editorial reviewed the downtown's many problems and concluded that what the city needed was "a real-life Batman to rescue this kid sister of Gotham."[5] As the twentieth century drew to a close, it appeared that only a superhero could save Philadelphia.

Philadelphia in the 1940s and '50s was a major manufacturing center, known as the "Workshop of the World." The city produced a wide variety of goods, including textiles, tools, beer, and huge naval ships. Major companies included Budd Manufacturing, which made railway and subway cars, and the Stetson Hat Company, but the city was also home to thousands of smaller operations, producing everything from tools to ice cream to hosiery. Center City, the downtown central business district, was surrounded by large swaths of industry, where workers and their families lived in close proximity to factories and warehouses. In Kensington, a historically working-class neighborhood north of Center City, for example, early twentieth-century immigrants from Ireland, England, Scotland, and Germany clustered together, establishing "ethnic villages" within walking distance of dozens of textile firms. By mid-century, many of their descendants remained there, and similar ethnic communities were in place along the city's rivers and major transit lines. Of course, Philadelphia in the first decades of the twentieth century was no urban utopia, but the problems it faced were very different from those currently plaguing the city.[6]

Philadelphia's population peaked in 1950 at over two million and then began a steady decline. In the decades that followed, the city's industrial base shrank as manufacturing jobs moved to the south, the suburbs, or overseas. This process, which actually began before World War II, continued throughout the latter part of the twentieth century. Between 1970 and 1990, for example, the city lost 65 percent of its manufacturing jobs, 52 percent of its construction jobs, and 40 percent of its transport and utility jobs. Meanwhile, the number of low-level service jobs, such as those in restaurants or retail stores, grew by 47 percent.[7] As factories closed down and jobs with benefits and security disappeared, residents fled. In Kensington, the population dropped by 36 percent in the forty-year period between 1950 and 1990, from 149,000 to 95,000.[8] In the formerly industrial neighborhoods that covered so much of Philadelphia outside of Center City, conditions worsened as jobs disappeared and homes were left vacant.

Philadelphia also experienced major suburbanization during the second half of the twentieth century: while the city population declined by 554,000 between 1950 and 2000, the region as a whole grew by almost 1.5 million.[9] This decentralization was heavily racialized. The city was 82 percent white in 1950, but by 2000 whites comprised only 45 percent of residents. In contrast, the percentage of African American grew from 18 percent in 1950 to 43 percent in 2000. Flight to the suburbs was also classed. As middle-class families left the city, median income fell; by 2000, Philadelphia was in the bottom quartile of large U.S. cities and had a poverty rate of 23 percent. Thirty-eight percent of households with children lived below the poverty line.[10]

Given these statistics about job loss and population change, it is perhaps not surprising that by the late 1980s and early 1990s, Philadelphia's city government was in crisis, facing growing budget deficits and deteriorating city services. As revenues fell, the city was forced to raise taxes, including the notorious "wage tax." These tax hikes appear to have further spurred flight and disinvestment. The city's fiscal problems were also exacerbated by costly labor contracts with its municipal unions.[11] Meanwhile, Philadelphia's suburbs, particularly more recently developed areas on the fringes of the metropolitan area, were thriving. For example, at the same time that stores throughout Philadelphia were closing, King of Prussia, a luxury mall located about thirty minutes to the northwest, expanded dramatically, becoming the largest mall on the East Coast.

Philadelphia's public spending skyrocketed during this period, as expenses associated with poverty, homelessness, drug use, and teen pregnancy grew. Crime was also a major problem; the murder rate peaked in 1990, with 503 homicides.[12] The city's situation became so dire that it attracted national attention. Bankruptcy loomed and stories in local and national papers described city offices running out of basic supplies and beleaguered officials coping with the rising tide of debt.[13] A story published in a Pittsburgh paper in the summer of 1991 summarized the city's grim situation, describing overgrown playgrounds, trash in City Hall, and crumbling public buildings. Residents are quoted complaining about poverty, crime, and the lack of services: "There are no jobs in this city and that's sad. Drugs everywhere. No cops. The homeless. People shouldn't have to live like that."[14] There is no doubt that the city was in deep trouble.

In 1992 Edward Rendell was elected mayor, with supporters hoping he could somehow find a way to stave off bankruptcy. In journalist Buzz Bissinger's *A Prayer for the City*, a portrayal of the first of Mayor Rendell's two administrations, he tells of two city officials working late into the night in the winter of 1992 to determine the exact state of Philadelphia's finances. After elaborate calculations, these officials were stunned to realize that that the city's projected gap for the next five years was $1.246 billion, "a budget deficit bigger than the entire budget of Boston or Houston or Baltimore."[15] Rendell himself was well aware of the severity of the situation. Writing in 1994, he recalled that as he was headed toward his inauguration ceremony, he was so worried about the city's precarious state he "almost told them to turn the car around."[16]

Of course, Philadelphians have done more than bear witness to their city's decline. Beginning in the 1950s, local civic, political, and business leaders, concerned about Philadelphia's ability to compete with the suburbs and other cities, invested considerable public and private resources in the downtown. Factories and warehouses were replaced with skyscrapers and office buildings, high-rise apartment buildings were built on the site of former slums, and historic—but crumbling—homes were refurbished for members of the middle and upper classes. The redevelopment of Society Hill, a neighborhood in the heart of Center City, exemplifies this steady infusion of resources into the downtown. As urban geographer Neil Smith described in one of the early articles on gentrification, Society Hill, which had been home to Philadelphia's upper class before the Civil War, had deteriorated significantly by the 1950s. Through concerted efforts on the part of private organizations, businesses, and public officials, shabby houses were purchased, restored to their colonial glory, and sold to professionals. By the first decades of the twenty-first century, Society

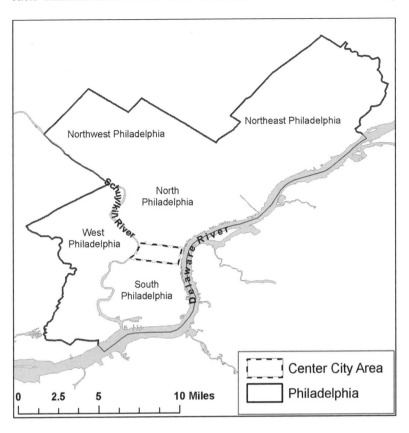

MAP 2.1. Philadelphia's Center City Area.

Hill had become one of the most affluent neighborhoods in the city.[17] In the 1970s and 1980s, city and business leaders strove to revitalize the city's retail scene (evident in the construction of suburban-style shopping malls in the downtown). Beginning in the early 1990s, Mayor Rendell focused on bringing visitors to the city. Thus, a massive convention center opened in 1993 in Center City, and new theaters and other cultural institutions were built in the years that followed.[18]

As a result, when the national economy began to surge in the mid-1990s, the infrastructure was already in place for a revival of the city's fortunes, particularly in Center City. The strong leadership and fiscal control wielded by the Rendell administration in the early 1990s, a tax-abatement on new construction, and growing national interest in downtown living, all sparked a real estate boom. Encouraged by the tax abatement, developers capitalized on Philadelphia's manufacturing past and converted old factories and warehouses into residences, such that huge factory windows and exposed pipes were "reborn as industrial chic."[19] As a result of these changes—new retail establishments, tourist and cultural attractions, residential developments, restaurants, and the refurbishment of public spaces—Philadelphia's downtown grew increasingly prosperous and desirable throughout the 1990s. In the words of CCD president Paul Levy, an avid booster of Philadelphia's local and national image:

> Philadelphia no longer exports manufactured products. During the Rendell administration, it redefined itself as a place that imports people and finds entertaining ways for them to leave their money behind. Building on the success of the convention center, the city in 1997 began to market itself aggressively as a tourist destination. This, too, has helped support the restaurant renaissance downtown and has boosted attendance at cultural institutions.[20]

These developments did not go unnoticed by local and national media. A series of *Philadelphia Inquirer* articles in late 2005 lauded the "renaissance" of the downtown area, explored strategies for maintaining the "momentum," and noted the spread to outlying neighborhoods. The *New York Times* published an article about young artists and professionals moving to Philadelphia in search of a more affordable lifestyle, and *National Geographic* called Philadelphia the "next great city."[21] Many factors contributed to the revitalization of Philadelphia, but the rebirth of the core downtown area that began in the 1990s owed much to the efforts of the CCD.

Business Improvement Districts: Channeling "Private-Sector Energy Towards the Solution of Public Problems"

In Philadelphia, as in other cities, federal divestment and the understanding of the challenges of the 1980s and 1990s as an "urban crisis" led city leaders to look to sources other than the government for help.[22] They sought out corporations and public-private institutions that could attract badly needed capital and embraced market approaches to urban revitalization. This strategy continued into the twenty-first century. Contemporary revitalization efforts thus generally involve private businesses and public-private ventures that focus on "historic preservation, consumer marketing, small business development, pedestrian access, and the cleanliness and safety of streets," in addition to projects designed to appeal to tourists, business travelers, and potential investors.[23] This kind of emphasis on physical appeal and consumption is consistent with the strategy of making urban areas more attractive to capital and to the professional-class residents, workers, and consumers that cities seek.

Business improvement districts, including Philadelphia's CCD, are among the most important players in this new approach to revitalization. They are private organizations, usually sponsored by local businesses, authorized by state legislation and local municipalities to levy taxes on properties within a specific geographic area in exchange for additional services to that area. During the 1980s and 1990s, BIDs emerged in cities across the country as organizations charged with promoting urban renewal, supplementing municipal services, and generally bringing the forces of the private sector to bear on the problem of urban decline. In a national survey of BIDs, public affairs scholar Jerry Mitchell found that nearly 60 percent were formed after 1990, following a period of major federal retrenchment in social spending and growing federal budget deficits.[24] They serve, in CCD president Levy's words, "sometimes as cheerleader, sometimes as quarterback—helping to boost office, hotel, and retail occupancy to new heights, while fostering a resurgence in downtown housing."[25] This metaphor is telling. It captures the impact BIDs can have on everything from marketing to policymaking.

By 2005 approximately a thousand BIDs were in operation in U.S. cities and towns. Typically BIDs provide such services as security, street cleaning, and marketing. The purpose is to maximize the assets and profits of their own members—the individuals, businesses, and organizations upon whose financial contributions they rely. While BIDs vary in size and efficacy, the more effective among them have been credited with reviving downtowns in cities such as Philadelphia, Cleveland, New York, and Milwaukee.[26]

Many BIDs, however, do more than market their neighborhoods or tidy the sidewalks and streets in their service areas. As "quarterbacks," they play a key role in shaping urban policy, influencing municipal decisions around tax, zoning, transit, and development issues.[27] Some BIDs participate more aggressively in these arenas than others, but all make decisions with an eye to improving their service areas' appeal to visitors, residents, and businesses. In *Sidewalk*, his classic study of New York City street vendors, sociologist Mitchell Duneier argues that the "importance of BIDs cannot be overemphasized in understanding the distribution of power in New York City."[28] Duneier describes efforts by two local BIDs to restrict the practice of selling books on the sidewalk, a campaign that began with behind-the-scenes lobbying and ended with the passage of a new city ordinance. Urban geographer Nathaniel Lewis traces the extensive involvement of BIDs in Washington, DC (one BID successfully mandated that all future construction include retail space, while others developed land-use strategies and brokered changes to zoning rules), and argues that municipal government in DC has "evolved into a more complex 'polycentric' system of governance, in which BIDs are now one actor."[29]

BIDs' ability to influence urban policy development derives from their unique status as private organizations with public responsibilities, operating in an era of chronic fiscal shortfalls. During the twelve-year period between 1980 and 1992, presidents Reagan and Bush sought to decrease or end funding for federal War on Poverty programs targeting urban areas, such as revenue sharing, urban development action grants, and community development block grants.[30] The funding loss to cities was extensive.[31] Jobs, training programs, and block grants were slashed as government funding disappeared. The Clinton administration created "empowerment zones" designed to spur new markets in impoverished areas by encouraging and rewarding private investment in communities that had been abandoned by capital but, bowing to entrenched political opposition and the federal deficit, did not craft a more ambitious agenda.[32] At the same time, welfare benefits came under attack. Because of inflation, new restrictions in payments, and benefit reductions, stipends for impoverished families from Aid to Families with Dependent Children (AFDC) declined significantly.[33] At the state level, significant retrenchments in AFDC and Medicaid continued throughout the 1990s. Thus, cities faced growing social problems such as homelessness, a rise in single-parent families, and an epidemic of crack addiction, with a shortage of resources, creating a need for organizations such as BIDS that could "fill the gaps."

During the 1980s conservative critics of government spending argued that depending on others for support was dysfunctional and unproductive and that individuals should avoid reliance upon charity or government. As organizations, BIDs embody a similar spirit. Rather than relying on local municipalities to provide services or improve the appearance of downtown areas, they aim to attack the problems themselves. Or, as an early proponent of the CCD said in his testimony before Philadelphia's City Council: "I see it as basically a self-help program."[34] Thus, in contrast to more distressed regions of major cities, which typically are dependent on federal, state, and local largesse for their survival, areas served by BIDs (particularly those with a critical mass of business capital) assume a mantle of independence and self-determination.

The trend, beginning in the 1980s, toward moving the locus of government responsibility to ever-more local levels was rooted in a broader critique of big government as inherently inefficient and heavy-handed. The underlying assumption—now generally treated as fact—is that smaller, more local organizations are better equipped to solve social and logistical problems. BIDs institutionalize this idea. They shift the responsibility for urban upkeep, marketing, and (in some cases) planning from local government to private entities. They are frequently described as "nimble" as well as effective. Unlike government agencies, they can move quickly to improve public spaces, reduce crime, solve service problems, and develop and implement short- and long-term revitalization strategies.[35] Proponents of BIDs often attribute their efficacy to their status as *private* organizations. According to Heather MacDonald, a fellow at the conservative Manhattan Institute: "The key to BIDs' accomplishments lies in their dissimilarity to big city government. They operate without civil service rules and red tape; most important, they negotiate labor contracts from a clean slate. They can hire and fire employees based on performance, not civil service status or other government mandates."[36]

As organizations founded by and for local businesses, BIDs are, of course, quite different from municipal government. They are suffused with market discourse and driven by market logic. From a BID's perspective, residents and visitors are "customers" whose business they seek and whose living, working, and shopping experiences they strive to make as pleasant as possible.[37] They assume that cities must compete with one another to survive, and that their survival is dependent on reducing government and labor "interference" and making cities as "business friendly" as possible. Equally important, they assume that the entire city will benefit from the economic growth resulting from business profits in a specific neighborhood or district. BIDs' prominence and power have opened the door to new partnerships and ways of funding and coordinating urban development.

Yet these organizations also have their critics. Criticism of BIDs tends to focus on their facilitation of gentrification and displacement: as areas served by BIDs become more attractive to tourists and professionals, they become less accessible or affordable for the rest of the population. As a result, BIDs can exacerbate social and economic disparities between the neighborhoods they serve and those that, lacking sufficient resources to support a BID, fall further behind. Moreover, BIDs are not subject to public scrutiny or accountability. Although they often operate like public entities, providing services and setting policy agendas, the people who run them are not elected, nor do they answer to any constituency beyond their dues-paying members. Also, while they take pride in their private-sector energy and efficiency, BIDs frequently are not fiscally independent. They often receive large sums in federal, state, and local grants, again raising questions about their accountability to the public.[38] Their chief virtues, a nimble responsiveness and efficient provision of designated services, come at a cost both to equity and accountability. Philadelphia's CCD, autho-rized by the City Council in October 1990 as a "special services district" with the ability to levy taxes on property owners in Center City, brings all of these elements together to provide a compelling example of both the strengths and limitations of this approach to "saving" cities.

The Emergence of the Center City District

By the late 1980s, a shortage of city services and increases in crime and homelessness had made Philadelphia's downtown dirty, unsafe, and unap-pealing to residents, workers, and shoppers, earning the city its "Philtha-delphia" nickname. This downward spiral, and the absence of any promise of support from federal or state officials, prompted the Central Philadel-phia Development Corporation (a nonprofit organization that had been working since the 1950s to promote economic development in Center City) to spearhead an energetic campaign to create a BID in Center City.[39] The founders of the CCD envisioned a private organization, authorized by City Council to levy taxes on properties, which would work closely with city government on downtown revitalization and other issues.

Testimony during City Council hearings on the proposed BID brought to life the sense that the city was teetering on the edge of disaster. City officials made repeated references to ongoing financial crises and over-whelming social problems. Explaining then–Mayor Wilson Goode's sup-port for the new district, a city official lamented, "At the precise time we want an improved quality of life to create opportunities for the future, we are choked by the spiraling costs of checking its decline."[40] City Council representatives spoke of the dismayingly low level of city services—the "twelve inches of dirt on my streets!"—and of ongoing problems with crime. According to testimony, the city had become a place where people felt unsafe, where the normal rules of behavior seemed no longer to apply: "the quality of life in Center City has deteriorated," and "the lack of cleanliness gives the appearance that Center City—or any part of the city—is not under control." The president of Philadelphia's Board of Realtors called Philadelphia's real estate market "comatose" and said housing values suffered from the perception that Philadelphia city government was ineffective. Consistent support for the new business district also came from the *Philadelphia Inquirer*, the city's major daily newspaper. Arguing that it was a "way to save Center City," the paper urged the legislation's speedy passage (and later provided enthusiastic coverage of the CCD's early accomplishments).[41] The creation of a new BID was thus presented to City Council as a way for Philadelphia to begin to reverse its decline. Center City would become a beacon of stability that would, in turn, help Philadelphia to survive.

There were some naysayers. The proposal to form the CCD was originally greeted with opposition from some Center City residents and business owners reluctant to pay additional taxes. Eventually, however, the plan was modified so that homeowners could avoid paying the extra charge, with their share covered by voluntary contributions from local institutions, such as churches and hospitals. Noting the minimal formal protest from the downtown, an *Inquirer* editorial explained, "With City Hall on the verge of bankruptcy, the old complaint that property owners shouldn't pay extra for services the city should be providing becomes increasingly pointless."[42] More sustained opposition came from businesses and elected officials in Northeast Philadelphia, who expressed concern that the police department's agreement to provide additional indirect services to Center City would end up harming law enforcement in their neighborhood. During public hearings, certain aspects of the proposal were questioned, but no one challenged the broader premise that the city was in desperate straits and needed all the help it could get. Likewise, no voices rose to question the notion that the city's survival depended on a vibrant, attractive downtown or that its best hopes rested with the private, rather than public, sector. The City Council's final vote on the legislation was 14-1. The sole "no" vote was cast by a representative from the Northeast.

What Does the CCD Do?

During the first year of operation, the CCD's budget was over $6 million, the vast majority of which came from levies on hotels, office buildings, and other large properties. The organization was charged with improving the safety and cleanliness of a 120-block area in the heart of Center City. It immediately hired a staff of "community service representatives" who, wearing distinctive teal-green uniforms, walked the streets to provide information to passersby and alert the police in case of trouble. It also hired sanitation workers, who swept and hosed down sidewalks and cleaned up graffiti. By 2005 the CCD had been reauthorized by City Council through 2025, and its yearly budget had grown to well over $13.5 million. In addition to a sizable administrative team, it employed approximately seventy sanitation workers and forty community service representatives. It also supported enhanced police coverage in the downtown area and assisted with crime tracking and mapping.[43]

Since its founding, the CCD has had only one president and CEO. Paul Levy is a tall, intense man with a doctorate in history from Columbia University, who taught in the New York City public schools in the early 1970s and worked for Philadelphia city government and other local organizations throughout the 1980s. As of this writing, Levy continues to head the CCD and is a prominent figure in the city. A profile in a local paper called Levy "the king of Center City" and "the most powerful guy you never voted for," noting that his annual salary (over $350,000) was approximately double the mayor's. Levy's name appears often in local and national newspaper coverage of Center City, and he speaks before national organizations on his work in Philadelphia. In 2006 Levy received the "Philadelphia Award," presented annually to the citizen who has "done the most to advance the best and largest interest of the community." A *Philadelphia Daily News* column applauded this choice, noting that "even the smaller touches he creates, like lighting the Parkway, are more than just little touches; they are illustrations of the ongoing story of a great city with an increasingly bright future."[44]

In addition to being one of the largest BIDs in the country, the CCD is also particularly ambitious and proactive. It has moved significantly beyond maintaining Center City as a "clean, safe, attractive, and well-managed public environment," to aggressive "research, planning and communications strategies that enhance the attractiveness and competitiveness of Center City."[45] The CCD's enhancement efforts also have included making changes to the downtown streetscape by planting trees, replacing light fixtures, and installing colorful maps and signs on street corners.[46] In short, with Levy at the helm the CCD rapidly transformed its role from provider of discrete services to significant player in market-driven urban revitalization processes.

Levy explicitly rejects the notion that the primary mission of BIDs is to supplement city services, arguing that this portrayal overlooks the "leadership many of these organizations exercise in shaping public policy and their emerging role in the governance of cities and regions." He notes, using language similar to that of "creative class" analyst Richard Florida, that BIDs began taking shape as the post–World War II population shift to suburbs increasingly threatened the vitality of urban centers: "In the highly competitive and mobile postindustrial economy, quality-of-life issues become paramount. Businesses, workers, and tourists have a wide range of choice, and they will go where the experience, options, and amenities are best."[47] BIDs, he maintains, provide services only as a means to a larger end, that of making cities more appealing and competitive. From Levy's perspective, organizations like the CCD serve a critical leadership function: "articulating strategic alternatives, forging coalitions for change, and successfully implementing entrepreneurial solutions to chronic urban problems."[48]

Key to the CCD's vision for Philadelphia is the attraction and retention of professional workers, particularly those who are in their thirties and forties, an age when they "have children, prosper in their professions, or succeed in their own businesses."[49] During this "prime" period, workers have more disposable income, buy more expensive property, start and grow more businesses, and contribute more to a city's tax base—all of which fuels economic growth. CCD publications frequently remind readers of the research on the relationship between urban economic development and human capital, noting that the presence of educated professionals in a city has been found to be the most important driver of rising incomes. In an interview, a CCD administrator explained:

And it was very clear that those cities in which incomes were going up significantly had two characteristics: they had a very high percentage of adults with college degrees, and they had a very high percentage of thirty-five to forty-four year olds. . . . Because at thirty-five to forty-four, people who started out in careers are seeing their incomes really rise at that point. People who have started business are succeeding. And to the extent to which you retain those groups in the city—one, you obviously just have higher-income people with purchasing power, but people who are forming businesses in a city are more likely to hire from within that city.

This focus on attracting educated people with disposable incomes to Center City was brought home to me in another way when I visited the CCD in 2005. The CCD is located in an imposing space in the heart of Philadelphia's downtown. Behind large glass doors framed in polished wood, the lobby boasts high ceilings, a Persian carpet, and professionally mounted displays of CCD projects. After being greeted by a friendly receptionist, I was ushered into the conference room. As I stood there, admiring the well-appointed space with its long polished table and artists' renderings of CCD projects, I noticed a drawing of a proposed (and now actual) riverside park. The text that accompanied the drawing of people walking, jogging, and relaxing on park benches described the park as a "tool for economic development" and "an outdoor amenity for students, knowledge workers, and visitors." There was no mention of other citizens who, while less central to the CCD's vision for the city, might also like to use the park.

Thus, in promoting Philadelphia, the CCD emphasizes amenities that are likely to enhance the city's appeal for companies and professionals who are weighing choices between different cities and between the city and the suburbs. According to a 2005 report, its efforts to promote Center City fall into three categories: communications, events, and retention and recruitment. The CCD uses advertisements in radio and print, newsletters, and its website to raise awareness about Center City's amenities and attractions.[50] A series of ads entitled "Living at the Center of Everything," for instance, trumpets the advantages of downtown living using images and text aimed at gays, empty nesters, and college graduates. The CCD also helps organize and promote events, such as outdoor concerts and the biannual "Restaurant Week," that "reinforce Center City as an exciting and vibrant place to live, work, shop and visit." The CCD releases several publications each year on topics including developments in retail, real estate, and employment; improvements to downtown public spaces; policy proposals; and extensive "State of Center City" reports. These publications draw from the CCD's own research and are professionally produced, with colorful maps, pictures, and other graphics, as well as the recognizable CCD logo. Many begin with a brief commentary from Levy describing Center City's progress or calling attention to particular challenges. Finally, to encourage commercial development and attract businesses, the

CCD produces and distributes brochures about the real estate market, collaborates with public officials in efforts to attract investment, supports public and private marketing efforts, and even sends its personnel to welcome new commercial tenants to Center City.[51]

The CCD's activities reflect the "trickle-down" assumption that downtown prosperity will benefit all city residents. As Philadelphia shifted from an industrial to an information economy, major growth occurred in knowledge industry and service-sector jobs, creating new openings in fields such as law, education, technology, financial and real estate services, and retail, leisure and hospitality. Many of these jobs were located downtown. Levy has argued that the jobs created in Center City went to residents from all parts of the city, explaining to a local reporter, for example, that in the early 2000s residents of the struggling North Philadelphia region earned $50 million annually working in downtown offices.[52] In addition, according to Levy, allowing the market to operate more freely in Philadelphia (by, for example, eliminating onerous taxes and regulations) would increase prosperity across the city and help address persistent poverty in a way that other sorts of government intervention do not: "But ultimately, the goal shouldn't be just to clear the land or build new housing, but to integrate the dispossessed into a market economy and let everything else follow."[53]

In touting the success of Center City since the CCD's founding, Levy has his choice of an impressive number of indicators. The area now has, among other improvements, less crime, a new arts-and-entertainment district and convention center, increased retail and restaurant business, and a boom in housing sales and construction.[54] Of course, the CCD's evolution coincided with broader trends—such as a growing interest in downtown living and a strong national economy—that brought prosperity to the area. However, with its marketing and policy work, as well as its physical improvements to downtown, the CCD unquestionably played a role in making Center City an attractive, vibrant region. In fact, the Center City of 2011 is so prosperous it is difficult to believe that only twenty years earlier it seemed on the brink of collapse.

Who Are the CCD's Customers?

Who lives and works in what the CCD calls "the vibrant 24-hour hub of Greater Philadelphia"? Beginning in the mid-1990s and increasing though the first decade of the twenty-first century, large numbers of professionals "flocked to Philadelphia's Center City to take advantage of job opportunities in the downtown core and a vibrant social and cultural scene."[55] It was one of only two parts of the city to experience population growth between 1990 and 2000, and evidence suggests that growth continued throughout the 2000s.[56]

As is so often the case with city neighborhoods, however, the labels are a little confusing. While the CCD officially covers only a 120-block area—the location of Center City's prime business properties—the label "Center City" is generally used in Philadelphia to refer to the entire downtown. This is the practice I follow in this book. Thus, Center City encompasses the CCD's service area but also reaches beyond it, stretching from the Delaware River to the east to the Schuylkill River to the west, and between Vine Street to the north and South Street to the south (see map 2.2). Many parts of Center City technically are not covered by the CCD, but they nevertheless benefit from the organization's broader marketing of Center City and from the amenities the CCD helped bring to the area.

A number of neighborhoods adjoining Center City also exhibited the same changes that marked Center City's revitalization, namely an influx of young, educated professionals and a rise in property values. In 2002 the Center City District released a report, entitled *The Success of Downtown Living: Expanding the Boundaries of Center City*, which documented the ways outlying neighborhoods were affected by Center City's growing desirability. Using real estate and census data, the report painted a vivid picture of a set of neighborhoods reshaped by gentrification and an influx of young professionals—the same "types of households drawn to the concentration of amenities that are animating downtowns across the country."[57] As map 2.2 shows, these areas are located directly to the north and south of Center City proper.

Philadelphians generally use "Center City" when speaking of the core downtown area, but the term sometimes also includes adjoining, gentrifying communities, a development that the CCD has celebrated as an indication of downtown's continued revival. Though I distinguish between the core and expanded Center City areas in my descriptions of Philadelphia, as we will see in chapter 4, the target audience for the Center City schools project included *both* residents of Center City and residents of the adjacent neighborhoods. Neighborhoods in the expanded Center City area were gentrifying rapidly, accommodating young families eager to live in the city but unable to afford homes within the traditional boundaries of downtown.

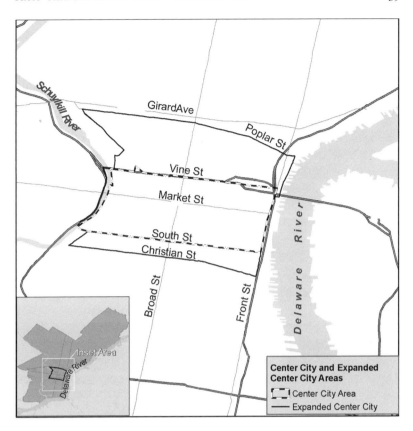

MAP 2.2. Center City and Expanded Center City.

In the early 2000s Center City's residents were a highly educated group. Whereas only 18 percent of Philadelphia's adults held college degrees, 67 percent of downtown residents did, placing the area just behind Chicago's downtown and Midtown Manhattan in the percentage of the population with college degrees. In addition, Philadelphia's downtown had *more* residents with graduate and professional degrees (36%) than did Chicago (33%) or Midtown Manhattan (33%). Over 30 percent of Center City's population was between twenty-five and thirty-four years old, an age group generally considered to be catalysts for downtown improvement because its members' disposable incomes fund the growth of such urban amenities as shops, restaurants, bars, and nightclubs.[58] The neighborhoods just north and south of Center City were also home to large numbers of

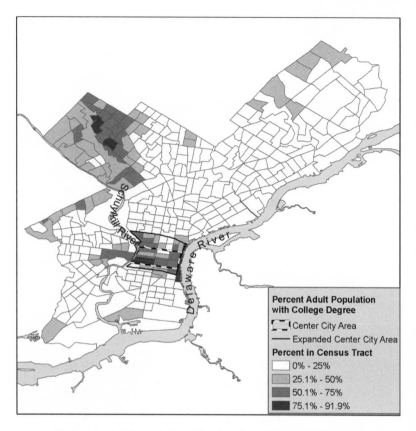

MAP 2.3. Percentage of adult population with college degree. Source: US Census, 2000.

college graduates. As map 2.3 shows, significant concentrations of college-educated adults were located in Center City and its immediate environs. In the areas beyond the expanded Center City region, like most of the rest of Philadelphia, far fewer adults had college degrees.[59]

Between 1990 and 2000, Center City saw a rise in the number of single-person households and in the number of married couples without children. While the number of households with children decreased between 1990 and 2000, this group—particularly families with young children—was on the rise after 2000. Indeed, between 2000 and 2010, the number of school-aged children in Center City increased by 16 percent.[60]

Given the higher percentage of college-educated adults in Center City and the adjacent neighborhoods, it is not surprising that incomes in the area exceeded those in the rest of Philadelphia. In 2006 the adjusted gross income in Philadelphia as a whole was $39,173. In every zip code in Center City and the expanded Center City, incomes exceeded the city average. For example, in the areas encompassing Rittenhouse Square and Society Hill (both in the heart of Center City), average incomes were $129,000 and $156,000, respectively. In the gentrifying neighborhoods of Bella Vista and Fairmount, just outside of Center City proper, incomes were lower than in Center City's core but were still nearly the double the city's median.[61]

Housing prices in this area rose far more rapidly than in the city as a whole. In 2002 the median sale price citywide was $60,000, reflecting a 20 percent increase since 1997. In contrast, the median sale price in several of the "hottest" downtown neighborhoods was over $350,000, reflecting a 300 percent increase in the case of one neighborhood.[62] By 2005, according to an analysis performed by the *Inquirer*, the median home price in parts of Center City had risen to as high as $450,000, compared to a citywide median home price of $120,000.[63]

The many uses and meanings of the term "middle class" is a recurring theme in this book. Much of the CCD's marketing (including the CCSI) targeted professionals, or "knowledge workers," trying to convince this group to live and work in the city. I argued in chapter 1 that professionals (or the "educated middle class" or "upper middle class") are significantly more elite than what is often thought of as the "middle class." The data presented here, about the large numbers of adults with graduate and professional degrees, and the differences in incomes and property values compared to the rest of the city, suggest that a significant portion of the residents of Center City, especially the areas in Center City's core, would be more accurately known as upper-middle class. Their families possessed higher levels of financial and cultural capital (as indicated by income and education levels) than many middle-class families, and they likely shared a host of class-related practices around consumption, recreation, and attitudes toward education. Making this distinction is important to understanding the politics of the CCSI. As I will argue in chapter 4, while those behind the CCSI saw it as a way of attracting educated, affluent *professionals* to the city, the initiative generated support among many civic and educational leaders in Philadelphia because it addressed their concerns about the city's shrinking *middle class*.

A focus on class should not preclude an understanding of the racial implications of urban revitalization. Center City was long a predominantly white region, but gentrification changed the racial composition of the adjacent neighborhoods. Whereas Center City remained only 8 percent African American between 1970 and 2000, black population in the expanded area (i.e., Center City and its adjacent neighborhoods) declined by 43 percent, from 22 percent to 13 percent (Center City District, 2002). Thus, the region's expansion and growing affluence coincided with displacement or out-migration of African American residents.

Enduring Divisions

Despite media attention to Philadelphia's comeback, the city's resurgence has been largely limited to the downtown and its environs. This form of uneven development, in which an increasingly affluent downtown and adjacent gentrifying communities are surrounded by deteriorating, low-income, largely minority neighborhoods, has been well documented in the urban studies literature and is captured in the "dual city" metaphor discussed in chapter 1.[64] Philadelphia, as a regional rather than global center, did not have the same concentration of extreme wealth that characterized New York City in the 1990s and 2000s, but it nevertheless experienced a growing polarization. One indicator of deep division is, as we have seen, the differences between the education and income levels and property values of Center City residents and those of Philadelphia residents in general. These data are consistent with the findings from a Brookings Institution study of middle-income households in urban areas that used 2000 census data to assess the impact of growing economic segregation on communities. In this study, Philadelphia was found to be rapidly losing both its middle-income households and its middle-income neighborhoods at the same time that the number of "very high income" and "very low income" neighborhoods was rising.[65]

For Philadelphia residents who lacked educational qualifications, the shift from a manufacturing to a knowledge-based economy was devastating. According to a 2007 report by a local organization focusing on workforce development, the city's labor force participation rate ranked 96th out of the country's 100 largest cities. Entitled *A Tale of Two Cities*, this report pointed to the large and growing chasm between the "city of prosperity," in which highly educated workers made good salaries and had only a 3.5 percent unemployment rate, and the "city of disparity," in which residents without degrees received low wages and faced an unemployment rate between 19 percent and 25 percent.[66] Like many of the CCD's publications, this report documented the connection between education and salaries and emphasized the need for a highly educated population in Philadelphia. However, *A Tale of Two Cities* also criticized the local approach to economic development for overlooking the importance of training and employing people already living in the city: "Largely missing from the broad public discourse on economic development strategies and taxes is the expansion of our wage base through the activation of our workforce."[67] The implication is that the city would do well to focus on *growing* (rather than importing) a skilled workforce.

In other words, the assumption that Center City's revitalization would provide widespread benefits has not been supported by the city's recent history. In the first years of the twenty-first century, Philadelphia was still among the most economically distressed and racially segregated cities in the country, and the gap between its rich and poor neighborhoods appeared to be growing. In this way, Philadelphia resembles other cities, where, despite the much-celebrated urban revival of the 1990s, poverty and high unemployment continue unabated.[68] In fact, early twenty-first century Philadelphia was a city with many worries, not least of them unrelenting migration to the suburbs.

The Great Exodus

Throughout this period of decline and (partial) revitalization, the issue of white and middle-class flight to the suburbs haunted Philadelphia. Philadelphia was not alone in this respect. For much of the twentieth century, federal policies both encouraged and subsidized flight to the suburbs, using low-interest, guaranteed home mortgages, racial criteria in lending, and the construction of highways to make suburban life affordable for vast numbers of working- and middle-class white families.[69] As a result, families across the country left urban centers for the suburbs, dramatically altering the course of urban history. Urban population decline was not experienced equally by all cities. Some cities, particularly in the West and Northwest, grew significantly in the past decades and continue to add residents. But for many others, particularly those that, like Philadelphia, had been manufacturing centers, the loss of population was extreme. Between 1980 and 2000, for example, a time when Philadelphia lost 10 percent of its population, Washington, DC, also lost 10 percent, Cleveland lost over 16 percent, Baltimore over 17 percent, and Detroit over 20 percent.[70]

Flight to the suburbs was not distributed evenly by race or class: for decades, the vast majority of the households leaving cities have been white and middle class.[71] In Atlanta, for example, white flight caused the city's racial balance to reverse over a twenty-year period, going from one-third African American in 1960 to two-thirds by 1980. The vast majority of the whites fleeing Atlanta were working or middle class, leaving poor residents behind.[72] Even in the 1990s, which is generally seen as a positive decade for US cities, the proportion of middle-income households in the 100 largest cities fell, while the proportion of low-income households rose.[73] This population shift and what it means for cities has been an object of concern in the United States for decades. Concern about suburban migration also tended to be heavily racialized, with commentators worrying that, in the face of a declining white population, minority groups would assume power in central cities.[74]

The "Cancer in the Pores of the City"

Philadelphia sustained significant loss in the latter decades of the twentieth century. Much of the exodus consisted of families leaving for the suburbs. As in many cities, middle-class class flight was largely—but not entirely—a white phenomenon. During the twenty-year period (1980–2000) when Philadelphia lost 10 percent of its overall population, its white population decreased by 30 percent.[75]

In the 1960s and 1970s, the large-scale movement of white families to the suburbs was seen by many within and outside the city as an indictment of Philadelphia's economic and social prospects and, particularly, of the "invasion" of African Americans into historically white neighborhoods and the accompanying racial tensions. In their 1991 study of Philadelphia, Carolyn Adams and her colleagues at Temple University noted that whites may have left for the suburbs out of racial antipathy or they may simply have been seeking better jobs. Whatever the case, the authors observe, during this period, "'white flight' became the metaphor for the emptying out of the city."[76]

Anxiety about flight to the suburbs reached a fever pitch in the 1990s. Both Mayor Edward Rendell (1991–1999) and Mayor John Street (2000–2008) made stemming the flow of middle-class families central to their agendas, as did many other local politicians and city organizations.[77] Mayor Rendell was particularly active on this issue: one of his few interventions into School District of Philadelphia policy came about when the school board was considering removing student admissions requirements for special programs and schools. Rendell convinced the board to leave them in place, arguing that removing them would cause more middle-class families, whose children were overrepresented in the district's most competitive magnet schools, to leave the city.[78] Rendell frequently referred to Philadelphia as a patient who arrives at the hospital with cancer *and* a gunshot wound. While he could fix the gunshot wound (the city's fiscal crisis), curing the cancer of continued job and population loss was another issue entirely.[79]

$175 Million

The "patient" continued to suffer after Rendell's two mayoral administrations ended, and people continued to worry. In 1999 the *Philadelphia Inquirer* reported that in the previous decade, the city lost 150,000 "taxpayers," whose average annual income was between $30,000 and $40,000.[80] To many Philadelphians, middle-class flight was dangerous primarily because of its impact on the economy. Middle-class residents spend money in shops and restaurants, they invest in local property, and they create a larger and more stable tax base. Indeed, the city's perpetual fiscal shortages and the choice its leaders regularly faced, between cutting city services and raising taxes, were often viewed as caused by the dearth of "taxpaying" citizens.

In 2001, three years before the launch of the CCSI, the *Philadelphia Inquirer* again addressed population loss, noting that "a fleeing population guarantees a declining tax base, which erodes the city's ability to address the very problems that chase residents away." The article continued:

> The fiscal impact of population loss can be summed up by a single number: $175 million. That is about how much wage-tax income the city lost last year—and will give up each year in the future—because the city's population slid about 10% between 1988 and 1997, while taxpayers' median annual taxable income dropped by an inflation-adjusted 14 percent.[81]

While sounding the alarm about overall population loss, this article noted that, from an economic perspective, it was the loss of the *middle class* that was particularly deadly.

In interviews about education and the city's future I conducted in 2005 with Philadelphia's civic, business, and educational leaders, the issue of flight to the suburbs (which my respondents more generally referred to as "middle-class" rather than "white" flight) featured prominently. Interviewees who praised the city's revitalization and improved national image nevertheless spoke tentatively about the future, noting that Philadelphia still faced many social and economic challenges. For example, in an interview held in the comfortable living room of his restored nineteenth-century rowhouse, an educator active in local civic affairs explained, "I don't think the city can really be thought to be fully in recovery until you're able to keep middle-class families here." Respondents like this one worried that whatever improvements the city had made could be reversed—particularly if the middle class continued to leave.

To these leaders, the sense that Philadelphia had to keep the middle class often seemed to be beyond question or explanation, because the alternative, a city without a strong middle-class base, was unthinkable. Thus an administrator with a nonprofit education organization remarked, "You cannot sustain a community with a high concentration of impoverished residents. Duh!" Similarly, an education advocate observed, "I don't think there's any doubt that Philadelphia needs to retain middle-class people. If there's anything the '70s and '80s have shown, it's that economic isolation is deadly for any kind of community." In this remark, the respondent evokes the city's most precarious era to argue that the city's dependence on a critical mass of middle-class residents is beyond question. The focus on the need to keep the middle class came to play a key role in shaping both the CCSI and the public response, as we will see in chapter 4.

In this chapter, I have begun situating the effort to market public schools in downtown Philadelphia in its local, national, and historic contexts. Like many other cities in the Northeast and Midwest, Philadelphia was hit hard by the mid- to late twentieth-century shift away from a manufacturing economy and the accompanying job and population losses. By the late 1980s, with Center City struggling to compete with emerging employment and commercial centers in the suburbs, business and civic leaders embraced a strategy for urban revival that had been gaining momentum in cities across the country: the business improvement district.

Philadelphia's CCD, the organization behind the CCSI and one of the largest BIDs in the country, was formed in 1990 and tasked with "saving" a downtown beleaguered by a host of problems. As a result of its efforts—as well as national trends that benefited downtowns in the 1990s and 2000s—Center City experienced a significant resurgence. However, the revitalization of downtown was accompanied by growing inequalities, as large sectors of the city remained essentially disconnected from the formal economy. Throughout this period, the issue of middle-class flight continued to plague Philadelphia, becoming an important symbol of the city's decline and the fragility of its more recent revival.

This chapter has identified three factors—a sense of crisis, the rise of markets, and growing economic and geographic stratification—that are important to the story I tell in this book about the effort to position a number of elementary schools as urban amenities. These factors help explain why Philadelphians believed their city's future remained precarious and why they were so concerned about attracting and retaining middle-class residents. It was this context that led many people to view the CCSI, which focused on the downtown area and its educated residents and used the marketing of schools to convince them to stay in the city, as a reasonable approach.

Yet, as a number of urban scholars remind us, there are always other options. Even within the constraints of economic competition, city leaders can be deliberate in planning for affordable housing, in involving diverse citizens in development decisions, and in distributing the benefits of economic growth more widely.[82] The CCD has been integral to reviving Center City—a revival that has indeed been beneficial to many in Philadelphia. However, the existence of continued and growing inequality suggests that in Philadelphia, as in other large cities, a market-driven, downtown-focused revitalization strategy, which places heavy emphasis on the resources and talents of middle- and upper-middle-class workers and residents, may not serve everyone's interests. As I will argue in chapter 4, the CCD's work with schools was an extension of its strategy for reviving downtown. Next, however, we will turn to Philadelphia's schools before the CCD's involvement, where similar dynamics of crisis, market solutions, and stratification were at work.

CHAPTER THREE

Institutions of Last Resort

Crisis, Markets, and Stratification in Philadelphia's Schools

If this is one of the flagship schools and we don't have a library, I can't imagine what is happening at other schools! —Grant Elementary School parent

Sue Anne, like Sharon, is a Cobble Square mother who went against the norm in her affluent neighborhood to enroll her child at Grant Elementary. In an interview conducted in a downtown restaurant, she described her continued trepidation about that decision. Because the School District of Philadelphia had a poor reputation in the city, Sue Anne worried that sending her child to a Philadelphia public school (even one that was generally well regarded) was risky. She knew this is what her neighbors thought as well.

SUE ANNE: I think that it takes—to tell someone that your kid goes to Grant. I think you're judged, in our neighborhood.

M: As what?

SUE ANNE: As either a social experimenter, which is probably the best thing they're thinking. [Pause] I just think, you're just—you're thought of as someone who takes chances.

Convincing parents like Sue Anne to "take chances" with their local schools was exactly what the Center City Schools Initiative (CCSI) aimed to do.

In this chapter, I turn to the School District of Philadelphia, a system wracked by ongoing crises and rescued (intermittently) by dramatic reforms. I show that a combination of academic failure, fiscal shortfalls, and market-oriented reforms initiated by state and local leaders made the district fertile ground for a partnership with a local business organization to market public schools to professional families. However, as Sue Anne's comment reveals, the effort to attract Center City families to the public schools faced many challenges. In addition to the low student-achievement scores generally seen in systems that serve a disproportionately low-income population, the Philadelphia school district, which served 185,000 children in 2004–5, had been the focus of years of bad publicity, a state takeover, and nasty battles between local and state leaders. Skepticism about the district, particularly in affluent neighborhoods like the one surrounding Grant, was so high that to send one's child to Grant was to risk, among other things, being "judged" by neighbors. This was the case even though the main alternative, sending one's child to private school, cost as much as $15,000 a year.

However, all schools in Philadelphia were not equal. The school district was a highly stratified system, a stratification that mapped onto divisions of race and class in the city. As a result, even in this context of systemic failure, some elementary schools had better reputations. Among these was a group of downtown elementary schools, locally known as the "Big Three," which included Grant, Hopkins, and Fairview (all Center City school names are pseudonyms).[1] But Grant's lack of a functioning library is a reminder that even in the most successful schools resources and facilities were still below many parents' expectations. This dearth of resources fed skepticism among middle-class families about the wisdom of sending their children to a neighborhood public school.

Public Schools in Philadelphia

The second half of the twentieth century was not kind to Philadelphia's public schools. As middle-class families left the city, the student population became increasingly low-income; the tax base declined, shrinking district funding; and school failure became endemic. The inequities between city and suburbs grew as links between geography, class, race, and school quality tightened. In 1963 48 percent of Philadelphia's public school students were white. Twenty years later, district enrollment was 27 percent white, 63 percent black, 8 percent Hispanic, and 2.1 percent Asian. By 2004, white enrollment had fallen to 14 percent of the district's student population.[2] Changing demographics significantly affected the city's approach to desegregation. In the 1970s and 1980s, Philadelphia tried to use voluntary choice programs and magnet schools to comply with desegregation mandates. Due in part to white flight from the city, these strategies were only minimally successful in reducing entrenched patterns of segregation.[3] By the mid-1990s, when the low percentage of white students in the district rendered meaningful integration unattainable, the focus of desegregation litigation shifted to ameliorating chronic underachievement in racially and economically isolated schools.[4]

The school district's difficulties during this period were exacerbated by a state funding system that did little to address fiscal inequities and failed to respond to the growing cost of public education.[5] In the 2004–5 academic year, the year the CCSI was first implemented, Philadelphia's total spending per pupil was $9,299. In contrast, suburban districts around Philadelphia spent as much as $13,000 or $14,000 per pupil; one spent over $17,000.[6]

Inadequate state support for Philadelphia's schools could be attributed at least partly to politics. Political strategist James Carville has famously described Pennsylvania as "Philadelphia and Pittsburgh, with Alabama in between."[7] Whereas Philadelphia is an overwhelmingly Democratic city, the rest of the state (excluding Pittsburgh) is more conservative. The interests of Pennsylvania's urban centers often do not align with those of its rural communities, and citizens across the state tend to be unsympathetic to urban problems. In the 1990s and early 2000s, Pennsylvania devoted a smaller percentage of state funds to public education than nearly every other state in the country: whereas other states contributed, on average, 48 percent of education funding, in Pennsylvania it was only 36 percent, leaving localities to raise the rest.[8] The consequences for urban districts—faced with increased costs associated with charter schools and growth in the special needs population—were serious. Many state officials also maintained that Philadelphia's schools were poorly run and inefficient and that the "stranglehold of the public system" was one source of school failure.[9]

Population changes and declining resources meant that Philadelphia's schools had fewer resources with which to educate an ever-needier population. Meanwhile, schools in Philadelphia's suburbs, with more resources and more affluent populations, flourished, a dynamic that was repeated in metropolitan areas across the country. While each new superintendent arrived in Philadelphia with promises of reform, the results were generally disappointing.[10] For example, in the early 1990s Superintendent David Hornbeck, a minister and leader in systemic school reform, unveiled the "Children Achieving" strategy, an ambitious standards-based model that received hundreds of millions of dollars from private foundations and the federal government.[11] After engaging in repeated battles with the state legislature over funding, and leveling charges that the state's funding formula was so unequal it was evidence of racism on the part of legislators, Hornbeck resigned in 2000. His resignation effectively put an end to Children Achieving. Ragged-looking banners bearing the reform's slogan, "Tell Them We Are Rising," continued to hang on some school buildings for years to come, reminding passersby of the demise of yet another bold reform.

The situation reached a crisis point in 2001, when, in response to mounting deficits and continued low student performance, the Commonwealth of Pennsylvania prepared to take over the school district. Before doing so, the commonwealth commissioned Edison Schools, Inc., a for-profit educational management organization (EMO), to conduct an evaluation of the district. Edison's report proposed that the city's 100 lowest-performing schools, as well as most central administration functions, should be contracted out to a private provider. As educational researcher Eva Travers notes in her description of the lead-up to the takeover, "While [the report] did not actually suggest that Edison itself should be the management company to take over the schools, the implication was hard to miss."[12] The prospect of a for-profit company running Philadelphia's public schools infuriated students, parents, community groups, and some local leaders. Student and community groups took to the streets in protest, waving signs proclaiming, "Our Schools Are Not for Sale" and "EMOs Must Go!" Meanwhile, Mayor John Street negotiated feverishly with Governor Mark Schweiker to work out a compromise that repackaged the plan as a "friendly" city-state takeover.[13] This arrangement gave the mayor more control than the original proposal had over the appointment of new district leadership, eliminated the plan to turn the running of the district's central office over to Edison, and committed the state to providing the district with a one-time infusion of $75 million.

In late 2001 the state replaced the school board with a five-member School Reform Commission (SRC). Under the terms of the compromise, three members of the SRC (including the chair) were appointed by the

governor, and the remaining two members by the mayor. Members were
expected to serve four-year terms. Governor Schweiker appointed James
Nevels, a businessman from the suburbs, as chair. Nevels immediately began implementing what became known as the "diverse provider" model.[14]
In early 2002 the SRC identified forty-five of the district's lowest-performing
schools and assigned them to private providers, including Edison and
other EMOs, as well as local universities and nonprofits. Opposition to
privatization continued during this period, and Nevels and other members
of the SRC fanned out across the city, holding public meetings at each
of the schools designated for private providers. In these meetings, they
hoped to answer questions, defuse anger, and generate support for the
plan. They were not always successful. I attended many of these meetings
and watched as irate parents confronted the SRC members, most of whom
were business and civic leaders unused to these sorts of open conflicts.
At one meeting, the SRC member's efforts to provide information and
reassurance were repeatedly shouted down by angry parents. Feelings ran
so high at that meeting that a uniformed police officer eventually placed
himself between the flustered SRC member and the parents.

Paul Vallas: The Pragmatic Hero

In the summer of 2002, the newly appointed SRC hired Paul Vallas, the
former CEO of Chicago's schools, as district CEO. When Vallas assumed
office, he was hailed for his pragmatism. In a city where ideological battles
raged over the role of the private sector, Vallas was seen as motivated more
by an interest in solving problems than in advancing a particular agenda.
He explained, "I'm for what works, whether private or non-private,"
a stance that alleviated some of the prevailing tensions.[15]

Vallas canceled a plan for Edison to help manage the district's central office and embarked on an ambitious reform agenda. In the first few
years of their administration, the accomplishments of Vallas and the SRC
included balancing the district's budget, implementing a standardized curriculum, improving teacher hiring practices, opening or planning to open
many new schools, and making capital improvements to schools. After
the takeover, scores on state tests rose and public perception of district
leadership—particularly Vallas—was quite favorable.[16]

Despite Vallas's reputation as a pragmatist rather than a proponent of
privatization, under his leadership the district embraced practices drawn

from the private sector. A study of civic engagement in Philadelphia's schools in the years following the state takeover concluded that this period was characterized by a steady "marketization" of the district. Drawing on a growing body of literature, the researchers defined marketization as "a term that encompasses privatization but also speaks to the ways in which policy makers and leaders promote market principles as the solution to a variety of educational problems."[17] Marketization is also characterized by an emphasis on schools' economic purposes, such as preparing students for the workforce or ensuring that a city can compete for new businesses and residents. In the case of Philadelphia, the district's new orientation was soon visible in a top-down corporate governance structure, an embrace of school choice and charter schools, a decision to contract out key services to an unprecedented degree, and an increased emphasis on customer service and public relations. SRC chair Nevels captured this shift in an article he wrote for Forbes magazine describing his work with Philadelphia's schools: "Should a public school be run like a business? In Philadelphia, the answer is yes."[18]

Under Vallas and the SRC, the school district moved toward the creation of educational markets in the city. Charter schools—once resisted by the district as a drain on its resources—were embraced as a means of providing additional options to parents and students. The district unveiled plans for the creation of at least twenty-eight small high schools, a strategy that reduced the number of students in large comprehensive high schools and also increased school choice. As Vallas explained during a visit to Grant, he believed that more options for families would mean more participation and confidence in the schools. He used his work with high schools as an example: "I feel that if I can expand the number of quality high school choices and improve the quality of the neighborhood high schools, this will go a long way toward changing the face of the school district and increasing parent confidence."

Vallas and the SRC also embraced partnerships with external organizations as a way of bringing resources to the school district and increasing involvement with the schools. The district established partnerships with local cultural institutions to create new themed high schools (such as the Franklin Institute's Science Leadership Academy), and worked with Microsoft to build the "School of the Future," which opened in 2006. Many Philadelphians viewed this growing web of relationships in positive terms, seeing such partnerships as evidence that the district was willing to reach outside its own organizational confines to solve problems and to draw on all available resources in the process. As one local civic leader remarked, "If Paul Vallas calls you, you get the feeling that good things are going to happen."[19] A key component of the new approach to partnerships was an emphasis on connecting organizations and institutions to schools within a particular geographic area, so that schools maintained closer ties to their immediate communities and local organizations developed a sense of investment in, and responsibility for, nearby schools.

Building schools that would appeal to middle- and upper-middle-class families was an important part of Vallas's reform agenda in Chicago.[20] He made his commitment to the same goal in Philadelphia clear. A district administrator who worked closely with Vallas emphasized how important this issue was to him:

> I think [Vallas] does really care about having—he listens to a lot of parents, and he really does care about having options for middle-class families. He understands what Paul Levy says, which is, people leave because they don't have anywhere to send their kids to school. I mean, he gets that, and I do think he's a believer in sort of, urban centers, and wants to keep people in urban centers, as—don't forget, he's sort of a former budget guy. So, he gets the economics.

The commitment among district leadership to attracting and retaining more affluent families to the public schools was clearest with respect to the CCSI (see later chapters). Vallas also referred to the goal in other contexts and was seen as generally supportive of any policies or programs that would advance it. For example, he frequently tied his expansion of school choice to his interest in providing more attractive options, including magnet schools, for families who might otherwise be likely to leave the district.[21] A 2010 article in a local paper noted that Vallas, "ever the politician," had been "on a mission to keep and attract middle-class families in the district," whereas his successor, Dr. Arlene Ackerman, was far less concerned about retaining the middle class.[22]

In the 2004–5 school year, the School District of Philadelphia's student population was 65 percent black, 15 percent Hispanic, 14 percent white, and 5 percent Asian. Seventy-one percent of the students were categorized as low-income. A new administration had taken charge, and a steady stream of reforms, including significant privatization, was underway. In other words, the campaign to attract Center City families to their local public schools was going into effect in a heavily poor, heavily minority district that had experienced major upheaval.

During this time, Vallas's boundless energy and political skills, in conjunction with Nevels's "unflappability," earned them some success in improving the district's image and establishing the legitimacy of the new governance structure.[23] However, the district continued to face major challenges. Enrollment in district schools, which had been on the decline for decades, sank even lower, as more and more middle-class and low-income families, whites and families of color, moved their children from district schools to newly opened charter schools.[24] Student achievement increased, but only slowly.[25] In fall 2006, with the district facing a budget deficit of $73 million (and the prospect of even larger shortfalls in the years to come), Vallas began to lose the support of the SRC and key city leaders, who blamed him for overspending and failing to adequately monitor the district's financial situation. After months of debates about Vallas's leadership and culpability, the SRC asked for his resignation in the spring of 2007.

A Perception Problem

In 2008 a columnist with the *Philadelphia City Paper*, an alternative weekly magazine, explained her reason for moving to the suburbs:

> The problem facing this city's leaders, assuming they want to attract people other than twentysomethings and emptynesters to town, is that for parents deciding where to settle down, Philadelphia rarely even comes into consideration. Philadelphia's public schools are seen as institutions of last resort, for folks who can't afford anything else or whose kids aren't smart or lucky enough to get into [magnet schools]. . . . The perception is that Philadelphia's public schools are just bad.[26]

Her phrasing is deliberately inflammatory, but it captures an important sentiment. Like urban schools across the country, Philadelphia's schools had a poor reputation within the city. The press certainly played a role in this. Even with the positive media attention generated by Paul Vallas's ambitious reforms, press coverage during the early twenty-first century was disproportionately focused on low test scores, school violence, and continued financial struggles. An *Inquirer* story from 2003 is typical.

Noting that Vallas had "instilled hope," the article went on to ask, "Will it work? Will test scores improve in a city where more than half of the students lack basic skills? Will the district climb out of the hole that landed it under state control and in a reluctant partnership with for-profit education companies?"[27] This sentiment—that schools were out of control and academically inadequate, that any progress was fragile, and that continued crises were to be expected—meant that many Philadelphia parents were reluctant to use the public schools.

In interviews conducted in 2005 with parents and civic leaders involved with the CCSI, I asked how the school district was perceived. I also solicited opinions about the relationship between the district's reputation and the effort to market schools to Center City professionals. The respondents identified a number of reasons parents hesitated to send their children to their local public school. These ranged from concerns about violence and uninspired curriculum to an aversion to the physical appearance of school facilities to a general sense that the Philadelphia public schools were just "not good enough." Consider the following comments from a high-level district staffer, a white woman, who was discussing the likelihood that her peers (young parents in Center City) would use even relatively well-regarded Philadelphia elementary schools:

> The people who I know who live in Center City, yeah, there are some people that move out [to the suburbs] because they can't afford to have two kids, live in the city, and go to private school. But they wouldn't send their kids to public school in Philadelphia in five years and probably not in ten years. So, for a lot of those people it's the difference between [local independent school] and moving to Lower Merion [nearby affluent suburb]. And I don't care how good [Center City public school] is, it's not going to be Lower Merion in five or ten years. Even if it's there academically, from a perception perspective, it's not going to be there. And there are some people, and nobody's willing to talk about this, but there are some people who aren't convinced that if they send their kids to a school with a lot of diversity that their kid's going to get the same education. I mean, there's lots of racial bias in this.

While expressing frustration with white parents who were reluctant to send their children to schools with large numbers of students of color, this respondent later acknowledged her own hesitation about using a Philadelphia public school for her two young children, for fear it would be unfair to them.

I mean, I'm the most likely person, profile of a person to do it. I'm staying in the city, I work for the district, and I highly doubt that in five years I would send my child to public school. It's this personal thing and I have this conversation all the time with friends of mine who are parents. It's like, okay, I'm willing to dedicate my entire life to this sort of experiment, but I'm not going to screw up my kid's education as part of this experiment. It's just not fair.

The comments of this staffer—and parent—capture the views of many in Philadelphia. There was a widespread perception that sending a child to one of the city's public schools would not be "fair" to the child because the schools could not be counted on to provide a high-quality educational experience.

As noted earlier, in 2004–5 71 percent of students in the School District of Philadelphia were categorized as low-income. To the parents I interviewed, this was worrisome. They believed schools serving overwhelmingly poor student populations were inherently troubled. Here is a middle-class Asian American mother (whose children attended Grant Elementary) describing her concerns about many Philadelphia schools: "But sometimes, unfortunately, in poor neighborhoods, the teachers don't care as much. Because the majority of the kids come from broken families. They're just sending their kids [to school] to get them out of the parents' hair so that parents can go to work or something." While there is no evidence that parents or teachers in low-income schools "don't care," empirical research on school composition generally confirms the assumption that disproportionately low-income schools are less effective than those with a critical mass of middle-income students.[28]

Parents were also put off by the undeniable shabbiness of Philadelphia's school buildings. Many of these were grand and old, but years of budget shortfalls had reduced maintenance to minimum levels. Heating and cooling systems often functioned sporadically, hallways and lunchrooms were dimly lit and shabby, and the paint on many walls, doorways, and window frames was peeling. Moreover, to prevent theft, metal grating covered the windows of all Philadelphia public schools. This hardly inspired confidence among prospective parents. As one prominent lawyer involved with the CCSI observed, many parents look at "this old rundown school, with graffiti on it, with grates on the windows, and a playground that's falling apart and say to [themselves], 'I don't know what's going on there. I don't care what's going on there. I can't get past what this place looks like!'" Even schools like Grant, that were relatively well regarded, were still encumbered by metal grating and unwelcoming entrances—an issue that, as we will see in chapter 4, the CCSI tried to address.

Philadelphia public schools were also perceived as plagued by high levels of violence. The 1999–2000 school year, for example, was marked by two high-profile events, the shooting of an administrator at a high school and a sexual assault in a middle-school hallway. Shortly after Vallas and the SRC assumed control of the district, they implemented a "zero-tolerance" policy, which included strong penalties for a number of infractions, including the possession of a firearm and the sale of drugs. Nevertheless, violence continued to be a problem. In 2006 a study of youth violence in Philadelphia sounded the alarm again, showing that the number of assaults in the public schools was rising steadily.[29] The vast majority of serious incidents occurred in schools serving overwhelmingly low-income student populations—schools to which most parents in Center City would never consider sending their children. Still, such events were frequent and glaring reminders of the challenges the district faced in maintaining order and ensuring safety.

Some Center City residents, particularly older, more established professionals, avoided these problems by sending their children to independent schools.[30] A city with Quaker origins, Philadelphia is dotted with "Friends" schools and has a vibrant independent school scene. In addition, many middle- and working-class families had a tradition of sending their children to parochial schools, partly because of their allegiance to the Catholic Church, but also as a way of avoiding the stigmatized public schools. Private-school attendance in the downtown area was quite high in the early 2000s, particularly compared to levels in the rest of the city. In Philadelphia as a whole, 23 percent of K-12 students attended private school in 2000. In contrast, in many census tracts in Center City, including the one where Grant was located, this was above 70 percent.[31] Even in the "expanded" Center City region (the gentrifying areas to the north and south of downtown where incomes were lower than in Center City proper), private-school attendance was above 40 percent in many neighborhoods. Other Center City families sent their children to one of the two or three charter schools with good reputations.[32] The rest chose to move to the suburbs in time for their children to enroll in one of the highly regarded suburban public schools.

Center City parents' practice of avoiding the local public schools saddened one white upper-middle-class mother I interviewed. In reflecting upon how few families from her neighborhood used Grant Elementary,

Judy, whose daughter was in kindergarten, said, with a frustrated look on her face,

> I was thinking about it, and out of all the moms and children that I've met since Lydia was born, say 100 children that she's friendly with—from synagogue, from the neighborhood, from the playground, from music class, from gymnastics class, from her whole group—there's only one other family that we were friendly with that went to Grant. Everybody else went to private school . . . or moved. In this city, it's private school or move out of the city.

The CCD was particularly concerned about parents like those in Judy's social circle. But skepticism about Philadelphia's public schools was not confined to the middle or upper-middle class. The rise of charter schools during this period is one indicator that parents without the means to use private schools or move to the suburbs also were seeking other options. In fact, many charter schools were founded by community organizations in low-income neighborhoods, where residents and community leaders were frustrated by the schools' continued failure.

Stratification in Philadelphia's Public Schools

Like all urban school systems, the School District of Philadelphia included both high- and low-performing schools. Take the high schools, for example. While the majority of the neighborhood comprehensive high schools had abysmally low student achievement and graduation rates and served overwhelmingly low-income populations, Julia R. Masterman Laboratory and Demonstration School (known locally as Masterman), the district's highest-ranked academic magnet, was consistently listed as one of the nation's best high schools.[33] Forty-eight percent of Masterman's students were white in 2004–5, 30 percent were African American, 15 percent were Asian, and 7 percent were Latino. Only 12 percent of Masterman's student body received free or reduced-price lunch. Though not quite as extreme, significant variation in percentages of low-income students, racial composition, and student achievement rates existed at the elementary school level as well.

Most of Philadelphia's schools were highly segregated along racial lines. In the 2003–4 school year, 109 of the city's 259 public schools were so segregated that 90 percent or more of the students came from a particular racial background. Of these highly segregated schools, 107 were over 90 percent African American.[34] Though test scores in most Philadelphia schools rose between 2002 and 2004, racial achievement gaps remained steady, with African American and Latino students scoring well behind Asians and whites. Schools where at least 10 percent of the student population was white were more likely to offer four or more advanced placement classes, to have more than half of the students achieve a score of proficient or higher on the state exams, and to have more than a handful of students identified as "gifted."

These differences were intertwined with issues of teacher quality. A 2005 report produced by Research for Action, a local educational research organization, found that teacher qualification and experience varied widely across the system. Philadelphia has long had a highly centralized system of teacher hiring, in which teachers with seniority have the first pick of available positions. The result, not surprisingly, was that more experienced teachers sought openings in schools with lower numbers of poor children, leaving the spots in the high-poverty schools for new teachers.[35] Not only were high-poverty schools disproportionately staffed by new teachers, once those teachers were in the system for a few years (and presumably had gained the knowledge of the curriculum and classroom management skills they needed to be successful), they generally moved to lower-poverty schools, leaving their positions to be filled by other new, inexperienced teachers.[36] As teachers accrued seniority, they often sought positions at one of the highly regarded schools in Center City.

The Big Three

Within this context of stratification and segregation, a few elementary schools stood out. They were not the only "good" schools in Philadelphia—there were some well-regarded elementary schools in West Philadelphia, for example, near the University of Pennsylvania's campus—but they had a citywide reputation. Grant, Hopkins, and Fairview (the Big Three schools) were all located in Center City and had, at least since the 1970s, been considered Philadelphia's top elementary schools and the ones most likely to appeal to middle-class families. In an overwhelmingly poor district, where 70 percent of the students were classified as low-income, the Big Three were significantly better off: 42–46 percent of students at these schools were low-income in the 2004–5 school year. In an overwhelmingly minority district, where two-thirds of the total population was African American, these schools had larger white populations (though the percentage of African American students was still significant, ranging from 39 percent to 62 percent).

Officially, the Big Three were neighborhood schools. They all had geographic catchment areas, meaning they served particular neighborhoods and all children living in those neighborhoods were entitled to attend the schools. Yet, historically, the schools had not filled with catchment-area children, partly because of population shifts in the city and partly because the neighborhoods they served tended to be affluent enough that many families sent their children to private school. As a result, they typically had openings for students from outside their catchment areas. Beginning in the 1970s, the district attempted to reduce school segregation through the use of a voluntary transfer process that allowed students to apply to a school other than their designated neighborhood school. Under this system, parents filled out a form known as the EH-36, requesting a particular school for their child.

Using the EH-36 process, thousands of students transferred to Center City schools over the years, hoping to avoid inadequate neighborhood schools.[37] Many well-connected city employees and elected officials also sent their children to one of the Big Three. According to a local education reform newspaper, for fall 2003 enrollment there were 1,553 requests for admissions to Grant, Hopkins, and Fairview, and only 60 acceptances. While these figures likely overstate the odds the applicants faced, they do provide a general sense of the schools' desirability among families in neighborhoods outside Center City.[38] In the 2005–6 school year, for example, only 33 percent of students in the Big Three elementary schools came from the schools' neighborhood catchment areas.[39]

Some examples from Grant Elementary help illustrate how important both school reputation and transfer opportunities were to families living in Philadelphia's low-income neighborhoods. As one of the Big Three, Grant received large numbers of transfer students, nearly 50 percent of its population in 2005.[40] Parents who transferred their children to Grant from low-income neighborhoods outside of Center City were forthright about their desire to provide their children with a better education. Rhonda, an African American mother living in West Philadelphia who worked as a mid-level manager in Center City, explained to me that she "went to the schools in [her] area, but wasn't really happy with them." Then she learned of the Big Three schools in Center City and thought they would be a better option. She toured all the schools and eventually chose Grant because she liked its diverse student population:

> Grant really to me represented more what I wanted my children to experience ... which is really having a lot of day-to-day interaction with children from other cultures. I didn't want them in a predominantly [white] situation, I don't want them predominantly in the black situation, I just wanted them to have a good mixture of different cultures. So, Grant was a good place to do that.

Rhonda's West Philadelphia neighborhood was predominantly African American, poor, and working class. Eighty-two percent of the students at William B. Mann, her neighborhood school, were low-income in 2003, and all but fourteen of the 593 students were African American—hardly the diversity she was looking for. Mann's student-achievement levels were much lower than Grant's. In the same year, 76 percent of Grant's fifth-graders scored "Advanced" or "Proficient" on the state math test; only 17 percent of Mann students did. The scores for reading were, respectively, 47 percent and 17 percent.[41] Thus, by moving her children to Grant, Rhonda attained a very different educational experience for them.

Sabrina, a health-care technician, is also an African American mother from West Philadelphia. Her children were slated to attend a neighborhood school similar to Mann. When I asked Sabrina why she transferred her three children to Grant, she explained that her mother, who worked as a janitor at another Center City school, had told her that Grant, Hopkins, and Fairview were the "top schools" in the city. Both of these parents thus attributed their decision to use Grant to its individual characteristics and reputation, and to its membership within this group of the "really good" Center City public schools.

Under the rules of the transfer process, parents indicated on the EH-36 form the name of their designated neighborhood school as well as the name(s) of the school(s) in which they would like to enroll their children. The form could be submitted as early as November 1 of the year before the academic year in which they wanted to enroll their children. According to School District of Philadelphia Policy and Procedures section 102.2, "Transfer into other than neighborhood school (EH-36)," all decisions about transfer applications were made by the Office for School Operations, which would then inform parents about the status of their request. Siblings of currently enrolled students generally received preference.

District written policy on the transfer process was frustratingly vague. In theory, all applications went through a lottery process based upon the number of projected spots at each school. Yet there was no transparency about the lottery process itself, nor was there an official date at which parents were to be notified of the results. At some point in the spring, parents received a letter informing them of the status of their request. But savvy parents quickly learned that a rejection from the district was not definitive. An additional "shadow system" was at work, which gave principals enormous discretion over school admittances. Not only could principals decide how many spots to make available to transfers, they also could choose whom to accept. The ability to "work" the enrollment system to admit the right number of students was an (unofficially) important part of a principal's skill set. Parents whose applications were rejected could visit the school and ask to meet with the principal. At that point, the principal would decide whether or not to accept the child. While the criteria for admissions were never made public, principals generally noted that they were looking for parents who would be supportive of the school.[42]

Donna, another Grant parent, described her experience with the EH-36 process and the shadow system. A middle-class African American woman, Donna lived with her husband and children in an "edgy" gentrifying neighborhood northeast of Center City. When I asked Donna why she chose to enroll her two children in kindergarten at Grant, rather than their neighborhood school, she was blunt: "I didn't want them to go to the school district school in the area that we live in—the school's a disaster!" She did not think Grant was perfect. She considered the arts programming inadequate, for example. Still, she saw the school as a significant improvement. Donna's EH-36 application was denied by the district, causing considerable stress for their family. She decided to take matters into her own hands and visit the principal at Grant over the summer.

> I spoke to her. I told her the situation. I pretty much *begged* her. I was like, "*You have to!*" And she wrote a letter [to the district], saying that, you know, she would like for the kids to come to the school . . . and then like a couple days later I got a letter saying that they were approved![43]

Getting her children into Grant, a school she considered good but not ideal, was so important to Donna that she was willing to plead with Grant's principal, a woman she had never met before. Donna's sense of desperation is an indication not only of Grant's status in the city, but also of the reality that she had no other options she judged acceptable for her children.

In the first years of the twenty-first century, the School District of Philadelphia was a struggling system, plagued by low-student achievement, persistent fiscal shortfalls, and significant policy turmoil. Its schools were often viewed as "institutions of last resort" by Philadelphians. Yet even in this context, certain schools stood out as more viable options, namely the elementary schools in Center City known as the Big Three. These, as we shall see in the next three chapters, were central to the CCSI's goals and successes. The district during the 2002–7 period (the years in which CCSI was developed and implemented) was a marketizing institution, a place where policies rooted in market logic and assumptions about education as a commodity resonated with key leaders' own philosophies. It was a place where arguments about the need to market schools and to use schools to attract and retain more-affluent citizens would find a ready ear.

CHAPTER FOUR

Revitalizing Schools

The Center City Schools Initiative

A generation ago, young professionals fled with their families to the suburbs. Philadelphia's public schools now have a historic opportunity to capitalize on a decade of positive change, to ensure the sustainability of Center City's remarkable revival and to retain a larger percentage of Philadelphia residents with college degrees.—Center City District, *Growing Smarter* (2004)

In November 2004 Grant Elementary School's Parent Teacher Organization (PTO) met, as it always did, just after the start of the school day in the school's shabby and infrequently used library. About a dozen parents (mostly mothers) sat around tables discussing fundraising, holiday gifts for teachers, and a new volunteer program. Halfway through the meeting, PTO president Sara, a petite, dark-haired white woman who lived in the affluent neighborhood surrounding the school, announced that the next agenda item was a new partnership between the Center City District (CCD) and the School District of Philadelphia. She turned to Sharon, another Cobble Square mother (introduced at the beginning of chapter 2) and asked her to explain. Sharon excitedly shared news of the CCSI, a project designed to market Grant and other downtown schools to families living in the area. Explaining that the mission was to "keep people in Center City and improve the schools," Sharon noted that the CCD was particularly interested in Grant because parents there were already marketing the school to other families in the neighborhood.

As a first step, she said, the CCD was organizing a group of architects to tour Grant along with two other schools (the Big Three described in the previous chapter). The architects would begin drawing up plans for extensive renovations that would make these schools more attractive to prospective parents. She continued, "The plan is to start with the three schools because we're the closest [to being considered viable by Center City families]. The other schools have a long way to go." Sharon asked parents to begin brainstorming about improvements that could be made to the school: "What we need is ideas. . . . Think big! Think additions to the building, central air!" While these renovations did not all materialize, the initiative did have a major impact on Grant over the next few years, bringing new resources and energy to the school and further solidifying its identity as one of the most desirable public elementary schools in Philadelphia.

Nearly a year after Sharon's announcement, I met with a CCD administrator and asked him about the origin of the initiative. I was curious to learn why the CCD decided to incorporate schools into its broader revitalization strategy. During the interview, this administrator explained that despite its years of engagement with civic and municipal affairs, the CCD had never before been involved with Philadelphia's public schools: "I am a person who spent the entire time doing this job through the nineties avoiding the public school issue. Just simply saying, 'Listen, we can go after empty-nesters. We can go after young professionals. Yes, it would be nice if the schools could be fixed, but we can live without it.' " Yet in 2004, he reported, demographic trends (a growing number of young professionals were choosing to live in downtown), new research on urban prosperity (studies had shown a link between an educated population and economic growth), and anecdotal evidence from young professional parents (who were concerned about their ability to remain in the city once their children started school) convinced him that ignoring the public schools was a mistake. The confluence of these three factors made it

> really clear that this was a very unique demographic that we had succeeded in capturing, and that all prior trends told us that we were at severe risk of losing. . . . And so you say, "If you've got all these young professionals here. Not only in their self-interests and in the self-interests of downtown employers, but in the interests of the vitality of the city . . . how do we retain that?"

Thus, the CCSI, an effort to further downtown revitalization by promoting public schools to professional families, was born.

This chapter tells the story of the initiative, from its origins with the CCD to its promotion into a partnership with the School District of Philadelphia, to its reception within Philadelphia's political field. As we have seen, Philadelphia's revival from its post–World War II decline was fragile and its school system was plagued by funding shortfalls and low student achievement. Here I describe the strategies the CCSI used to draw middle- and upper-middle-class families from Philadelphia's revitalized downtown into the schools. The initiative was an effort to "rebrand" a subset of Philadelphia's public schools to distance them from the rest of the stigmatized school district. This process was intertwined with the privileging of an already advantaged population and small group of schools. It is important to note, however, that the relationship between the CCD and the School District of Philadelphia was complex and multifaceted. The school system as an institution was not simply overcome by market principles. Rather, as this chapter shows, the partnership between the two organizations elevated market principles and altered institutional policies and practices in both subtle and obvious ways.

To understand how civic and educational leaders in Philadelphia grappled with this initiative and the tensions it raised between ensuring educational equity and retaining the middle class, I draw on interviews conducted with dozens of local civic actors about their views of the CCSI.[1] Many interviewees were concerned the initiative would exacerbate existing inequalities in the city, with some arguing that efforts to market schools to a subset of the city's population were misguided and ignored more equitable and systemic policy solutions. Yet for many others, such inequities were justified. To them, continued middle-class flight represented an existential threat to the city. Not only would an increased middle-class presence promote economic growth, but the social, cultural, and financial capital of middle-class families would catalyze widespread school improvement.

"Public Schools Can Change the Value Proposition of Downtown Living"

In spring 2004 the CCD announced "a new initiative aimed at engaging Center City business leaders and residents in an effort to market and expand the range of educational choices available to the growing population of young professionals and parents of school-age children in Center City."[2]

A CCD report, entitled *Growing Smarter: The Role of Center City's Public Schools in Enhancing the Competitiveness of Philadelphia*, was released in November of the same year. That report outlined the challenges facing the city and showcased a strategy designed to propel the downtown, and Philadelphia as a whole, forward.

First, according to Growing Smarter, Center City had become "the preferred residence for the region's young college-educated adults— future parents of the region's school children."[3] These highly educated young professionals comprised a population critical to the city's economic prospects. Second, the real estate boom in Center City and adjacent gentrifying neighborhoods, and the movement of young professionals into Center City, brought an increase in the number of young children born in Center City throughout the late 1990s and early 2000s. Third, many of Center City's professionals (about half, according to the 2000 Census) left the city once they reached age thirty-five. When the CCD surveyed young professionals about their plans, the most common reason given by people who expected to leave the city was the need for better schools.

To the CCD, these developments suggested a particular opportunity: "Public schools in Center City can capitalize on this historic convergence of demographic and real estate trends and help Philadelphia retain a significantly larger percentage of young *knowledge workers*, a group key to efforts to enhance the competitiveness and prosperity of Philadelphia." Unlike other cities with revitalizing downtowns but a scarcity of school options, the report continued, Philadelphia was fortunate in that Center City was already home to three K-8 public schools in the core area, as well as Masterman, the city's highly ranked, academic magnet secondary school. Not only were schools in place, but parents in the area were already "lobbying for change and marketing to their peers."[4] The next step was convincing young professional families, particularly those who were unable to pay for private schools and might be tempted by the suburbs, to give Center City public schools a try.

To accomplish this task, the CCD turned to a set of market strategies that had served it well as it worked to revitalize Center City throughout the 1990s and early 2000s. As noted earlier, the CCD's approach to transforming Philadelphia's downtown was well aligned with national trends in urban redevelopment. These included using a variety of incentives and amenities to lure residents and businesses to revitalizing areas, and recreating downtowns as centers of the new information and service economies. While public schools were different in many ways from such urban amenities as beautiful parks, attractive streetscapes, or posh shops, it seemed likely that the same "entrepreneurial model" that brought visitors and new residents to city neighborhoods could entice them to consider the public schools:

> But to capture highly mobile young professionals accustomed to exercising a wide range of choice in all aspects of their lives, public schools must compete on a more equal footing with the quality and customer focus of local private schools and with suburban school districts. This means embracing an entrepreneurial model in which principals are encouraged to see their primary role as attracting and retaining Center City families by delivering a high-quality educational experience.[5]

The report went on to explain how the CCD planned to improve schools' physical appearance (or "curb appeal"), enhance customer service, collaborate with the district to bring all public schools in the extended Center City area together into one new administrative unit, and give Center City residents priority in admissions to all Center City public schools.

"And So We're Quickly Viewed as a Partner"

As a private organization with no official ties to the public schools, the CCD could not accomplish these goals on its own. In order to market schools effectively and create the policy changes leaders believed would make the downtown schools attractive, the CCD needed a partner—the School District of Philadelphia. While, as noted earlier, the CCD had historically been reluctant to work with the schools, by 2004 the time seemed right for the development of a new relationship. Not only was the school district implementing ambitious reforms and improving its reputation, but district leadership seemed likely to be more receptive than previous administrations. The School Reform Commission (SRC) was chaired by James Nevels, a prominent businessman, and the district's CEO, Paul Vallas, was known to embrace market models and be concerned about middle-class flight. In an interview a CCD administrator explained, "And it just luckily really coincided with a School Reform Commission, Nevels, and Vallas, who are really willing to make significant change."[6]

Leaders at the CCD met with Vallas and other high-level district officials multiple times about the project. At these meetings, the district agreed to most, if not all, of the CCD's proposals for the scope of their relationship and the accompanying changes to district policy. The administrator continued, "When we first sat down with Vallas . . . it was 'yes' to everything, and we're going, you know, 'this can't be real!'" Specifically, the school district agreed to the partnership, created a new administrative unit (the Center City Academic Region) bringing together all schools in the broader Center City area, adjusted its admissions notification timeline to make it more competitive with independent schools, created a new transfer policy, and shared its enrollment data on students and schools with the CCD.

In the process, the CCD enjoyed excellent access to school district staff and to Vallas himself. For instance, in fall 2005 Vallas and CCD president Paul Levy appeared together before a meeting with several hundred representatives of the home construction industry. The conference, entitled "The Learning Curve," was sponsored by the local Building Industry Association, an organization that promotes residential development in the city, and was intended to bring developers up to date on Philadelphia's schools. Levy gave a speech in which he described a conversation with Vallas about the procedure the district followed to notify students of their acceptance into a specific school:

> We sat at the table with Paul and said, you know, you give parents a choice but you don't tell them until August whether they're getting in. Meanwhile, a private school requires a non-refundable deposit by March first. Like that, the policy was changed! The public school will notify parents by February fifteenth, so public schools are competitive with independent schools.

Vallas nodded decisively as Levy spoke, confirming his account. In an interview an administrator with the new Center City Academic Region similarly noted the cooperative relationship between the leaders of the CCD and the school district: "I know Mr. Vallas is very, very committed, and he's met several times, of course, with Paul Levy and also with [another administrator with the CCD]. I know they have, you know, direct access to him."

Because the majority of Philadelphia's students were poor and the majority of its schools low-performing, the school district took a political risk when it embraced the CCD's proposals to bring additional resources and attention to an already well-functioning group of schools. The reasons for taking such a risk had much to do with the power and status of the CCD.

Describing the alliance between Vallas and Levy, one district administrator involved with the early development of CCSI noted, "Paul Levy's very powerful. Paul Levy is the person who said, 'We need to do this.' Paul Vallas bought into it." The CCD's partner organization, the Central Philadelphia Development Corporation (see chapter 2), had a membership list that included hundreds of local organizations, ranging from major law and architectural firms to banks, developers, universities, and prominent nonprofits. An entity run by and for businesses, the CCD spoke with a loud voice in the city, and had a reputation for setting ambitious goals and getting them accomplished.

However, as political scientist Clarence Stone observed in his seminal work on city politics, urban political power is less a matter of "power over" and more a matter of "power to"—the power to forge coalitions among various entities to pursue specific goals.[7] In Philadelphia the CCD's power was not such that the school district automatically complied with its demands. Rather, because it was a downtown business organization, the CCD had the ability to make connections and provide incentives that were sufficiently attractive to secure the district's interest in a partnership. The leadership of the School District of Philadelphia felt it needed the CCD because of its status and because of the financial resources it could help generate.

The CCD's ability to create partnerships and achieve its policy agenda was enhanced by its members' ties across the city, including with school district leaders. For example, one prominent attorney affiliated with the CCD had worked with former-governor Tom Ridge's administration around the legislation creating the School Reform Commission. In the process, he came to know several high-ranking district administrators well. When this attorney became involved with the initiative, such relationships were invaluable. In our interview in a Center City restaurant, he told me that he spoke to one administrator "sometimes daily about all kinds of things" and would also contact "Paul" (Vallas) and his senior staff when necessary. Invoking the status of his law firm, he noted that he had "pretty good access to community leaders" and that he could "get on the phone" with most local college and university presidents "and have the call returned or speak to them right then." SRC chairman Nevels, who was an investment banker, made a point of reaching out to the business community. Daniel Whelan, a state-appointed member of the SRC and the former president of a large Philadelphia corporation, also had close ties to local business leaders. As a result, when the CCD began to consider working with the public schools, it already had in place a network of relationships that allowed it to move ahead quickly.[8]

Whereas Ed Rendell, Philadelphia's mayor during the 1990s, was known for promoting Center City development, John Street, the mayor during this period, was more identified with the "neighborhoods," or the low-income areas outside of Center City. Nevertheless, the mayor's office, which had been only minimally involved with Philadelphia's schools in the years following the 2001 state takeover, also worked behind the scenes to push the CCSI forward. In an interview, an official within the mayor's cabinet observed that, because of Mayor Street's highly publicized interest in redirecting the city's development resources toward low-income neighborhoods, there were "all sorts of, you know, good political issues" that would prevent the mayor from being a visible supporter of the CCSI. She explained that the mayor's administration could not "take the lead on this" because it would be seen as counter to his citywide agenda. Nevertheless, this official, with the mayor's support, spoke with Levy early in the CCSI's lifespan and facilitated the relationship with the school district. A CCD administrator later confirmed this account, remarking that this official's "under-the-radar" efforts "smoothed the way" for the CCD's own work.

The benefits the CCD had to offer the school district helped solidify the partnership. While Vallas and the SRC had made progress in improving the district's reputation since the days of the state takeover—when its failures were local and national news—Philadelphia's schools during this time still needed to prove themselves to a skeptical audience, both locally and at the state level.[9] The CCD provided the district with important symbolic resources, lending its credibility to Vallas and the SRC. When district leaders announced the Declaration of Education (an ambitious set of goals for Philadelphia's schools), Paul Levy was a prominent supporter. Describing the early days of the initiative, before it had been formalized, a CCD administrator told of the growing relationship between the two organizations:

> So we did a lot of things for the district in the summer of last year [2004]. They were making a large public show of their Declaration of Education, and Paul Levy showed up there to publicly endorse them. He did a lot of public endorsement of the school district. And so we're quickly viewed as a partner. . . . And that was really the beginning of the evolution of the relationship.

The early stage of the initiative coincided with a round of contract negotiations with the Philadelphia Federation of Teachers, in which district leadership attempted to negotiate major concessions. In a show of support, Levy, the head of the Chamber of Commerce, and other local dignitaries stood with Vallas and SRC members at a press conference announcing the district's intentions. The district's press release describing the event included a quote from Levy supporting the proposed changes to the contract.

For the school district, the ability to lay claim to a partnership with the CCD was politically useful because business involvement in Philadelphia's schools had been fairly minimal at that time. Moreover, the development of a partnership fit with the district's own interest in pioneering public-private collaboration.[10] The significance of this relationship was clear in spring 2005, when a district administrator visited a PTO meeting at Grant to discuss the CCSI and the relationships she envisioned between the CCD, the school district, and Grant parents. At that meeting, the administrator spoke repeatedly of the myriad benefits the CCSI would bring to schools like Grant and was excited by the opportunity to partner with the CCD: "Here, the business community came to us and said we can't do this without you. This is very unusual! Usually we have to beg the business community to be involved. That the business community has come to us is awesome!" Thus, in partnering with the district in this way, the CCD helped provide legitimacy for the district's policy goals, furnished backing for a major political struggle (with the teachers' union), and lent its status to an organization still laboring to improve its own standing in the city.

Besides these symbolic and political gains, the perennially underfunded school district stood to gain material benefits from working with the CCD. Though the CCD did not contribute money to the district, it did sponsor the Center City Schools Fair (discussed in chapter 7), which allowed the district to highlight its elementary schools. It also coordinated efforts to publicize and market downtown schools, assisted individual schools with raising funds, helped secure funding from large corporations, and organized volunteers and donations from local businesses. As well, the CCD—through the publicity generated by the initiative and its own connections—helped the district form partnerships with local organizations that could bring other resources (such as curriculum support, instructional materials, new programs, and volunteers) to the schools. Finally, it provided assistance to the district on other issues, including real estate matters and strategies for "rebranding" the new location of the central administrative office to make it more appealing to staff members.[11]

Unquestionably, the CCD-district partnership brought significant advantages to both parties. But because the district was a public institution—one charged with serving all children in Philadelphia—this partnership also created challenges. People close to the CCSI expressed concern that any sign that the district was directing public resources disproportionately toward Center City would attract the ire of local activists, politicians, and community groups. Describing an early meeting with district leadership about the initiative, an administrator with the CCD acknowledged that the district's core constituency faced far greater social and economic challenges than the Center City families he was interested in. He explained, "And in some sense, what we were talking about could be seen as a diversion from their really important mission. I think, to their credit, they fully understood that they could and should pursue both." While he argued that the two goals (of ensuring equity and increasing the middle-class presence) were not mutually exclusive, he was aware that they represented a worrisome contrast. Indeed, there was some political backlash, an issue I take up later in this chapter. But despite this criticism, the campaign to attract professional families to Center City schools moved forward.

Marketing Urban Public Schools

Whereas the growing influence of market principles on the public sphere is often spoken of in fairly abstract terms, the CCSI provides an opportunity to see how the intersection between market mechanisms and a public institution actually played out "on the ground," resulting in changes to district institutional structures, policies, and practices. These included modifications to the district's administrative structure, new admissions policies, and a sophisticated marketing campaign. In describing these components, I begin with the administrative changes and then move to an analysis of the ways the CCSI tried to "rebrand" downtown public schools.

During this period, the School District of Philadelphia was divided into "regions," groups of schools within a particular geographic area. Each region was its own administrative unit: a regional superintendent was responsible for managing the schools and supervising the principals in the region. Before the CCSI, schools in the Center City area fell into several different regions. In fall 2005, as a part of the campaign to recruit Center City families into the schools, the district created the Center City Academic Region, consolidating all twenty schools in the downtown area.

In a letter to "Center City Region Stakeholders," the chief academic officer of Philadelphia's schools noted that this new region was a way for the district to "underscore its commitment to this initiative." While the CCSI's marketing focused entirely on the elementary schools, the region itself included elementary, middle, and high schools. Though some of the schools in this region, which included the Big Three Center City elementary schools, were fairly strong academically, the region also encompassed schools with high levels of poverty and lower student performance.[12] At six of the region's thirteen elementary schools, 80 percent or more of the students were classified as low-income in 2005. With the exception of two academic magnets, the five secondary schools in the new region similarly served overwhelmingly poor and minority student populations.[13]

The district's next step was more complicated (and more controversial). Prior to the CCSI, admissions to Center City elementary schools (as to all elementary schools) went first to students within the "catchment area"—meaning the neighborhood immediately surrounding the school. Any remaining available spots were then opened to other students. Using the EH-36 voluntary transfer process, students from across the city participated in a lottery to secure admission to the school of their choice. Because some of the Center City elementary schools, notably the Big Three, were considered to be better options than most Philadelphia schools, they historically attracted hundreds of applicants each year hoping to avoid their own low-performing neighborhood schools.[14] The CCSI altered this process significantly. Beginning in 2006 (and affecting admissions for the 2006–7 and 2007–8 school years), under a policy entitled the "Neighborhood Catchment Area Admissions/Transfer Policy," students within the Center City Academic Region had priority over students from other parts of the city in admissions to all Center City elementary schools, including the desirable Big Three.[15] In other words, the Center City Academic Region became a "secondary catchment area." (Students already enrolled in a school, as well as their siblings who applied to the school in the future, would not be displaced.)

Another change was less dramatic but still important, both symbolically and practically. Before the initiative, parents who hoped to transfer their children into a school outside of their catchment zone learned about the outcome of their application in late spring, and sometimes not until summer. As the CCD administrator (quoted earlier) noted, this delay created problems for parents who were choosing between public and private schools, because the private school deposits were due in February and

March. Even parents who may have preferred Grant, for example, over one of the local independent schools would have to "play it safe" and put down their deposits, often several hundred dollars. By the time word came from the district that their children had been accepted to Grant, it would be too late—parents were already committed to the private school. To alter this pattern, the district moved up its notification date, informing parents by mail in mid-February whether or not their children had been accepted to their school of choice.

Besides the organizational restructuring involved in creating a new academic region and changing admissions policies, the other components of the initiative were largely marketing strategies designed to raise the profile and appeal of Center City elementary schools. These were the province of the CCD. First, the CCD launched a marketing campaign (a new website, fliers, postcards, newsletters, and public events) to inform downtown parents about their educational options. In October 2005 it sponsored the Center City Schools Fair, held in the city's convention center to showcase the area's public, private, and charter schools. Over a thousand parents attended the event and, according to the CCD, attendance at school open houses increased dramatically following the fair.[16]

Second, the CCD took on the task of improving the "first impressions" the schools made on parents. Describing these efforts as enhancing "curb appeal," the CCD planned both minor improvements to landscaping and playgrounds and more significant renovations to school buildings. As noted earlier, the CCD sponsored a tour of the Big Three elementary schools for local architects; these architects then volunteered their time to design plans for improvements to the buildings.[17] The CCD also worked with parents to raise funds for other improvements to the schools' infrastructures, such as the "cybrary" (a high-tech multimedia library) that was eventually installed at Grant.

Noting the contrast between public and private schools in this realm, the CCSI strove to make the schools more "customer friendly." The new CCD-sponsored website was one way of accomplishing this, because it made it easier for parents interested in particular schools to access information. A CCD staffer was also instrumental here, serving as a liaison between parents and the district. This staffer, a friendly woman with a professional demeanor, had experience in both education and business. She distributed her phone number to parents, helped plan fundraisers and other events, answered questions about district policies, and passed along parents' concerns to district officials.

The CCD and the district leaders further communicated to school administrators the importance of treating parents as valued customers and attracting and retaining Center City parents. This was a change. Historically treatment of parents by district employees varied widely, with some educators and administrators embracing parents and others treating them with disregard or barely veiled hostility. As a frequent visitor to Philadelphia schools, I had often had the experience of standing in a school's reception area, waiting uncomfortably for one of the secretaries to notice me and then flinching inwardly at her unfriendly greeting.[18] Principals were often similarly unwelcoming. In an interview conducted in the office of the new Center City Academic Region, an administrator explained her expectations regarding principals' treatment of parents. She smiled as she spoke, but her tone was forceful:

> They have to be warm and inviting. They have to be able to reach out, you know, forge partnerships. And, if that's going to happen, in our schools, the principal has to be the one to make that happen. They have to model the behaviors that, you know, we expect in others. How do you make people feel special? And that's something that I would expect from every principal in our region.

In a meeting before the beginning of the school year, this administrator informed all downtown principals that they should focus on attracting Center City families. Her directive was later applauded by the CCD as a "big, important message!"

Noting that she attempted to model excellent customer service for her principals, this regional administrator said she was quick to give out her email address to parents and that, in her new position, she received more emails from parents than she had in her past position in a much poorer part of the city. This approach was evident when, in spring 2005, she met with the Grant PTO to discuss the parents' role in selecting a new principal for the school (see chapter 5). At this meeting, she emphasized her willingness to work with parents throughout the process, reminding them several times that she would be "at their beck and call." Thus, principals in the new Center City Academic Region were expected to be more than instructional leaders: like this administrator, they had to "sell" their school to professional parents and provide them with exemplary customer service.

The initiative also involved the cultivation of "institutional partners," relationships with local organizations and institutions that brought resources and opportunities to the schools and complemented each school's "signature" (the unique identity the district and CCD were trying to create for every school in the new region). This kind of partnering was a particularly important piece of the initiative because Center City is home to such a rich array of museums, cultural organizations, and businesses. For example, Center City schools could partner with a local science museum to enhance science programming or with a theater around arts instruction. Partnerships with local businesses could also "help underwrite some of the curricular development" involved with creating more attractive schools. In an interview, an administrator with the new region told me that pursuing these partnerships was an important part of her job, because they were a way of bringing resources to schools and helping schools to be more effective.

A parent navigating the CCSI website could—and still can as of this writing—visit each school's page and, for many of the schools, see an impressive list of partners, ranging from local theaters and art museums to corporations and nonprofit organizations.[19] For example, the page for Hopkins Elementary, one of the Big Three and also one of the highest-performing elementary schools in the city, lists nineteen partners, including several theatrical organizations, a university museum, and a local college of art. Not only does Hopkins's long list imply additional resources and opportunities for students, it also signals to parents that the school is a place where interesting people and organizations are making exciting things happen.

Rebranding Center City Schools

Many Philadelphia public schools had websites in 2005. For the most part, these were idiosyncratic and amateurish, generally created by a tech-savvy parent or school staffer, and updated infrequently. Some had pictures of the school and students, while others had generic images (e.g., a pencil, an apple, an open book). They had little information, and links often did not work. In contrast, the schools targeted by the CCSI had professionally designed websites, uniform in appearance and linked to the Center City Schools homepage.[20] They were designed to provide parents with a "customer-friendly virtual front door," a first introduction to a special kind of public school. Such distinctive websites were emblematic of the CCD's goal of creating a new "brand" for the Center City schools, one that distanced them from the district and emphasized their membership within a more elite group.

The target audience for this rebranding was middle- and upper-middle-class parents in the expanded Center City area, residents who needed to be convinced that Center City schools were competitive with their other options, including private or suburban schools. When a CCD administrator compared the visual appeal of public and private schools, he had these parents in mind:

> And you walk into [certain select private schools] and it's like, "Wow! This place is alive! I want to go here." Right? Walk into some public schools and your heart sinks. . . . The landscaping around Grant is dead. I mean, wake up, the building has got to be alive. It's got to be vibrant! The parents have got to feel, "I want to take my child in here!"

He did not want flowers around the school merely because they created a more positive environment for the students; instead, flowers would make the school appealing to discriminating adults and, hence, better able to compete with private schools for such families.

Flowers also mattered for what they symbolized, which was the development of a new identity for the Center City schools. In her study of urban lifestyle magazines, sociologist Miriam Greenberg argues that a city is "produced not only materially and geographically but also in the social imagination and through changing modes of cultural representation."[21] She describes how civic and business leaders strive to create new or altered images of their cities ("urban imaginaries," in her words) to make them more appealing to potential residents, visitors, or businesses. Though it targeted a set of schools rather than an entire city, the same processes—of using subtle and not-so-subtle representations to create a new identity—are evident in the CCSI's strategies for marketing Center City public schools.

A first, critical step in this process was the development of institutional distance from the rest of the school district. The distinctiveness of downtown schools had to be more than just an impression. It had to be written into the very structure of the district. As a CCD administrator explained to me, this was behind the CCD's request that the district alter its organizational structure to create a region of schools that would "think differently," provide exemplary customer service, and have distinctive signatures and a "system of school choice."

The CCSI further developed the new identity of its schools by creating symbolic distance from the rest of the district. This "rebranding" (in the words of a CCD administrator) would shift their identity from "School District of Philadelphia" to "Center City" schools. As Greenberg notes, branding as a marketing strategy deliberately creates connections, operating on emotional and subconscious levels, between the goods being marketed and broader conceptions of lifestyle and identity.[22] In this case, the branding of the Center City schools was an effort to reshape the ways customers (meaning parents) understood the schools and to change the images they associated with them. The goal was to replace an inner-city identity with one based on the schools' location in the affluent downtown area.

As a subgroup with a distinct identity, Center City schools were to operate differently from the rest of Philadelphia's "inner-city" schools. Parents from Center City were to be treated as valued customers, both during the choice process and after they had enrolled their children. CCD and school district staff repeated this emphasis on parents as customers often during the course of my research, noting in many cases what a major paradigm shift it was for the district. Thus one CCD administrator observed, describing experiences with the School District of Philadelphia years ago, the district had long been "a public school bureaucracy that simply was not customer focused." The CCD made the special treatment for downtown parents clear when it advertised the shift in the admissions policy on its website, in publications, and at public events. According to one school administrator, parents were very aware of this difference: "I feel that the message out there to parents is that if you live within the Center City district, you'll get preferential treatments to which school you choose to go to. I think that message has been clear. Parents really are jumping on that."

The very existence of a CCD administrator whose job it was to work with these parents was evidence of the enhanced service they would receive. This was apparent in early 2005 at a meeting of Grant's PTO, when about ten parents gathered in the library and discussed issues ranging from volunteering in the lunchroom to bullying. Toward the end of this meeting, George, a white, dark-haired Cobble Square father, dressed in a conservative sweater and khaki pants, spoke up. He referenced the new Center City schools website and the CCD's interest in "giving Center City people more options." George described a conversation he had had with a CCD administrator who had asked for his thoughts about a proposal from the district to make changes to a prestigious magnet high school. While the other parents listened attentively, George explained that not only did this administrator hope parents would communicate with her ("she would like to hear from us!"), she also suggested they email their opinions directly to CEO Vallas. And, he said, she had made it clear she was willing to use her leverage and contacts to make sure parents' views were heard: "She knows key people. If people are upset, she'll talk to Vallas." Smiling with satisfaction, he concluded that she must have been sincere when she said she wanted to hear from him, because she gave him both her work and home phone numbers. Several other parents smiled as well, nodding their agreement. Thus, in contrast to the school district, which was widely perceived as a cumbersome and uncaring bureaucracy that had little interest in parents' concerns or opinions, the Center City Academic Region was a place where downtown parents could count on superior treatment.

The CCD administrator's practice of handing out her phone numbers, asking for feedback, and promising to pass it along to Paul Vallas was more than just a matter of customer service. An example of the ways the CCSI altered institutional policies and practices, it signaled recognition (on the part of the CCD and school district) of middle- and upper-middle-class parents as customers whose status entitled them to special privileges and access to top district leaders. It is also evidence of the development, within a district that served tens of thousands of families, of privileged channels of contact between Center City parents and district leadership, channels that parents used to great effect (see chapter 6).

The plan to create a signature for each school was another example of the larger effort to generate symbolic distance between downtown schools and the rest of the district. A school's signature was a characteristic or emphasis that would identify it as unique. For example, because of its diverse student population, Grant could be known as an "international" school, while another downtown elementary school might focus on the arts, and still others on math or science. In contrast to an all-school theme, which would entail a much more intensive and programmatic focus, the development of signatures was largely a marketing strategy. According to district and CCD staff, signatures would make the schools "distinctive," giving the CCD's marketing efforts something to "showcase." This would help "foster choice and product differentiation among downtown schools."[23] By creating unique signatures at each school, the CCSI also enhanced the perception that these schools were different from other neighborhood schools. After all, schools in the rest of the district did not have signatures.

Funding the Initiative

The CCSI was funded largely by two grants, both awarded in 2005. The first was from the Pennsylvania Department of Education for a total of $250,000. The application prepared for this state grant lists the school district as the recipient but notes that the bulk of the funds ($243,000) would go to the CCD for contracted services involving "promotion/public relations/advertising/ [and] enrichment."[24] The second grant, for $350,000, was from the William Penn Foundation, one of Philadelphia's largest philanthropies. The CCSI project was evaluated as part of a larger application to William Penn from the CCD (for $1,250,000) to underwrite a set of initiatives that included improvements to a major parkway, the regional transportation system, and the Delaware waterfront. Taken together, these initiatives would "lay the groundwork for future investments in the downtown and ultimately help create a quality of life that will strengthen Center City as a competitive place to live, work and visit."[25] The funds from the state and the William Penn Foundation paid for the salary of a CCD administrator charged with coordinating the initiative, contracts with architectural consultants, the school fair, and the marketing campaign. The CCD donated its services to support the marketing effort, manage staff, and run the website.

While the CCD was the force behind the initiative, the school district also invested significant resources in the partnership. Not only did the district dedicate an entire staff to the newly created academic region, but Vallas personally hired a consultant (a Center City parent) to spread the word about the CCSI in the downtown community, solicit corporate partners for Center City schools, and plan special events related to the initiative.[26] According to a CCD administrator, the district's investment in the project ran to hundreds of thousands of dollars. Additionally, the administrator chosen to serve as superintendent of the new Center City Academic Region, who had previously held the same position in a much poorer part of the city, was experienced and highly qualified. Her reputation within the district for competence and discretion was excellent, which made her an appealing choice for the new region, particularly because the position would be high profile and would involve navigating tricky political terrain. Speaking positively of the new superintendent, another district insider observed, "And part of the reason why they gave her that job is that it's so tough and they know she can do it." Unlike the costs associated with hiring a consultant, assigning this superintendent to the Center City Academic Region may not have resulted in additional expenses to the district. However, given her positive reputation, the transfer was a way of redistributing resources to benefit the new region.

Benefits and Beneficiaries of the CCSI

The money spent on Center City schools was a worthwhile investment, the district and the CCD argued, because keeping professional families in the city and involving them in the public schools would benefit Philadelphia *as a whole*. In their application to the state for $250,000, the CCD and the School District of Philadelphia asserted, "The number of people that may ultimately be served by this project is unlimited, as this project will help enhance and sustain the economic base in Center City by maintaining and enriching the residential population, which in turn will help the economic base of Philadelphia." The school district made similar claims in its own documents, noting that Philadelphia as a whole would prosper economically when more downtown families were recruited into the schools. For example, a letter from the school district to "Center City Region Stakeholders" used language very similar to that of CCD brochures: it began by noting Center City's "amazing renaissance," spoke of the importance of retaining downtown residents, and concluded that the CCSI would benefit all Philadelphians.[27]

The CCD also envisioned educational gains from the initiative, claiming in Growing Smarter that it would "expand the base of involved, pro-education parents committed to further improvements in all Philadelphia's public schools." In an interview, an administrator with the CCD explained this reasoning further. Noting that the vast majority of children in Philadelphia's public schools came from low-income families, he continued, "And there is no public bureaucracy that can really pursue quality if all its constituents in that system are people who have no other choice. I mean, how you hold the system accountable, is people with choice exercise influence." In other words, not only would the infusion of middle-class families lead to a more prosperous city, it would also help create a better school system.

"Should They Get Preferential Treatment?" The Politics of the CCSI

The claims of the district and the CCD are compelling, but they overlook a central point: the *marketing* of Center City public schools was deeply intertwined with the *privileging* of Center City communities and schools. The ways in which this happened are discussed at length in chapters 5, 6, and 7. Here, however, it is useful to inventory the equity issues raised by the CCSI.[28]

In a city struggling with the legacies of postindustrialization, including the economic devastation of many of its neighborhoods, the CCSI targeted an already revitalized area. In a city with large numbers of poor residents, it targeted middle- and upper-middle-class families for special treatment and privileges. In a system with insufficient resources, the initiative channeled additional resources and attention into historically high-performing schools. In a system with thousands of students stuck in failing schools, the initiative made it more difficult for students from outside Center City to attain access to well-regarded downtown schools. Taken together, these aspects of the CCSI suggested to many Philadelphians that it contributed to the stratification of public education in the city. Below, I draw on data from interviews with local civic and educational leaders to examine both critical and supportive views of the CCSI. (The policy was also hotly contested within the school district's central office. I discuss this contention and the impact on the initiative's "life course" in chapter 7.)

The perspectives considered here demonstrate that how a problem is framed shapes, both directly and indirectly, the solutions that are proposed. They further show that notions of the "greater good" that policy solutions could pursue are highly variable. For critics of the CCSI, Philadelphia's educational problems were tied to larger inequalities. Any effort to solve those problems that could create new stratification was inherently misguided. In contrast, supporters of the initiative saw middle-class flight as the key problem. To them, reversing that dynamic would be better for everyone.

"We're Creating the Haves and the Have-Nots"

Opposition to the initiative tended to focus on changes in the transfer policy that made it more difficult for students from outside Center City to enroll in high-performing elementary schools within the region. Nearly everyone interviewed, including those who were generally supportive, expressed some concern about restricting access to Center City schools for students from other parts of the city. The issue was consistently raised in newspaper coverage, meetings, and other public events and conversations related to the CCSI, with the potential for inequity most often understood in terms of the possibility that spots at Center City schools would be reserved for more advantaged students.

Accordingly, many local civic actors criticized the initiative because it seemed unfair to disadvantaged students. According to one leader of a citywide parent organization, "And what's happening, again, is we're creating the haves and the have-nots." In a letter to a local newspaper, a member of Philadelphia's City Council called the preference for Center City parents a "setback for school choice [that] should alarm city families seeking access to Center City's most sought-after schools." Noting the large number of students in Center City schools who transfer from other parts of the city, she continued:

> Getting Philadelphia's children from worse-off regions into those desirable schools just got that much harder. What is left for those children who can't get by the new admission priorities? They risk being stuck at the bottom end of Philadelphia's unequally performing district. In spite of the district's welcome efforts to equalize educational opportunities, the city's schools are hardly on an equal playing field. . . . Given these realities, it's clear that poorer families with fewer resources now face fewer choices.[29]

To these critics, the initiative was problematic because it would limit access for students most in need of high-quality educational options, thus interfering with what they saw as education's primary purpose: providing all students with equal opportunity.

Whereas the student population in most Philadelphia schools was overwhelmingly African American or Latino, the Center City schools, especially the Big Three, attracted significant numbers of white students. These schools were often seen as beacons of racial integration in an otherwise segregated district. Opponents of the CCSI argued that the initiative could undermine this diversity. In meetings with the district, local education advocates warned that because Center City had so few black residents, the new region could become predominantly white if minority students from other parts of the city were denied access to the school. Fears of resegregation prompted one community organizer to call the transfer policy "racist and classist," while an African American educator, describing conversations he had had about the initiative, observed with disgust, "Most people think it is the most racist, most ill-conceived notion!"

To many critics, particularly education and community activists, the initiative was problematic for another reason as well: it ran counter to their belief that positive change begins with a collective approach to social problems. Noting that the transfer policy allowed parents in gentrifying areas around Center City to move their children out of the lower-performing schools in their neighborhoods and into the Big Three elementary schools, one education advocate remarked laughingly, "That's not my vision of how people come to recognize we're all in the same boat together!" He continued:

> We've got to do better at making sure that there are opportunities all through the system. And what's disturbing, I guess, about this is it's always squeaky wheels that get the grease. It's those people who . . . put the energy into fixing something up, that they get something back for that energy. But [what] you would like to see them get back is that *everything* gets fixed up, or a lot, and they're included. But if they're the only ones that get the stuff, it's not healthy.

He noted the possibility that rather than leading to improvement for all, middle-class involvement could result in the channeling of even more resources to middle-class children, positioning them as "the only ones that get the stuff." The parent leader quoted earlier also spoke passionately about this issue: "Any child in the city that's not getting the services, it impacts on every child in the city. And when we create the haves and have-nots, again, it doesn't matter what race, religion, part of the city they live in, we're doing a disservice to all of our citizens and our children." To this parent, inequality mattered both because it was unjust and because, ultimately, it harmed everyone.

Critics of the CCSI often placed the government at the center of their vision for a more equitable solution to educational problems. For example, in an interview, a journalist with an alternative newspaper identified resolving the inequities in state educational funding as the first step in tackling Philadelphia's challenges:

> I think obviously the long-term solution is more funding across the board. You don't have to be depending on outside donors for stuff that middle-class parents, or any parents, would see as basics. But—if what we're saying is that our schools don't appeal to middle-class parents because they don't meet basic standards and [through] the funding of a business partner, we're going to get three of our schools, or twenty of our schools up to basic standards, I don't know how you can—I mean, it seems like an unacceptable strategy on its own.

He criticized the idea of a two-tiered system in which only some schools are "good enough" for middle-class children and envisioned a more universal improvement strategy. Given their interest in treating all students equally, these critics saw the school district—rather than individual parents or a private organization—as the only entity with both the responsibility and the capacity to ensure school quality and equity for all citizens. They further implied that policies that take the onus for providing these things away from the school district will inevitably have inequitable outcomes. These criticisms offer an important counternarrative to the assumptions underlying the CCSI about the efficacy of market strategies and the "trickle-down" of economic and educational benefits. Yet viewpoints such as these were largely overshadowed by the consensus within the city about the danger of continued middle-class flight.

Keep the Middle Class!

The concerns many Philadelphians felt about ongoing middle-class flight (see chapter 2) shaped their responses to the CCSI. The need to retain the middle class was treated as an obvious "fact" that needed no real explanation beyond an occasional reference to the Philadelphia of the 1970s and '80s, a time when the city seemed likely to collapse under the weight of massive job and population loss. This powerful discourse highlights the slipperiness of the term "middle class." The CCSI explicitly targeted "knowledge workers," and, as discussed in chapter 2, many of the families in Center City would be more accurately labeled upper-middle-class. Yet supporters of the initiative invariably treated it as a way of preventing *middle-class* flight.

Many shared the enthusiasm expressed by a business leader and former state official during an interview in his downtown office. Describing the CCSI, he exclaimed, "I think it's brilliant! . . . For Center City to thrive well into the future, the middle class there has to feel like these schools and these classrooms are ample and attractive and staffed by the right people—you'll really help repopulate the city!" In praising the initiative, he linked the presence of middle-class families with Center City's economic future and then with a "repopulation" of the entire city. Though he did not say so explicitly, his comments (and others discussed here) implied that the size of the city's population was less important than its class character. When he said "repopulate the city," he meant with middle-class residents.

Concern about middle-class flight was so powerful that even those school district officials and representatives of advocacy groups who worried about the CCSI's implications for educational equity reiterated the importance of keeping middle-class families in the city. In these interviews, respondents often prefaced their critique of the initiative with a nod to the problem of middle-class flight. For example, one district official's initial response to the CCSI was positive:

> When I first learned of it, just the concept, I thought it was a good idea to help retain the middle class in Philadelphia. . . . And I get, this is difficult for me, because . . . I get the whole choice aspect and to be able to throw public schools into the choice for middle-class, Center City parents, I think is a big thing.

Though this administrator later expressed skepticism, it was tempered by her belief that the city really did need to retain middle-income families. A long-time education activist responded to a question about the initiative with a sigh, observing, "This used to be so much easier when I was so sure of everything!" She went on to explain that an increased middle-class presence would be better for the city and the schools, even though the consequences for other students worried her. Whereas she might have, in the past, opposed the initiative on equity grounds, she was unwilling to take such a stance now because of her concern about the exodus of middle-class families.

A city official, also wary of the equity issues raised by the initiative, explained his support by pointing to the contributions middle-class families make to the city. He described the middle class as the "glue that keeps the city together . . . the real folks that are going out there and they're spending money in restaurants and keeping neighborhoods alive and vibrant." His comments position middle-class families as playing important social functions—they provide social solidarity, "the glue" that holds communities together, and make neighborhoods feel vital. In making this point, he further distinguished between members of the middle class and wealthier residents. In his view the latter do not count as "real folks," nor do they contribute to neighborhood vitality. Indeed, he noted that a city divided between the "richest of the rich in a brand new condominium and the poorest of the poor" would be dysfunctional. Thus, the middle class not only contributes to economic stability, it also keeps the city vital and "real."

An educator active in local politics and community affairs similarly linked the presence of middle-class families to the economic health of the city. He was supportive of the CCSI precisely because it would help retain this important constituency.

> I think you have to be able to retain middle-class, tax-paying people, if you can. That's the story of Philadelphia, that it's lost all those people for fifty years, so, I can't help but think it's generally a good thing, if you can retain more young families. The kids grow up here and feel a connection to the place, the parents keep living here and maybe working here, paying taxes here.

This educator pointed to Philadelphia's recent history of decline to argue in favor of measures designed to keep the middle class. In addition, like many others I interviewed and much of the local media coverage on the issue, he emphasized the important contributions the middle class made to the city's tax base.

Recruiting middle-class parents into the city's schools would also, many argued, catalyze widespread school improvement, because middle-class parents would be more effective voices for school improvement than the low-income parents traditionally served by the district. In essence, these supporters agreed with the CCD that large bureaucracies improve only when individuals and groups being served by the system place pressure on it around their (or their children's) needs. They felt that because urban school systems have historically served a low-income, largely disenfranchised population, the necessary pressure had been missing or ineffective. By bringing more affluent (and, hence, more powerful) people into the school system, the CCSI would increase the demands for performance, forcing the district to do a better job educating all students.

For example, the head of an educational nonprofit argued that those students in the new region who were not affluent would benefit from an influx of affluent parents who would be able to push for school improvement:

> What I see is an effort to, not just provide decent schools for Center City parents, the people we think of, traditionally, as Center City—more upper class— but people who are in the region. So the question is: Can you lift all those using the political leverage of those Center City parents, to help create reforms that make that an attractive region for all parents?

In referring explicitly to Center City parents' "political leverage," she claimed that these parents would be able to promote more substantive school improvement than other parents. Similarly, an education advocate who was skeptical about the CCSI because of its implications for equity nevertheless agreed with the initiative's efforts to bring a more powerful constituency into the system:

> In some ways, it's exactly the way you hope school improvement will work. The theory is that consumers will say, "Hey, I've had it. I want something different! Fix it for me!" . . . And that's all good and it starts with concerned parents saying, "I need services, I need quality." And a demand for quality is something that there hasn't been enough of in this city.

Low-income parents had not forced the district to "fix it" in the way that this new group, with its higher expectations and sense of entitlement, could.

A local newspaper made the same point in an editorial expressing support for the CCSI and the accompanying change in enrollment policy:

> The choice plan will make it easier for the district to attract affluent—and white—families in Center City. And the problem with that is . . . what? The painful truth is that white, affluent kids don't use the public schools. And the district has suffered politically as a result.[30]

This editorial acknowledged that the new transfer policy advantaged people living in the Center City area. However, its headline ("What Choice Does the School District Have? Effort to Attract White and Affluent Students Is Necessary") made the editors' position on the equity issues clear: the cost of *not* having this affluent constituency was more than the district could afford. According to this line of thinking, the schools would improve only when they served a population advantaged enough to advocate successfully on behalf of its own children and generate political (and, hence, financial) support for the system. And while other students may be affected by the necessary "accommodations," that cost was outweighed by the possibility of bringing about a greater good.

In addition to being more politically powerful, supporters argued, middle-class parents would also be more involved members of school communities. Speaking at an SRC meeting in favor of the new transfer policy, a Grant parent explained, "We need parents that will show up to plant flowers, to control the chaotic playground and the newly erected jungle gym. . . . We are convinced that if more local parents had a better chance of sending their children to Grant the numbers of involved families would increase."[31] This parent's comment about "local" (i.e., Center City) parents exemplifies the expectation that such parents would improve the schools, thereby justifying their special treatment.

Finally, a number of civic actors expressed support for the CCSI because, by bringing more middle-class families into the system, it would increase racial and economic integration in the schools, a contrast with those critics who claimed the initiative would lead to greater segregation. Explaining her efforts to promote the initiative, a former city official commented, "And last but not least, it is one of the only ways I know to get true economic and racial integration into schools. I don't know how else to do it. I mean, there are very few places that you can do it." In this context, racial integration was a matter of adding more white students to the system. Because the district had, proportionately, so few white and middle-class students, it was unrealistic to expect the schools to be racially or economically integrated anywhere except in Center City and the handful of other areas with significant numbers of white and nonpoor students. For this reason, a local newspaper columnist also wrote favorably about the CCSI, citing research on economic integration showing that low-income students do significantly better in schools with more middle-income students. Noting the disproportionately low-income population of Philadelphia's schools, she concluded, "If families with choices continue to opt out of public education, the preference policy won't improve that sad poor-to-middle-class ratio. It'll just shift it from one school to another. And that's not progress. It's just rearranging deck chairs on a sinking ship."[32] In contrast, she suggested, when middle-class families are involved in public schools, they prevent that ship from sinking.

Taken together, these arguments in support of the CCSI, like the consensus about middle-class flight discussed in chapter 2, position the middle class as crucial to the city's future. Middle-class families are the "glue that holds the city together." They are the "taxpayers" who will secure Philadelphia's economic fortunes. And, with respect to the schools, they are the "pro-education" parents who can avert disaster.

Imagining the "Middle Class:" Obscuring Class and Race Distinctions

Yet just as scholarly and popular conversations about social class in America often lump people with very different incomes, education levels, and social practices into one, all-encompassing "middle class," so too did the discourse around the CCSI conflate the middle and upper-middle or professional classes. In fact, whereas the CCD's literature on the initiative referred to the importance of attracting professional "knowledge workers" to the city, when its president gave a presentation about the initiative to a meeting of representatives from the building industry, he too used the terms "middle class" and "middle income" to describe the group who would benefit from the initiative. This tendency may have made the initiative more politically palatable. It is unlikely that the many people who spoke positively of the CCSI as a means of attracting and retaining the middle class to the city would have been as sympathetic to a policy that gave special advantages to a more elite population.

Some respondents, however, did challenge the assumption that the CCSI's target was the middle class. A community and education activist, who was critical of the initiative, observed:

> I mean, the issues of race and class in Philadelphia are, like most urban centers, fairly extreme, and not talked about most of the time. So, for example, even the question of Center City being a place to attract middle class, primarily white folks, doesn't make sense, because most middle class people don't live in Center City. . . . Downtown is thriving, but it's mostly thriving with *professionals*.

This advocate points to the growing polarization of race and income in Philadelphia to distinguish between professionals and the middle class and to argue that Center City was home to a more advantaged population. Even supporters of the CCSI noted their concern that Center City would become affordable only to the most affluent families: "I don't know how many three- and four-bedroom apartments you have in Center City that are priced so that a family can afford them. . . . There's so much you can't afford in Center City. I've been a lawyer for twenty-five years and I can't afford it!" While this lawyer saw the rise in real estate values as a problem for the CCSI because it decreased the number of potential "customers," his comments also demonstrate his perception that Center City's population was becoming increasingly elite.

Though most people who interrogated the class status of Center City residents called them upper-middle class or professionals, a former city official took the opposite position. She contrasted the pool of future Center City public school students with the "rich kids," noting, "These aren't rich kids. The rich kids are going to private school, trust me." Thus, the question of the class status of the initiative's targets was by no means a settled one, reflecting both the highly contested nature of class labels and the general murkiness with which Americans think and talk about social class. In fact, even those who emphasized the advantaged status of the Center City population referred often—and in the same conversations—to the CCSI as a way of retaining "middle-income" families. Such rhetorical slippage, which happened again and again in interviews and in media coverage, underscores the power of this refrain and its role in helping to justify the initiative.

Supporters of the CCSI also generally spoke in terms of class rather than race. Though interviewees talked comfortably about the need to keep the middle class, none explicitly stated that the city needed to keep white families. This is striking given the demographics of the downtown area and the city as a whole: the city of Philadelphia is home to a large black middle class, but in 2000 Center City and its surrounding neighborhoods were 76 percent white and only 13 percent African American, and there were no initiatives targeting neighborhoods with large numbers of middle-class black families.[33] Thus, while not presented as such, the initiative was designed for a population that was both professional and largely white. It is possible that this discursive focus on class rather than race was due to the policy itself, which explicitly targeted people of a certain occupational (e.g., class-related) status, in contrast to desegregation policies that highlight race. However, the extent to which the discourse around the initiative focused on class rather than addressing issues of racial segregation also suggests another way in which "middle class" served a masking function: it allowed people to express their concerns about "white flight" without actually using those words.

The use of "middle class" rather than "white" in describing the population moving out of the city is particularly interesting given historian Robert Beauregard's finding—in his study of media coverage of urban decline—that for much of the twentieth century, discussion of suburban flight was heavily racialized, with commentators bemoaning the migration of whites from cities.[34] The focus on class in Philadelphia is presumably related to two factors. First, as sociologist William Julius Wilson noted as early as the 1980s, middle-class flight to the suburbs is no longer a wholly white phenomenon: African Americans who can afford to also leave urban neighborhoods.[35] Second, Americans have grown more sensitive about articulating racialized sentiments since the 1960s and '70s. Thus the racial reality that the Center City knowledge workers targeted by the CCSI were overwhelmingly white was hidden by a seemingly benign interest in the "middle class."

The CCSI was designed to attract professional families to public elementary schools in Philadelphia's downtown area. Though the project began within the CCD, the district collaborated because of shared policy goals and the resources and status it stood to gain from partnering with a prestigious business organization. The initiative positioned schools as an urban amenity, and the CCD marketed the Center City public schools in much the same way it marketed Philadelphia's unique cultural scene or business opportunities.

Central to the marketing campaign was the explicit and implicit privileging of professional families. They were explicitly privileged by a new policy giving children living in the affluent downtown and surrounding gentrified neighborhoods priority over children from other parts of the city in admissions to high-performing downtown schools. The marketing campaign advantaged middle- and upper-middle-class families in more subtle ways as well. It institutionalized a focus on these families as valued customers and instituted privileged channels for communication with district and CCD administrators. The CCSI further brought additional resources, programming, and attention to key downtown schools.

In this chapter, I also drew on interviews with dozens of local civic actors in order to probe Philadelphians' views of the initiative and the tensions it brought to the surface between providing equal educational opportunities for all and promoting the city's economic development. Because the CCSI directed resources and opportunities toward an already advantaged part of the city, it angered some who were concerned about the consequences for low-income and minority students. Many of the civic and educational leaders interviewed, however, situated their responses in the context of on-going middle-class flight and the danger this flight posed to the city's social and economic health. They focused on the potential economic and educational benefits, arguing that the city was in such a state of crisis it could ill afford to ignore middle-class interests. The discourse around the need to keep the middle class obscured important distinctions of class and race, which likely helped make an initiative that served an overwhelmingly white area, populated by significant numbers of upper-middle-class families, more politically acceptable.

It is true that a greater commitment among the middle class in Philadelphia to the public schools would be beneficial. It is also true that an increase in the number of middle-class households in the city would improve the city's economic outlook. However, the privileging of that population fostered by the CCSI moved the district away from its mission of providing equal educational opportunity to all students. CCD and school district administrators, as well as supporters of the CCSI, did not openly acknowledge the connection between giving special treatment to some families and routine treatment to others (although, as will be discussed in chapter 7, some district employees were critical of the CCSI for that very reason). However, to paraphrase George Orwell's *Animal Farm*, one outcome of the CCSI was an ideological environment in which "all families are equal, but some families are more equal than others."[36] This chapter has suggested how such a context was created, showing the ways in which the intersection between the CCD and the School District of Philadelphia reshaped institutional priorities, altered official policies, and gave rise to new relationships and practices. The next two chapters examine these processes within the walls of one elementary school.

"This Is Not an Inner-City School!"

Marketing Grant Elementary

Mom, my day was SO GOOD it was from down to here [pointing to ground] up to outer space, and past that, past that, past that, and past that—that's how good it was!" is our Kindergarten son's excited mantra that he exclaims every day that I pick him up from school at our neighborhood public school, Grant Elementary. . . . That's a big deal for us—I've lived in the neighborhood for the most part of 18 years and we were not certain where our two children would go to school. In fact, we were originally on the fast track to private schooling for our oldest, our 5 year old. And then we had our second child. Well, you do the math. (Doable, yes, but one must pick their battles.) . . . You can see it in the parks and playgrounds – you can see it all around Center City. More people are choosing to stay. Grant needed to add a third Kindergarten because we've had more neighborhood kids this year. . . . So, I welcome you to check it out. You never know, you may find it out of this world! —Newsletter, Center City neighborhood civic association (2004)

In 2003 a story in a local newspaper profiled Grant Elementary School and told of the middle-class and upper-middle-class mothers who appeared at playgrounds, community centers, and other neighborhood spots to promote the school.[1] It described a community meeting in which these parents explained—to an audience comprised largely of professionals—that the school offered all that local private schools did, without the expensive tuition. At this meeting, parents noted that, by avoiding paying tuition in private elementary schools (averaging around $15,000 annually), parents could save so much money that an Ivy League education would be "sort of free!" By 2010, seven years later, Grant had been featured several more times in the local and national media, always in articles touting the "return" of middle-class families to urban schools.

The wide hallways and spacious, though timeworn, classrooms of Grant Elementary provide a useful venue for understanding what efforts to market urban public schools to middle- and upper-middle-class families look like on the ground level. It is in these spaces that the infusion of market ideas and practices—from the belief that schools should promote economic growth, to the emphasis on certain parents as valued customers, to the very act of marketing a school—took on real meaning. During my years of fieldwork at Grant, hallways, classrooms, and meeting spaces were home to debates about the future of the school, struggles between differently positioned parents, and tensions around race and class, as well as the everyday business of a large public school. The campaign to attract more middle- and upper-middle-class parents to Grant actually predated the larger effort to market Center City schools but was intertwined with it in many ways. Grant was one of the Big Three schools targeted by the CCSI, and key Grant parents were involved in the project from its earliest stages.

Like deciding where to buy a home, the decision parents make about where to send their children to school is a critical moment in the social reproduction process, with parents attempting to choose schools that will advance (or at least maintain) their children's class status.[2] With respect to middle-class parents, then, it was not enough to simply inform them about the unique offerings of a particular school. Administrators involved with the CCSI, as well as parents hoping to increase middle-class participation in the schools, had to convince skeptical parents that Grant and other Center City public schools were deserving of their trust. They had to show that, unlike other "inner-city" Philadelphia public schools, these were up to the task of preparing middle- and upper-middle-class children for future success. The consequences of doing this were more complicated than one might expect.

The campaign to attract Center City families to Grant touched upon two underexplored tensions operating at the school and in the broader education and policy fields. The first is the tension between the well-established benefits of economic integration and the negative framing of low-income families inherent to economic-integration discourse and policies. The second is between the intimacy and sense of community implied by the notion of the "neighborhood school" and the accompanying exclusion of those who are not part of the neighborhood. In both cases, what is often seen as

socially and educationally beneficial also involves significant marginalization. Because a central argument here is that in this context middle-class
families became more desirable than working-class families, the chapter
ends with a discussion of the experiences of four parents (two upper-middle-
class and two working-class) as they enrolled their children at the school.

Introduction to Grant

Grant Elementary is located in Cobble Square, a beautiful neighborhood in downtown Philadelphia, home to some of the city's most influential citizens. Imposing brick townhouses, with glossy paint on their
front doors and windows framed by large black shutters, line the leafy
streets. Many of these houses proudly bear such relics of the neighborhood's colonial past as plaques between the second-floor windows (signi-
fying that the eighteenth-century owners had purchased fire insurance),
metal "bootscrapers" by the front steps, and "busybodies" mounted near
third-floor windows (small pieces of angled mirror allowing residents to
peer outside without being seen). Some townhouses have been broken
into apartments, but most are single-family homes. Historical markers are
scattered throughout the neighborhood; they draw attention to notable
former residents, the architectural significance of certain structures, and
locations of historical events. While much of Cobble Square is residential,
the neighborhood is also home to many shops and restaurants and to a
hospital. Real estate values in Cobble Square far exceed those in the rest
of the Philadelphia region. In 2002, two years before I began my research
at Grant, the median sale price in the neighborhood was $477,500, nearly
six times the city's median value and the highest in the city. By 2008 the
median sale price had risen to over $1,000,000.[3]

Cobble Square covers approximately thirty city blocks. According to
U.S. Census data, in 2000 Cobble Square was 3 percent African American,
3 percent Asian, 2 percent Latino, and 91 percent white. Grant's catchment area is nearly twice that size, encompassing neighborhoods to the
north and west that are less affluent, including one with a large Asian
immigrant population. The residential population in Grant's overall catchment area was 9 percent African American, 13 percent Asian American,
4 percent Hispanic, and 75 percent white.

Grant serves nearly 500 students from kindergarten through eighth
grade. Its three-story building has a formidable, castle-like façade, with

metal security grating (present on all Philadelphia public schools) covering its windows. While Grant's setting—in the midst of blocks of townhouses—is quite lovely, it is flanked on one side by a large swath of asphalt that at one point contained only a basketball hoop or two and a parking area for teachers and visitors. There is no grass. This area, where students congregate before and after school and for recess, was improved during the course of my research by the installation of a new play structure. On the school's other side, trees shade a courtyard where planters and benches create a more inviting space, although these fixtures share the area with a large metal dumpster and banged-up plastic trash cans. The dumpster, the relatively barren grounds, and the grates on the windows remind passersby that, despite Grant's idyllic location, it is still an urban public school maintained by a district with minimal resources to spare on appearances.

When I began my fieldwork in 2004, 471 students attended Grant.[4] Forty-three percent were Asian American (many recent immigrants or the children of immigrants), an additional 43 percent were African American, and 11 percent were white; 46 percent of students were eligible for free or reduced lunch.[5] Long known as one of the best schools in Philadelphia, Grant had experienced waves of middle-class involvement in the past, particularly from families living in Cobble Square. However, at the time of my study few families from the Cobble Square neighborhood actually sent their children to the school, with most opting for one of the local private schools. In 2000 76 percent of students living in Cobble Square used private school.[6] Because Grant had a good reputation in Philadelphia, hundreds of students from across the city applied for admission each year.[7] In 2005 (before the CCSI's transfer policy went into effect), 49 percent of Grant's students were transfers from other schools, with the other half coming from within the catchment area. Transfer students at Grant, as at the other desirable downtown schools, were largely African American and from lower-income areas.[8]

As students moved through Grant, the few from Cobble Square—and the more high-achieving students in general—often left for private and magnet schools. The most prestigious magnet school in Philadelphia begins in fifth grade, so many students remained at Grant only through fourth grade. As these students exited, there were more openings for transfer students. The result was a striking contrast in the racial composition of the grades that was apparent to me even as I walked the halls of the school: the lower grades had significant numbers of white students and the upper grades were nearly entirely black and Asian American.

In 2004 and 2005, Grant's principal was an African American woman whom I call Ms. Ashton. A long-time district employee who had been at Grant for a year when I began my research, Ms. Ashton had a rigid and unfriendly manner and had earned the enmity of many parents and teachers. As will be discussed later in this chapter, Ms. Ashton was replaced in 2005—after a contentious principal selection process—by Ms. Fordham, a white woman from Center City.

Most schools in the School District of Philadelphia have low levels of achievement. Many do not "make" Adequate Yearly Progress (AYP), which means that student achievement scores are not improving at the rate mandated by the federal government under No Child Left Behind (NCLB). Even Grant, one of the district's "gems," struggled to keep its scores up. The school made AYP on the state-mandated tests in 2002 and 2003 but did so only sporadically in the following years.[9] Nevertheless, as I have explained, it was seen as one of the city's best elementary schools because of its location within Cobble Square and history of solid academic performance.

Diverse and Desirable

I visited Grant several times a month for over two years. I attended meetings, walked the halls, visited classrooms, and chatted with parents before and after school. Grant's classrooms during this period were a little shabby, with mismatched furniture and peeling paint. But they were also bright and airy, had big windows, polished wood floors, and lots of storage. Displays of student work, such as essays about a class trip to the zoo or subtraction worksheets adorned by smiley-face stickers, broke up the long hallways. Some of the displays, with corners faded and curling, obviously stayed up for quite some time. The wall facing the office boasted an elaborate mosaic of student-made tiles. Classrooms seemed orderly, and most rooms were arranged in the traditional fashion, with students in rows and the teacher standing at the front. Students passing through the hallways were generally decorous, remaining in line and talking quietly, and friendly and respectful of adults.

Students, teachers, and parents at Grant took pride in the school's racial and ethnic diversity. As a frequent visitor, I too was struck by this diversity and by how well the different groups seemed to get along. For example, observing a class of fourth-graders in the schoolyard, I noticed that not only did the student population include whites, African Americans, and Asians, but that individual social groups—such as the trio of girls that walked past me giggling—were also diverse. Though Grant is physically large, it did not have the anonymous feeling that plagues many big schools. Teachers seemed to look out for the students and to enjoy interacting with the children and their families. In fact, teachers at Grant tended to remain there for many years. Because the district's staffing policy allowed teachers to choose schools based on their years of seniority, teachers at Grant generally "earned" their position by serving in other schools first.

Teachers' positive rapport with the students was apparent in the hallways before and after school. The following incident from my fieldnotes in the spring of 2004 is typical:

> This morning, as I was coming into Grant for a PTO meeting, I got stuck behind a crowd of students making their way up to the classrooms. As I neared the top of the second flight of stairs, I saw that the "traffic jam" was caused by a young Asian girl, probably a kindergartner, struggling to pull a suitcase on wheels (it looked like that was what she used instead of a backpack) up the stairs. She was very young and small and the suitcase seemed so unwieldy, I was surprised she'd gotten as far as she did. Another little girl made some halfhearted attempts to help her, but she was determined to do it by herself. She was just wrestling the suitcase up the last step as I reached her. I noticed a teacher standing at the top of the stairs, also watching the little girl and smiling. I caught her eye and we laughed together while the girl, pulling her suitcase behind her, trotted off down the hallway.

The teacher did not bark at the girl or yell at her to hurry up, even though her struggles with that suitcase were making it harder for other children to make it up the stairs. Instead, she appreciated her determination. Like other teachers at the school, she was able to take the time to notice and value students' personalities and achievements.

Grant's PTO

My research at Grant focused on the school's Parent Teacher Organization (PTO), an active organization with over 100 official members and a smaller group of about ten to fifteen parents who set the agenda and did the bulk of the work.[10] I targeted the PTO because it was a key vehicle for the pursuit of different visions for Grant's future. The PTO had a great deal of power within the school, and because PTO meetings brought together a relatively diverse group of parents, all of whom were interested in "improving" the school, these meetings became a site for contestation among the parents about who mattered, whose voice should be heard, and what sort of school they were striving to create. The only parents' organization at the school, the PTO generally served as the vehicle through which parents interacted with the school district and the CCD.

Grant's PTO met at least once a month for an hour or so. These meetings were held just after the start of the school day in the school's shabby library, a room with torn yellow shades covering the windows and dusty shelves filled with books dating back to the 1950s.[11] Anywhere from five to twenty parents attended these meetings, and teachers and the principal sometimes visited to discuss particular issues, such as a new program or curriculum changes. The PTO also hosted occasional other visitors as well, including "reps" from various fundraising programs (e.g., candy or wrapping paper sales) and administrators from the school district's central office. For the regular monthly meetings, Sara, the PTO president and a Cobble Square mother, wrote up a brief agenda. Regular meetings covered such topics as the PTO's budget, fundraisers, grant applications, the status of special PTO projects (e.g., the new playground), school performances and trips, gifts for teachers, and the purchase of school and classroom supplies. During the course of my research, the PTO also held numerous supplementary meetings: smaller officers' meetings (to which I was occasionally invited), and sessions for planning special events, mapping out big PTO projects, or dealing with particular tasks (such as helping to select a new principal).

At these meetings, parents—mostly mothers and an occasional father—sat around tables arranged in a loose U shape.[12] Usually about half of the attendees were white and half were African American. Few Asian parents attended the meetings. While black and white parents often sat together, the seating was sometimes more racially divided, with, for example, the African American parents clustered at one end of a table and the white parents at the other. Some parents were casually dressed, in jeans or exercise clothing, and others, clearly on their way to work, wore suits. One mother, a health-care technician, often wore surgical scrubs. White parents from Cobble Square generally dominated the meetings, though several African American parents were also vocal. For the most part, the meetings were friendly and businesslike. They were run in a casual but orderly way, with PTO president Sara presiding. At times, however—as will be apparent in this chapter—the meetings became tense, with parents openly disagreeing with one another, expressing their frustration with muttered asides, or exchanging angry or bemused glances with one or another parent they saw as an ally.

"Transfers" and "Neighborhoods": Explaining the Terms

Who attended Grant during this period? Whom did parents and administrators hope to attract to the school? What were the differences between these groups? The answers to all of these questions involved important distinctions of race and class. Yet at Grant, as is so often the case in racially and economically diverse environments, most people were reluctant to speak openly about race and class. This was particularly true of PTO meetings or other group settings, in which participants hoped to avoid open conflict or uncomfortable conversations. As a result, geography became a stand-in for social position, and parents and educators used the terms "transfer" and "neighborhood" as shorthand labels for groups of students and families. As an observer, it quickly became apparent to me that such labels were enormously significant and that they referred not only to where families lived or how they attained access to the school but also to their class and (to a lesser extent) racial status. With respect to the CCSI, the labels also indexed the differences between the customers the initiative targeted and those it did not.

For students who lived within the school's immediate catchment area, admission to the school was automatic. Grant was their neighborhood school, and their parents could enroll them at any time. For students from other parts of the city, the process was much more complicated. Among Grant parents and educators, the term "transfers" generally referred to all students who came to the school from outside of its catchment area, either through the normal transfer process or under the provisions of NCLB, which allowed students to transfer out of failing schools. While apparently straightforward, the term referenced an essentially stigmatized group—the students who did not really have a "right" to be at the school and whose presence impeded the sort of change many middle-class parents sought. Though Grant had long had large numbers of transfer students, the positioning of them as negative appears to have been related to the marketing campaign and intensified over the course of my research.

In contrast, "neighborhoods" (or "neighborhood students," "neighborhood families," or "Cobble Square families") referred to students and parents from the school's immediate environs, Cobble Square, not to all students within Grant's catchment area. Because Cobble Square is a predominantly white neighborhood, it is tempting to assume that "neighborhood" was a code word for "white." In reality, however, "neighborhood" indexed broader social status, namely membership within the middle- or upper-middle class, rather than a particular racial (or even geographic) identity. For example, two of the PTO parents, Donna and Lisa, who generally joined with Cobble Square parents on issues in the school, were African American and middle to upper-middle class. Neither lived within the Grant catchment area, yet they tended to agree with the Cobble Square parents about the need to attract more neighborhood families and were seen as part of that faction. As one Cobble Square mother explained in an interview, discussing a disagreement within the PTO that pitted neighborhood parents against other parents and referring to Donna and Lisa by name, "I look at them as neighborhood people. You know what I mean?" The fact that certain parents were considered "neighborhood," regardless of their actual address, makes the symbolic nature of the term clear. That African American mothers from outside of Cobble Square could be "neighborhood" mothers by virtue of their class status and position on particular issues is evidence that the term was used to identify parents of higher class status, whatever their race.

Donna and Lisa actually took on a certain symbolic importance within Grant's PTO: their allegiance with the neighborhood parents was taken as evidence that the tensions among parents at the school were not racial—a dynamic many PTO parents fervently hoped to avoid. In an interview conducted in a Center City café, Sue Anne, a Cobble Square mother who worked in finance, concluded a discussion of conflicts within the PTO with the observation that it would be easy to misconstrue these tensions as being rooted in racial differences: "I really don't think it was about race, but was it not for [Donna and Lisa's] presence, it could easily have been interpreted that way, and even framed that way." Sue Anne was worried about the prospect of the PTO becoming racially divided and relieved that these two African American women often sided with the (otherwise all-white) neighborhood parents. She continued,

> Okay, so they don't live in the neighborhood, but—I don't know if, I think they're perceived as people who—you know, because they are part of—see again, people keep on saying it's neighborhood versus not-neighborhood, but I don't really think it's that.

When I asked Sue Anne to clarify her comment, she explained that she saw the tension as not simply one of "neighborhood versus not neighborhood" or even as rooted in racial differences. Rather, she saw it as a matter of social class:

> I think that the neighborhood versus non-neighborhood thing represents the class issue, because the neighborhood is a specific class, it's no other class but that class. It is not at all diverse in any way, and so it can represent race, but it's not that. And they sit there as shining examples of that, and I'm so glad that they're there.

As Sue Anne notes, the fact that Donna and Lisa were seen as "neighborhood parents" defused the racial tension somewhat, moving the focus to social class, which was less inflammatory.

In fact, the terms "neighborhood" and "transfer" appeared to serve an important masking function, allowing parents to talk about race and class without actually using the words. Working-class parents could speak derisively of the "neighborhood parents" in interviews (and, occasionally, meetings and conversations) in a way that may have been difficult for them to do if the only words available to them were "affluent, mostly white mothers." Or parents and teachers could argue that "transfer students" were behavior problems without seeming to target African American students. In addition, the term allowed professional parents to speak of their own status indirectly, to say, "x will look good to neighborhood parents," without making any mention of social class—that is, "upper-middle-class parents like me would like x." This term, then, obscured the extent to which parents were actually leveraging their class status when they advocated for particular changes or improvements. While this language may have enabled parents to sidestep some conflicts, it did not alleviate the tensions that existed between the two groups. Thus one long-time Grant teacher noted that PTO meetings were places where, though race itself was never mentioned, racial differences were very important: "Even though it's carefully expressed and not on racial levels, everybody gets it."[13] The "it" here is the powerful influence of race on dynamics within the school.

Grant's catchment zone also encompassed a large Asian immigrant neighborhood, and significant number of children from this neighborhood attended the school. While clearly not transfer students, Grant's Asian students also did not receive the "neighborhood" label commonly applied to children from Cobble Square. Because parents from that area only rarely appeared at PTO meetings, they did not play much of a role in the events featured here, and their voices are largely silent in these pages.[14] Interestingly, while the lack of Asian representation at PTO events came up occasionally at meetings, no one ever accused Asian parents of not "caring" or used the sort of critical language that so often characterizes conversations about low levels of parental involvement in urban schools.

When tensions brewed between different groups of parents, the Asian community remained largely, if not entirely, removed. A white neighborhood mother, reflecting later upon her experiences with racially charged interactions, noted as much:

> I have never felt so much racial hostility in my life as I did there in the school! And it's the black community. It's not the Chinese community . . . it's not them that are making the trouble.

Here she compares the school's largest nonwhite groups, implying that the African Americans were problematic and the Asians reasonable. This positioning of Asians, especially Asian immigrants, as the "model minority" is nothing new, of course.[15] Nor is the hostility directed at the African American community. Thus, Asian students and their families played a curious role at the school: they were not members of the desired neighborhood group, but neither did they carry the sort of stigma associated with the transfers.

Terms like "neighborhood" and "transfer," with all they implied about class and status, were also related to a larger dynamic that transcended Grant but was manifest in particular ways at the school. This was a discourse around class that positioned middle-class families as inherently virtuous and low-income families as deeply dysfunctional.

"They Care!": Economic Integration and the Discourse of Class

In the previous chapter, I argued that concerns about middle-class flight were an important factor in Philadelphia's political scene and suggested that people spoke of the need to "keep the middle class" in such a way that it tended to justify privileging an already advantaged population.[16] While the broader discussion of the need to keep the middle class in the city often had something of an abstract nature to it—constructing a sort of idealized and monolithic middle class on the verge of fleeing—the discourse about the middle class that circulated at Grant was much more immediate, and it had clear consequences in shaping parents' status at the school.

The strength of this discourse was apparent when district CEO Vallas visited a PTO meeting to talk about his reform agenda and plans to build a new playground at Grant. This meeting, held in the school's auditorium, attracted about forty people—mostly parents and a few teachers. When a former parent raised the issue of neighborhood families choosing private schools over Grant, a PTO officer jumped up and responded triumphantly, "Next year we have twelve families from the community enrolling!" Her news was greeted with a round of applause, with several Cobble Square mothers smiling and nodding (though, as I learned later, not all parents shared this enthusiasm). Similar events occurred often enough for one African American middle-class mother to comment upon it, noting wryly that many within the PTO assumed that by attracting "rich white parents . . . our lives are going to miraculously do a 180."

The belief that middle-class parents would improve the school had several elements. First, many of my interviewees mentioned the resources middle- and upper-income parents could bring, from actual fundraising to various enrichment programs. As one Cobble Square mother said in an interview, "Because those parents aren't spending $15,000 a year [on private school tuition], so when their kid's kindergarten needs a $2,000 computer, they just write the check." Another parent, also from the neighborhood, noted that she and her husband had "resources to share with those that don't have," including the "the ability to give, you know, a few hundred dollars, or even a couple, a couple thousand dollars, to give to the school for something substantial. For whether we give them money or we do some serious fundraising." In a chronically underfunded school district, these additional resources were badly needed.

A second major function people believed middle-class parents served was to use their social and cultural capital to "work the system" and bring resources to Grant. One parent observed, in a conversation in a Cobble Square coffeeshop, that parents with education have "networks" and "know how to get things done." In an interview, a working-class African American mother who did not live in the catchment area noted, in a matter-of-fact manner, that she did not have the "connects" that the Cobble Square parents did, which was why she did not run for the position of PTO president. She spoke positively, though, about parents who could use their connections to the school's benefit: "And if you can bring those

fruits to the school, please do that, because it's all about the children."
Though this parent was willing to devote large amounts of time and energy
to the school, she felt unable to play a leadership role because she lacked
valuable social connections. Research on social capital and home/school
relationships has shown that middle-class parents have rich stores of social
capital they can choose to activate with respect to their children's education, findings that resonate with these parents' perspectives.[17]

In talking about this issue, parents and educators' remarks are consistent
with the literature on economic integration, which indicates that middle-
class parents and children can bring resources to schools and "raise the
bar" for other students.[18] However, conversations at Grant also embodied
the more troubling side of the economic integration literature, its implicit
and negative positioning of working-class and poor families, particularly
African American families. Such comments underscore Lipman's assertion
that the expectation "that low-income students will benefit from exposure
to middle-class students is fundamentally a cultural deficit argument about
students of color."[19] The underlying assumption is that whereas middle-
class families have much to offer, low-income families have far less.

Hitting the Floor: Chaos, Order, and the Middle-Class Ethos

Many parents and educators further hoped an increase in middle-class
families at the school would have a transformative impact on its culture,
helping to create a new "middle-class ethos" at Grant.[20] In contrast to the
disorderly "inner-city" school, a school with a middle-class ethos would be
one in which students generally accepted the teachers' authority, followed
the rules, and, with their families, were invested in the broader project of
achieving academically and attaining the appropriate credentials. This was
important because, though Grant was relatively safe and high-performing
compared to the bulk of Philadelphia public schools, it was nevertheless
an urban public school and did not consistently convey the sense of order and industry that many parents, particularly Cobble Square parents,
sought for their children.

Parents often expressed concerns about discipline issues and criticized
the administration for tolerating a level of disorder they found unacceptable. The majority of Cobble Square parents had children in the younger
grades. The older grades, where behavior tended to be louder and more
boisterous, and where classes contained fewer white students, seemed
threatening to them, as did, at times, the overall climate at the school. In

describing her continued hesitation about Grant, Sue Anne told me the following story about walking her daughter, a kindergartner, to her classroom one morning:

> I walk Sara in the class, walk her into the school, and it's chaos. Or, it's not chaos, but it *feels* like chaos. Lots of older kids come in late, security guards [saying], "Get your butt up there!" you know, up the stairs. . . . It's—it just feels like a public school. *An inner-city public school.* When you walk in the door, [when] you're outside of the confines of the kindergarten classroom, when you're in the middle of kids moving around in the hallways—I have never had that experience in my lifetime. My husband has, but I haven't. One time we walked in, and I don't know, someone dropped a whole stack of books. I almost hit the floor and covered my head! *I almost hit the floor and covered my head.* . . . Yeah, literally, I thought like, that was gunshots and I needed to get me and my daughter down on the floor as soon as possible.

Believing she had heard gunshots, she sought to ensure her daughter's safety.

> And I looked at Sara—you know, first I jerked and I looked around, and I went like this and like [mimics ducking low and covering her head], then I'm like, where's Sara? And she's just standing right in front of me, and—she hadn't even noticed, she looked around and she's like, "What's—what's holding you up, Mom?" She walks up the stairs and skips into her room.

Though there had never been an incident of gun violence at Grant, Sue Anne continued to feel nervous in the building: "Would this have to happen thirty times for me to stop feeling that way? Maybe. So it doesn't feel safe, is part of it." It is quite possible that one reason a rowdy start to an elementary school day made Sue Anne uncomfortable enough to worry—even subconsciously—about gunshots was the fact that almost all of the older students in that crowded stairway were African American. On some level, Sue Anne may have associated such students with widely held stereotypes about urban street violence. Regardless, to these parents, what they saw as unruliness did more than disrupt student learning; it also communicated a lack of control that seemed dangerous and conflicted with their ideas about how schools should operate.

In addition, many parents and teachers assumed that Cobble Square children would be stronger academically. Here is one Cobble Square mother talking about the role her eight-year-old son, Simon, played in increasing achievement:

> The fact that our kids are higher performing, brings up the test scores, enhances the performance of the schools, for what that's worth. And I think it's a shame that the school has to be evaluated on the kids' test scores and that has to reflect on the school's reputation but it does. And so, you know, I'm glad Simon does his little part.

While she offers a critique of testing, she also assumes that children from families like her own will improve the school's scores. The comments of one teacher, who was sympathetic to the CCSI, attributed this achievement difference to Cobble Square parents' greater support for education:

> [I]f the neighborhood children came to this school and it's an affluent neighborhood and it's caring parents, then all the parents that send the children here would care about their children, the education, and maintaining Grant to where it's a very good learning environment.

Supporters of the CCSI assumed that middle-class children, through their higher academic achievement and more orderly behavior, would have a positive impact on other children. They, and their parents, would help alter the negative dynamics frequently associated with urban schools, creating a safer, more productive environment. A Grant administrator explained that it would be beneficial to the school if more Cobble Square children attended because it "would help the diverse population in everything. You know, academics, behavior, helping the students be better citizens." Thus, middle-class families were constructed as civilizing agents and low-income children and parents as the symbolic Other who embody and are responsible for the chaos and dysfunction that characterize so many "inner-city" schools.

In discussing this dynamic, Center City parents referred to a sort of "snowball" process, in which neighborhood parents benefited a school simply by sending their children there because their family's involvement attracted other, similarly advantaged families, who then made the school even better. Here is one mother explaining her thinking about using Grant:

> I think though by going, by being there, by saying you do it, that's some sort of testament. It's a passive one, but it's still something. So I can say that is a contri-

bution to trying to recruit people. If someone asks, I tell them, and I say it in an enthusiastic way, because I do think it's a good thing to do.

When this mother spoke of "people" (i.e., the people sending their children to Grant or the people being recruited), she was not referring to parents in general; instead, she was referring to "people" like herself, who would be choosing Grant instead of a private or suburban school. Comments like hers underscore the transactional element implicit in much of the discourse about the need to attract the middle class: these families were valuable because of what they brought to the table, namely, the financial, cultural, and social capital schools need.

Legitimizing the Discourse: District Officials and the CCSI

District officials shared this belief in the importance of attracting more affluent families. In a visit to the school in spring 2004, district CEO Vallas made several references to the need to keep the middle class. He explained this was why he wanted to increase funding for gifted classes, because the dearth of such programs was one reason "why parents with means left." At this same meeting, the PTO president thanked Vallas for his decision to give Grant over $100,000 to build a new playground.[21] Vallas immediately observed that the district's efforts to upgrade schools (with playgrounds and libraries) and make them more physically attractive were all part of the "campaign to get more in the community [i.e., Cobble Square] to send their kids here." Another Cobble Square mother jumped in at that point, informing the crowd that she had met with staffers from the district's Office of Facilities and "the ball [was] already rolling" on the playground project.

This connection between upgrading the school and attracting a particular population did not go unnoticed, especially because resources in the district were so limited: in several interviews, parents and teachers observed that the play structure, completed in 2005, was a direct result of the district's desire to make the school more appealing to professional families. "That's the way it was presented to us," one teacher explained in an interview. When I asked her if she could think of other examples of physical improvements the district had made as a part of the effort to market Grant, she mused, "That's the only thing—no, that's not true, we did get the play-yard resurfaced out there. We did get a mural painting in the lunchroom. And the school has been painted—areas that hadn't been painted have been painted, that kind of thing." Another teacher also noted the fresh paint the school had received: "The principal's office was painted recently and we've got a new office floor. I've been in—this is my twentieth year of teaching and I've never had that done all at one time ever, in any school that I've been in." For both teachers, the contrast between the district's usual slow pace and its speedy upgrades at Grant was evidence that the district was serious about making the school more attractive to Center City families.

The conviction that more middle-class families means a better school may well exist in any economically integrated school setting, even in the absence of an explicit marketing campaign. The fact that this senti-ment predated the CCSI and is related to a larger set of assumptions about the virtues of the middle class suggests this is the case. Rather than creating this discourse, then, the CCSI legitimized prevailing assump-tions about middle-class value. It made attracting these families a clear policy goal and the strategies schools could use to accomplish this goal a reform priority and important topic of conversation within the school. As well, the CCSI made the number of Center City families enrolling in the schools an indicator of its success, institutionalizing their status as desired customers.

Contesting and Complicating the Discourse

While this perspective on the benefits of middle-class participation was powerful, it did not go uncontested, particularly among African Ameri-can teachers and parents. For example, whereas many parents and edu-cators spoke of the additional resources middle-class parents brought to the school, several working-class parents of color commented that new resources automatically followed middle-class families. In this way, their analysis was similar to that of the African American residents in Elijah Anderson's study of a gentrifying neighborhood, who believed that an influx of white (and middle-class) residents would lead to better law en-forcement, garbage collection, and other city services.[22] Janet, an Afri-can American mother of two young children at Grant, echoed this view: "When you have the more affluent parents you do get more resources, that's just a given." Later in our interview, she said Grant parents were successful in advocating for an additional kindergarten teacher because the system favored schools like Grant: "they get results here because more tax dollars are spent here." Similarly, another African American mother noted that only schools that served more advantaged populations—"the people with money," in her words—received special programs, such as a visit from a local television personality. For these parents, the link between parental class status and school resources was more ambiguous than it was for the middle-class parents: whereas the Cobble Square parents saw increased resources as coming from *their ability* to donate or raise funds, these parents seemed to believe *the system* favored schools serving middle-class populations.[23] This represents an important critique of implicit assumptions about middle-class efficacy.

In addition, several African American parents and teachers questioned the assumption that an influx of neighborhood families would create a more positive school environment. For example, whereas some of the white parents and teachers noted that middle-class parents were more involved with their children's education than working-class parents, the two African American teachers I interviewed refused to make any generalizations about parents based on race, class, or geography. Thus one teacher of older children observed, "There's been years that we've had families that are not from the Grant area and they've been very active. So I think it's very hard to point one way or the other" and further noted that she had "never met one parent that doesn't want the best for their kids." The other African American teacher I spoke with said she had not been at the school long enough (she had been at Grant for three years and a teacher for twenty) to draw any conclusions.[24] Thus, whereas the dominant narrative, particularly as it was expressed by white parents and educators, included normative assumptions about the ways behaviors vary by class, some African Americans at Grant strove to interrupt this, emphasizing commonalities across all parents and students and attributing the success of middle-class families at least in part to a system that channels resources toward the already advantaged.

This alternative perspective gained little traction, however. In interviews and private conversations, although parents and educators sometimes prefaced their comments with concerns about making generalizations, they were largely quite quick to offer a host of reasons Grant would benefit from an increased middle-class presence. The result was a normalizing order in which middle- and upper-middle-class families assumed enhanced value at the implicit and explicit expense of other families.

Again, there is little in parents' and educators' comments that is not supported by the large body of research on mixed-income schools. But assumptions about the benefits of a significant middle-class presence at the school, which may seem abstract and unimpeachable when backed up by data and published in a journal or report, take on a very different meaning during day-to-day interactions in a diverse school. Such assumptions attribute a host of virtues to the Cobble Square parent sitting on one side of the table at a PTO meeting, devalue the transfer parent sitting across from her, and attribute an overwhelmingly negative set of traits—from incompetent to uncaring—to the transfer parent who, for whatever reason, did not attend the meeting. Thus, while Cobble Square parents publicly celebrated the enrollment of "neighborhood children," more extensive conversations about the reasons for attracting middle-class families were conducted in private. Yet, as I show in chapter 6, working-class parents were well aware of how they were positioned by these conversations.

Symbolically and Institutionally Excluded: Transfer Students and Their Families

The CCSI and the marketing of Grant communicated multiple messages about the inferior status of the largely working-class and African American transfer students and their families. These families were the implicit Other against which middle-class virtue was compared. They were explicitly not the customers to which Grant was being marketed, and they did not fit within the new identity being forged for the school.

During the 2005–6 school year (before the new transfer policy), 237 students transferred into Grant from outside of the catchment area, making up 49 percent of the student body. Of these transfer students, 180 (or 76%) came from schools outside of the Center City Academic Region. Seventy-one percent of out-of-region transfers were African American, and 64 percent of all African American students at the school were transfers from other regions.[25] Sixty-nine students (38% of out-of-region transfers) came from schools that had been identified as chronically underachieving and served large numbers of low-income students. Most of the others came from schools in West and Southwest Philadelphia, both low-income, African American areas. These were students hoping to escape unsafe and low-performing schools in their communities. As one father who transferred his son to Grant explained at a PTO meeting (during a discussion about discipline issues), "I grew up in North Philadelphia where there is lots of violence. I brought my son here to·get away from violence." As well, many transfer students (approximately 100) came to Grant under the federal NCLB legislation; these were students whose original schools had failed to meet certain standards and who, as a result, were entitled to attend a nonfailing school. Though data on the percentage of transfer students who were low-income are not available, it is reasonable to assume, from the regions and schools to which they were originally assigned, that the majority were poor or working-class.

Transfer students were often seen by CCSI supporters, especially PTO parents, as a liability to the school. They were the group in need of the civilizing influence of the middle class, the group whose behaviors were to be countered by the school's developing middle-class ethos. This was particularly the case around discipline issues, as transfer students were frequently perceived by both educators and parents as the major source of discipline problems at the school. For example, one neighborhood parent, speaking at a meeting with the district CEO, attributed bullying problems at Grant to transfer students. He said, "We have a lot of diversity here, bringing kids in from troubled areas. But this creates problems that need extra attention." Similarly, a teacher of younger children was critical of students transferring into Grant: "I don't know what happened in their other schools . . . [or] maybe it's their upbringing. And they come here and they don't respect authority, they don't respect anyone. And they don't respect themselves. And that brings about all of the problems." This teacher expressed concern that the behavior of such students, who "come from an area where they're not well trained," would discourage other Cobble Square parents from enrolling their children at Grant.

Parents were also attuned to this issue. In an interview in a Cobble Square café, Donna, a middle-class African American mother, was explicit about the connections she saw between race, transfer status, and behavior: "The people who are being bused in, the people who are doing the bullying and in the upper classes [at the school] and all that, are predominantly black people." Patricia, a working-class African American mother, spoke earnestly about this association and her desire to show, through her first-grade son's behavior, that all transfer students were not behavior problems.

> We're good parents, and we would send him there and make sure that he respects the other students, does what he's supposed to do. That's what we send him there for, to get an education. Not to act like a fool. So, you know, if you

get more parents that have kids like that and can send them to the schools, to show these other parents that live in the neighborhood that, everybody's [from outside of the neighborhood] kids are not bad or, you know, are not going to disrupt the school or tear up the school.

This mother did not disagree that some transfer children were discipline problems—"some kids can go a little bit, you know, overboard with a lot of stuff that they do," she noted—but it was important to her to make it clear that other families from outside of Center City were serious about education and good behavior.[26] While I do not have data to assess the validity of this association between transfer students and discipline issues, it was clearly the case that, as in most elementary schools, behavior problems were more frequent among the upper grades; at Grant, these grades did include a disproportionate number of transfer students.

The children who enrolled at Grant through NCLB (the "choice kids") were even further stigmatized. According to both educators and parents, their enrollment presented a challenge to the school. A teacher in the younger grades explained that the students transferring under NCLB represented "a very difficult population." She continued, "These are children who come with almost like a record of having left this school and that school, and behavior problems, and these have been some of your major problems in the schools." Another teacher echoed her point, noting the challenges such students presented to Grant's resources:

> Because we're not technically an at-risk school, we don't have a lot of surplus of personnel or manpower to do a lot of the services or interventions that a child who is two or three years below really needs or requires. So . . . that puts added pressure on our staff, because now you have the children who are on grade level, the children who are just learning English, the special ed children who are inclusion, and then you might have the choice [NCLB] child who is sitting there. And the choice child could, in reality, be lower than the special ed kid.

She continued, describing the implications for teachers: "So now you have all the accommodations and interventions that you have to do, and that's difficult to do when you have thirty-two kids in the classroom. So I think that's what the teachers are a little bit frustrated about." Teachers also spoke wistfully about Philadelphia schools whose principals had managed the enrollment process in such a way as to deny spots to NCLB students: "I know in other schools they've managed to keep out the school choice kids."

Parents at Grant displayed a similar range of perspectives on the NCLB students. Some expressed concern that, because they had so many needs, the school did not have the resources to serve them very well, and others argued that they brought too many behavior problems and negatively impacted the school. One Cobble Square mother was particularly blunt: the NCLB students, she remarked to me in a casual conversation, "screwed up the school big time."

Like the transfer students, children in the upper grades were reputed to be behavior problems. These grades were often viewed more negatively in the school, particularly within the PTO, which was dominated by parents of younger students. An administrator connected these behavior problems to the different make-up of the upper grades:

> And the sea-change in the school in the upper grades, sixth, seventh and eighth grades is where you see the change occur. . . . This first grade is wonderful, everyone is fabulous. And third, fourth grade, it just starts. And by sixth, seventh, eighth, you just see a change in the make-up. . . . Well, many of our kids go to Masterman or other magnet schools, or private schools. After fourth grade, we lose a lot of them. So you do start to see the change. . . . So you see the differences in seventh and eighth grades. And many of my Cobble Square neighborhood kids, families, are not up there.

As one Cobble Square mother told me, the reputation of the older students for bad behavior was discouraging to parents thinking of keeping their children at Grant. Though she had been very happy at Grant thus far, she thought the upper grades were "a little different" and "rougher" than the younger grades.

In essence, the upper grades—perceived as the sites of major discipline problems and more heavily populated by African American and Asian students—did not fit into the identity Cobble Square parents were trying to promote, the image of Grant as a neighborhood school with a solidly middle-class ethos. Thus, their existence became a marketing problem, a challenge to parents' and the CCD's efforts to symbolically distance Grant from the rest of the "inner city" district. The school's open house, which was held to showcase Grant to prospective parents, provides a good example of the sort of "impression management" to which Cobble Square parents were driven by this problem. When I asked a white teacher about the impact of the campaign to attract neighborhood families to the school, she used an incident that occurred at the open house to highlight what she saw as the marginalization of older, African American students.

> I'll give you an example. We have a sixth grade—both sixth grade classes are very difficult. . . . The teacher was lining them up outside on the day of the open house [and the students were loud and disorderly]. And the two parents who were running—and this class is predominantly black, I would say, black and Asian. And you know, it was two white parents who were running the open house, and they came *flying,* and they said, "You've gotta get these kids in the building! The parents are coming!" And so, I mean it was obvious: they're black, these white parents are coming.

The students, she noted, were not immune to the parents' concerns:

> The kids are not stupid. They know. . . . They knew that these potential parents were coming. They knew that they were putting on a show, you know. And that it would be seen as, "You're not as important." And why? And I mean, it doesn't take—people get to that conclusion before they can think of words.

Later, a Cobble Square parent recounted the same episode, expressing frustration that the teacher had not removed the students. She also included a description of the incident—"Ms. Ellis left her loud, out-of-control class in the lobby as guests were arriving"—in a memo to the principal as an example of what she saw as unfortunate faculty apathy around attracting downtown families.

As an observer at the open house, I noticed a similar phenomenon. The parent leading the tour in which I participated took her group into several kindergarten, first-, and second-grade classrooms but did not visit a single upper-grade class. When I asked her about this over coffee a few weeks later, she said it was because the classes were so "awful," the students were "not model citizens," and the "clientele of the upper grades would not be appealing" to the parents looking at the school. Though this parent attributed her concerns to student conduct rather than race, these episodes demonstrate that, from the perspective of parents interested in attracting downtown families, the lower grades—with their more diverse classrooms and orderly students—were an asset, while the upper grades—with their mostly African American and Asian American students and more challenging behaviors—were a liability.

Parents' sense that some students were more "marketable" than others, and the inherent conflict between that perspective and the school's job of serving all students equally, represents an important tension that emerged in this context from the application of market mechanisms to a public institution. After all, the Cobble Square parents were responding to a very real aspect of the school choice process. Research on school choice—as well as the parents' own experiences—provides ample evidence that parents use race and class to select schools, with white parents much more likely to select schools that are mostly white.[27] As well, middle-class parents were concerned about the disorder they perceived as inherent to any urban school. Given these issues, it is not surprising that parents hoping to attract professional families to Grant believed prospective parents would be deterred by the sight of an unruly, largely African American group of students. They were probably right to be alarmed, as it is likely that such an image would be enough to discourage many white middle- and upper-middle-class parents.

The "It" School: Selling Grant Elementary

Parents marketed Grant in neighborhood playgrounds, praising the school while their children swung on the swings or raced around the climbing equipment. They had casual conversations in local stores and coffeeshops; identified and recruited parents they thought might be interested; and introduced themselves to reporters from the city's daily papers, hoping to interest them in a story on Grant's accomplishments. They also wrote articles for area newsletters, spoke at local preschools, put flyers around the neighborhood, and held multiple open houses. As one Cobble Square mother noted enthusiastically, these efforts successfully created a "buzz" around the school:

> We had that amazing, you know, open house, and people came from all over. And people stopped me and said, you know, "I've been on other tours, and this is just such a great tour. You guys have so much energy, you're doing so much, and we've got so much momentum, that people are calling it like the 'It' school," because we as parents have marketed it so well. You know, writing articles and fliers and just getting the word out.

Marketing language infused conversations about these efforts and the school in general. Parents, educators and CCSI administrators referred to creating a new "brand," improving "first impressions" of the school, making the school more "customer friendly," and convincing parents to "buy into" Grant; parents often described their work as a "public relations campaign."[28] Though such efforts predated the CCD's involvement, the initiative brought resources and greater sophistication, and there was near-seamless continuity between the CCSI and the neighborhood parents' agenda for the school. At Grant, as with the CCSI in general, these efforts revolved around the creation of a new identity for the school, one that overcame the broader association with the school district and "inner-city" schools. In this case, the new identity was one of a downtown, neighborhood school serving a sophisticated, high-status community.

At the early stages of the initiative, Grant parents often spoke of their efforts to attract neighborhood parents, explaining they hoped to make Grant "the kind of school that it needs to be to cater to Cobble Square." With the growing involvement of the CCD, the pool of desired families expanded to all those living in the broader Center City area. However, the demographics of the targeted population remained fairly stable: professional parents, largely white, whose default school-choice decision would not, without significant persuasion, be the neighborhood public school.

Rebranding Grant

Despite Grant's relatively good reputation, it was still, as many parents noted, a "tough sell." This was particularly the case because, compared to other high-performing downtown schools (i.e., the other two of the Big Three), it had lower test scores and a smaller percentage of white students. Responding to this concern, and perhaps to their own ambivalence about the school, Cobble Square parents used any opportunity they could to mark Grant's identity as different from Philadelphia schools in general. A conversation among a group of Center City parents at a PTO meeting provides a good example of how deliberate parents were in managing Grant's reputation. At this meeting, five mothers, all from Cobble Square or its adjacent neighborhoods, sat around a table in the library. The conversation, which had been fairly desultory as the PTO president made routine announcements, quickly became heated:

PTO president Sara moves to a district-produced report on school violence.

SARA: This report has all the serious infractions for 2002–3 broken down by school. Grant had only five incidents of severe problems, putting it in the top 20 percent in the district. Three of the incidents led to transfers to disciplinary schools, two to lateral transfers. Should we publicize this? This is a great record, people should be made aware of it.

LESLEY [leaning forward in her chair]: Why do this?

KATE: To publicize Grant.

SHARON [emphatically]: To me, five incidents would make me say, "'bye Grant."

[Lesley and Maria nod, exchanging glances.]

LESLEY: Academic achievement is something to praise, not safety.

MARIA: Something about it sounds backhanded. Five kids? What did they do?

SARA [reading report]: Violations: assault on teacher, threats, weapons . . .

SHARON [shaking her head and speaking firmly]: We don't want to publicize this!

SARA [with a worried look on her face]: But compared to others . . .

SHARON: Compared to the war zone! We don't want to even talk about this issue. It will only scare people.

Sara agrees and the conversation moves on.

These parents were cognizant that the population they were hoping to attract to Grant would expect their children's schools to be safe, would view any sort of violent incidents with alarm, and would need to see Grant as wholly different in this regard from the rest of the district.

A year later, Catherine, another Cobble Square mother, expressed the same sentiment to me in an interview. She described a conversation she had with the principal, Ms. Ashton, about unresolved bullying issues at the school. In this conversation, Ms. Ashton claimed not to have known about the bullying problems—a claim Catherine dismissed—and further incensed Catherine by using references to other Philadelphia schools to try to minimize the issue. Catherine recalled this incident with evident frustration. Her voice rose and she leaned forward, gesturing sharply with her hands.

I said, "Well, you know, people are feeling their kids are being bullied and harassed. [These issues are] not being handled, and they're going to leave the school." And Ms. Ashton said—well, basically it boiled down to, she had no idea any of this was happening, which was a lie. And, she said something like,

"We should be lucky, other kids, in other schools, are being shot, we should be lucky." And I was like, "What are you—what are you on? What are you, joking?" I was like, "Yeah, granted, our kids aren't getting shot. Yeah, and granted, this is a good school, [but] this school can be way better than it is."

Because the school district as a whole had such problems with violence, it was important to parents to show that Grant was different. And, as Catherine made clear in her interview, it was unthinkable for the school to be included in the same category as other Philadelphia schools.

One way of managing the school's identity was to emphasize its membership within a cadre of elite schools, a strategy that created the same sort of symbolic distance from the district that the CCD's branding (discussed in chapter 4) was intended to promote. With the growing prominence of the CCSI and the introduction of the Center City Academic Region, parents sometimes adopted the initiative's language, speaking proudly of Grant's identity as a "Center City school." The initiative itself was a selling point, evidence that the school was special and the focus of additional attention and resources. At the school's open house in the fall of 2005, a parent spoke about the CCSI, explaining that Grant's planned cybrary (a library makeover involving the addition of state-of-the-art hardware and software) was one result and predicting that capital improvements and other "big changes" would follow.

The creation of a new image for Grant also involved implicit and explicit appeals to status—essentially attempts to show that "the right sort of people" sent their children to Grant. These efforts were important because social ties played a key role in parents' school-choice decisions, and Center City parents felt more comfortable choosing Grant if they could point to "people like them," or of even higher social status, who had made a similar choice.[29] For example, in the spring of 2006, a Cobble Square mother trying to recruit other neighborhood parents told me about a cocktail party at her house she was planning for these parents. She explained that she would invite other "presentable" parents, as well as such notables as Paul Levy and Paul Vallas, and concluded, "I can't imagine that I can't throw a cocktail party that won't convince at least some of these people!" This parent drew from her own ample stores of financial, cultural, and social capital (she owned a beautiful house, was a gracious entertainer, and had a large network of friends and acquaintances) to show parents that hers was an affluent family that had deliberately chosen the school. This was an effective strategy. As another parent, who had enrolled her child at Grant the previous year explained, this same mother's efforts to recruit her were successful *because* her high social status was so obvious: "I was just sort of impressed that a Cobble Square person would send their kids to the school. I mean that's definitely impressive."

Other examples of these implicit and explicit shows of status included a newspaper article about parent organizing at Grant that, in naming the parents involved, indicated their educational or professional status (one had a master's degree in education, another was a lawyer, and a third was a former teacher) and an opera concert held at the school (one of the parents was a professional opera singer), which a number of parents attended in formal evening garb. By far the most dramatic example, however, was a special event held in fall 2005 to raise funds to update the school library. This elegant party, planned by a Cobble Square parent with assistance from the CCD, was held at a historic property in Cobble Square often used for weddings and high-profile fundraisers. Tickets for this event cost $100 each. At the party, waiters passed hors d'oeuvres while guests drank white wine and strolled through rooms decorated with period antiques, sumptuous curtains, and elaborate chandeliers. While the opera concert drew a relatively diverse set of parents and children, attendees at this party were predominantly white and professional. The event also featured an auction, in which several bids exceeded a thousand dollars. As a special favor to one of the parents (and to show his support for Grant), district CEO Vallas served as the auctioneer, making jokes about how much money parents were spending. The event raised over $40,000 in a single night. All of these efforts, linked as they were with material wealth and high social status, served to distance Grant from the stigma of the low-income district. They allowed parents to show that it was a school that served a more advantaged population, had ties to an affluent community, and had been chosen by people who—in contrast to the majority of Philadelphia parents—had other options for their children.

The presence of large numbers of Asian American students also played a role in Grant's rebranding. Parents and educators spoke of the school as diverse and international, and the fact that the student population was not simply divided between black and white appeared to be part of Grant's appeal. The stereotyping of Asians as the "model minority" was certainly at work here as well.[30] For example, when a charter school opened nearby, many parents and administrators were concerned that it would draw Chinese students away from Grant. One parent explained, "The charter school that's going to open is definitely—it's definitely going to hurt us. Because

you know, we like this diversity, um, I like what Asian families stereotypi-
cally bring to the table, which is, you know, [being] hard-working."[31]

A Special Kind of Neighborhood School

A final piece of Grant's new identity was its (re)construction as a neighborhood school. Although only about half of Grant's students actually
came from the catchment area, and a much smaller number came from
its immediate neighborhood, parents, administrators, and CCD staff all
spoke of their goal of making Grant into a neighborhood school. In doing so, they invoked notions of an idealized community, where families
know other families and the school is a center of community life. Both the
Cobble Square parents and the CCD embraced this vision of Center City
schools as integral parts of vibrant, cosmopolitan neighborhoods.

A CCD postcard, with a picture of a father walking with his son in a
schoolyard populated by children of various races and ethnicities, held out
the following promise:

> Walking your kids to school. Taking lunch in the front row of the school play.
> Personally introducing them to Philadelphia's theater, art, music and history.
> Center City schools offer you the opportunity to be more involved in your chil-
> dren's lives through the unique shared experiences that come from working,
> playing, living and learning right here.

Both the visuals and the language of this postcard include several interesting class markers. The parent pictured is a professionally dressed, white
man. Parents are assumed to have the interest and cultural and financial
capital to "personally introduce" their children to Philadelphia's culture
and history. They are also assumed to have enough autonomy at work to
"take lunch" during a school play. The wording and images here are thus
indicators of both the population to which the CCD was appealing and the
message it intended to convey about its target audience—that the people
who would be considering the schools have the status and inclinations the
postcard implies and would value being part of an urban community.

At the school's open house, several parents from Cobble Square ex-
tolled the virtues of their "neighborhood school," linking it to a downtown
lifestyle. As one parent said, "I am just thrilled to be here. I am so happy
with our decision to come to our neighborhood school. I love the city lifestyle. We walk everywhere! I always feel like I'm on vacation." For these

parents, the construction of Grant as a neighborhood school suggested an "urban village" of sorts where families of similar status and sophistication experienced the best of city life.

The notion of a neighborhood school has long had appeal in the United States, calling up images of rural, close-knit communities, where neighbors share the same values and look out for one another.[32] As one Grant parent commented, reflecting upon her interest in making Grant a "true neighborhood school," there is something very special about having neighbors who are involved in the same school. Not only does that provide a "support system" for school improvement efforts, it also means parents have someone to call when they forgot a lunch or cannot pick their child up from school. In a neighborhood school context, children's friendship networks are more local; they can continue to play with their school friends after they come home. And, as the CCD postcard suggested, the prospect of a companionable walk to school is compelling, particularly in the current context of long commutes and hectic schedules.

Research on the importance of parental involvement and school-community connections supports the prevailing wisdom about neighborhood schools. Parental involvement is critical to academic achievement, and it is likely easier for parents to attend various school events if the school is close to home.[33] According to a Grant administrator who had previously worked in the suburbs, when students live in the neighborhood it opens up a myriad of options for family involvement:

> And we are planning here to do some type of a reading activity in the evening, to try to bring some families together. So we're working on that, but I do think more of that would happen if it were more of a community school. And I only say that from my background being in the suburbs. . . . [W]e'd have a winter carnival on a Saturday and there would be activities and games for kids to do and crafts for families to buy. It became more of a neighborhood and a community. Where you don't really have that here.

Such activities could lead to stronger and more positive relations between school and community, relationships that are essential to sustained school improvement.[34]

In addition, scholars are increasingly recognizing the importance of school-community connections and the powerful intersections between school and neighborhood transformation. This interest in neighborhood schools is "embedded in widespread assumptions about the power of the neighborhood as a potential source of school improvement and school quality. Neighborhood schools are expected to boost community attachment to schools, encourage resource sharing, and increase parent involvement and social capital."[35] Thus, in arguing for the value of making Grant a neighborhood school, parents and educators were certainly not alone.

Yet the notion of the neighborhood school has another history as well. It has been invoked in opposition to desegregation policies, with critics arguing that busing children to schools in different neighborhoods has negative consequences for education and community. This stance goes back to the early days of integration and was the logic behind many of the decisions that rolled back desegregation. In a historical analysis of the politics of busing in Chicago in the 1960s, Danns found that opponents often argued that interfering with neighborhood enrollment patterns was disruptive to families and communities. However, "underlying many of their arguments was the fact that some lived in communities that excluded blacks and some resented the fact that the Board of Education now sought to bring the very people they had moved away from into their neighborhoods."[36] Though the discourse at Grant was significantly less contentious than that surrounding busing controversies, dynamics at the school reflected the same tensions. Because Cobble Square was a largely white neighborhood—and Center City as a whole was predominantly middle- and upper-middle class—cries for Grant to become a "true neighborhood school" essentially excluded, both symbolically and materially, the predominantly African American and working-class families who did not live within the neighborhood but wanted access to the school.

Contesting Grant's New Identity: The Case of the Principal Selection Process

Grant's identity as a unique neighborhood school serving a high-status community did not go uncontested—particularly by people aware of the exclusionary possibilities. Some teachers, for example, were skeptical of parents' efforts to "rebrand" Grant. Earlier in this chapter, I discussed an incident at the school's open house, in which a teacher's decision to leave her (in the words of a Cobble Square mother) "loud, out-of-control class" in the yard just as a group of Center City parents was entering the building attracted the ire of several Cobble Square parents. One of these mothers later told me that she had expressed her concern to the teacher, to which the teacher responded angrily, "You need to face facts. You need to stop trying to make this school something it's not! You need to face reality about what this school is." This teacher's angry response implied that parents like her were ignoring Grant's status as an urban public school serving a diverse, often-challenging population.

An incident at a PTO meeting in the spring of 2004 made the contested nature of Grant's identity quite clear. At this meeting, attended by about a dozen parents, Sara, the PTO president, discussed her (and other parents') dissatisfaction with Ms. Ashton, Grant's principal, explaining that Vallas had asked for feedback about her performance. Sara recounted a conversation she had with Ms. Ashton in which the principal claimed to have been "handpicked" to lead the school because of her experience in inner-city schools. Sara saw this as an example of Ms. Ashton's lack of fit with the school, exclaiming, "This is not an inner-city school! This is a Cobble Square school!" (Notably, this conversation occurred at a time when only a few dozen, at most, of the students at Grant were from Cobble Square.)

Janice, a working-class African American mother from another part of Philadelphia, stiffened when she heard this, crossing her arms and assuming a disapproving expression. When she saw me looking at her, she shook her head and said, in a low voice to herself and those around her, "This is not a Cobble Square school. Not all the kids come from Cobble Square. They come from all over, North Philly, South Philly, West Philly." A few other parents, including a white husband and wife sitting near me, looked at her sympathetically and gestured to her to speak up. Janice did, explaining in angry tones that she did not agree with the term "Cobble Square school." She was interrupted, however, by Ms. Ashton's voice on the intercom system, reading the morning announcements. When the announcements were completed, Sara began again to discuss concerns about Ms. Ashton. Though a few (white and black) mothers whispered that Janice was not finished talking, Sara either did not hear them or chose to ignore them. The mothers exchanged glances with Janice but did not persist, while Janice continued to talk under her breath.

The areas Janice mentioned, North, South, and West Philadelphia, are all heavily African American, poor or working-class parts of the city. Thus, it appears that Janice's frustration with the "Cobble Square school" remark was rooted in her sense that it excluded the many African American transfer students whose families were less affluent than those in Cobble Square. While she had chosen to transfer her child to Grant because of its superior reputation, Janice resented the notion that Grant was somehow *qualitatively* different from other Philadelphia schools, especially because this difference—as articulated by the Cobble Square parents—meant emphasizing its association with an affluent, white community and rejecting its connections with a city system serving large numbers of low-income African Americans. The way Janice was silenced—either intentionally or unintentionally—at that meeting also demonstrates the power of the Cobble Square parents to set and control the PTO's agenda.

The disagreement over Grant's identity and its future came to a head at the end of the 2004–5 school year. Over the previous year, a number of Cobble Square parents had capitalized upon Vallas's interest in Grant and communicated with him repeatedly about their dissatisfaction with Ms. Ashton, whom they saw as obstructionist, overly bureaucratic, and incapable of marketing the school. Complaints about Ms. Ashton were not limited to this group, however: several low-income African American mothers also expressed frustration at her rigidity. Teachers too were generally quite unhappy with the way she treated them. Toward the end of her tenure at Grant in the spring of 2005, Ms. Ashton had few supporters.

Though many parents were frustrated with Ms. Ashton, Cobble Square mothers clearly took the lead in convincing the district to replace her. Their activism in this regard alarmed many African American parents, who worried that the Cobble Square parents were assuming too much control over the school. At one meeting late in 2004 (seven months after the meeting in which Janice objected to Grant's designation as a "Cobble Square school"), PTO president Sara again expressed her concerns about Ms. Ashton, referring this time to the many complaints she had heard from teachers about Ms. Ashton's behavior toward them. When she did, several African American parents at the meeting objected, saying that the PTO should not get involved with a "teachers' issue."

Sara moved on but later in the meeting returned to the topic, reiterating that Vallas had asked for her input on Ms. Ashton's performance. She proposed writing Vallas a letter describing some of the frustrations parents and teachers had shared with her. To protect the identities of those who had confided in her, she suggested keeping the letter private. While the white parents in the room seemed satisfied with this plan, a number of African American parents protested, objecting both to involving the PTO in disputes between Ms. Ashton and the teachers and to the prospect of a "private" letter. Donna, an African American mother who often sided with the Cobble Square parents, became so angry that she stood up and proclaimed, "If the letter is going to go out from the PTO and I'm not going to see it, I have to say I don't want to be a part of the PTO!" Others in attendance applauded. The Cobble Square parents quickly backpedaled. "Well, let's not throw the baby out with the bathwater," soothed Sharon, and the issue was dropped.

In an interview a few weeks later, Lisa, who had been one of the parents objecting to Sara's plan, explained her reason for responding so forcefully:

> As an African American woman, when you see a group of white people coming after you, you feel like you're going to get lynched. That's a reality. . . . We are a very peculiar people, and we will rally behind our own. Look at OJ, look at Michael Jackson. That's the way it goes. That's the way it goes. You're going to lynch one of our own? I don't care what he's done!

Racial tensions ran high among parents throughout that winter and early spring, with many African American parents rallying around Ms. Ashton and criticizing the Cobble Square parents' efforts to remove her.

The tensions between parents during this time were more than a struggle between different racial groups about power or racial loyalty; at a fundamental level, they were about what kind of school Grant would become. This became clear in the spring of 2005 when the district announced it would be moving Ms. Ashton to a position in the central office and selecting a new principal for Grant. District administrators who visited the school during this period told parents that, because of the CCSI and the school's new status as a *Center City* school, a parent (as well as a representative from the CCD) would serve on the committee that interviewed candidates and made final recommendations to the district. When district administrators explained the process for selecting the principal and suggested that parents elect their representative at a PTO meeting, parents immediately began to clash about how best to do that, with the neighborhood and transfer parents forming opposing camps.

While parents' disagreements during this meeting and in the weeks that followed focused on the process for electing their representative, it quickly became clear that a number of transfer parents were worried that white Cobble Square parents would end up choosing the new principal. Thus, when the Cobble Square parents wanted to move quickly to elect a representative for the principal selection committee (arguing that whoever showed up for a particular meeting should be the ones to vote), transfer parents resisted, afraid that without wide participation a Cobble Square parent would be elected. This contention persisted through one special meeting after another.

Cobble Square parents were frustrated by what they saw as unreasonable opposition to their involvement in such an important process. They believed the transfer parents had unnecessarily injected race into the issue. In an interview in a local deli conducted several months later, a Cobble Square mother spoke angrily about the parents who had opposed her membership on the committee to select the new principal: "I was told that the 'sisters' [i.e., black women] would never allow a white woman to be on that committee . . . because they didn't feel like a white woman could represent their interests." Transfer parents who were vocal during this period believed that the neighborhood parents had a particular and exclusive agenda for the school. A transfer mother I interviewed during this time explained that many parents were "fearful," believing the Cobble Square parents had "their own agenda" and did not "care about anyone else." They knew neighborhood parents hoped to promote Grant's identity as a neighborhood school, an agenda that implicitly excluded families like theirs and was rooted in—and legitimized—a discourse about class that they found marginalizing.

A district administrator, who heard about these tensions from a contact at the CCD and was concerned that they were escalating, intervened and suggested that two PTO officers (Sara, who was white and from Cobble Square, and Janice, who was black and a transfer parent) serve as representatives. After that, the controversy died down somewhat. Yet several parents' comments after the fact showed that they hoped the new principal would embrace neither the identity for Grant promoted by Cobble Square parents nor the special treatment for middle- and upper-middle-class families such an identity indicated. At a PTO meeting held in the evening (to attract more participation) and focusing on parents' expectations for the new principal, Kim, an African American transfer mother, was explicit about her concerns:

> We want someone [for principal] who is interested in making the school the best. Someone who doesn't care who is here. . . . We want a principal who can treat everyone of different classes equally. Watch how he responds to Sara and Janice. Is there a difference?

In an interview held a few weeks later, Rhonda, a middle-class African American transfer mother, made a similar point: "Everybody needs to be up on par with this. Every parent needs to be addressed and culturally respected in the school." These parents envisioned a school in which families would have the same value, no matter their race, class, or residence, and the principal would have no need or desire to cater to particular groups.

Despite these parents' protests, the more powerful group at Grant—the middle and upper-middle-class Center City parents working with the CCD—appeared to have "won" the battle over Grant's identity, or at least a significant early round. Among the people who applied for Grant's principalship was Ms. Fordham, a white Center City resident who had long been involved in local business, was friendly with an influential Cobble Square mother, and had previously worked as a principal in the suburbs. After interviewing all the candidates, the principal selection committee agreed on its two top choices and, believing that because Ms. Fordham had such powerful connections she was already likely to be chosen by the district, deliberately did not include her in their selection. In later conversations, representatives explained that they thought Ms. Fordham would do a good job at the school but they liked the other two candidates a bit more, particularly because they had experience in Philadelphia schools. In making the final decision, district administrators—possibly influenced by the CCD and the voice of a powerful Cobble Square mother[37]—nevertheless overrode the committee's recommendation and chose Ms. Fordham.

Ms. Fordham was attractive and charismatic. She wore expensive suits and jewelry and had many ties with local community and business leaders. As one participant in the selection process, who expressed concerns about Ms. Fordham's lack of experience in Philadelphia schools, said, she was chosen because she had status, connections, and was a good salesperson; from the CCD's perspective, "she was perfect." Once in her position, Ms. Fordham spoke often about the importance of making Grant a neighborhood school, introduced herself to prospective neighborhood parents, and actively recruited several Cobble Square families—although she also maintained that the school's mission was to serve *all* its students well. At PTO meetings and when she spoke at the school's open house, she gave the impression of an energetic, engaging principal who was willing to work closely with parents.

Tensions within the PTO, which had come to a head during the selection process, died down, and the parents returned to more everyday tasks, such as planning fundraisers and special events. Yet the social divisions within the school remained. White Cobble Square parents continued to be valued customers, while the African American parents of transfer students maintained their diminished status.

"I've Never Felt So Recruited in My Life!": Parents and School Choice

What did all of this mean for parents as they engaged in choosing a school for their children? Here I will describe the ways the market at Grant—shaped as it was by the CCSI and the discourse of middle-class value—affected parents during the school-choice process. To do so, I will focus on the experiences of four Grant mothers (all actively involved in the school), chosen because their stories are representative of general patterns found at the school, in which professional families were heavily recruited and transfer families had to manipulate administrative channels to secure admission. Whereas proponents of choice policies often assume all parents will be equal players in the educational market, this was not the case here. Instead, a family's class status determined its position. And this positioning was legitimized, as we have seen, by the expectation that middle-class families would be an asset to the school.

Catherine and Sue Anne are both white Cobble Square mothers, professionals with at least college degrees, and relatively affluent. Both are married. When I asked Catherine and Sue Anne (in separate interviews) about their choice process, they told fairly long, involved stories about comparing public, private, and (in Sue Anne's case) parochial and charter schools. Grant was attractive to them because it had a good reputation, was located in their neighborhood (which enabled them to walk their children to and from school), and was free. Both parents said they were reluctant to use private schools because they had more than one child and the tuition would just be too high. For Catherine, who is an educator, part of the appeal of coming to Grant was the opportunity to work with other parents to improve the school, particularly around literacy, which was her specialty.

Both parents recalled being heavily recruited by other Cobble Square parents, and both understood from this that their status at the school, as affluent Center City parents, would be special in some way. For Catherine, because she wanted to help improve Grant, this was a major selling point. In choosing Grant she was influenced by another neighborhood mother who, referencing the expectation among school and district leaders that parents like her would make the school better and the leverage this gave her, told Catherine she had such influence that "they'll do anything I want them to do!" Sue Anne had a similar experience. Describing multiple conversations with Grant parents, being stopped on the street and at the playground, and fliers stuffed in her mailbox, she exclaimed, "I've never felt so recruited in my life. . . . Like, I felt like if I had been an athlete, maybe I'd have gotten a car!"

Despite their children's positive experiences at Grant, Catherine and Sue Anne expressed ongoing reservation about the school's academics and climate and continually emphasized keeping their options open. Sue Anne and her husband reminded each other often that they could always move their child to a different school, and Catherine, dissatisfied with Grant's academic climate and her own involvement in the PTO, eventually put her child in private school. (This reliance on the "exit option" will be discussed in chapter 6.) Because they lived within the catchment area, they did not have to struggle to gain admissions to the school. In fact, their original encounters with the school were as highly prized patrons who could always withdraw their patronage if they were not satisfied.

Kim and Patricia's experiences were different. Both African American, they lived in low-income parts of the city that were outside of Grant's catchment area. Kim was a single parent; Patricia's husband was a soldier serving in Iraq. At the time of our interviews, Kim had a bachelor's degree and Patricia had almost completed her degree, but neither was working outside the home. In contrast with Catherine and Sue Anne, Kim and Patricia praised the school's programs and believed it deserved its good reputation. They chose Grant as a way of escaping the low-performing schools in their neighborhoods. In an interview conducted on the floor of her living room (the room had only one chair), Patricia spoke critically of her neighborhood school:

> I have a school right up the street, and when they come [out at the end of the day], they're wild. I mean, it's wild, and it's like, what are the parents doing at home? . . . Every time they're coming out of there, it's a fight. Most of the time it's a fight. . . . Instead of just going straight home to do homework or whatever they need to do, they're just wild.

Patricia and her husband debated sending their son to parochial school but were advised by his preschool teacher (and, later, her hairdresser) to try to get him into one of the good Center City elementary schools. A family friend, thought to have "pull" at the school, promised to get their son into Grant, but his help turned out to be insufficient. Their first encounter with the principal, Ms. Ashton, was quite negative. As potential transfer parents, they tried to enroll their child in the school in the spring of 2004. Patricia explains:

> When we first took the paperwork down there, Ms. Ashton did come off with like a little bit of an attitude. . . . She was like, "Well, I'mma tell you right now, we are only accepting for kindergarten, but you have to fill this out first." And it was like the *way* she said it to me. So I instantly got an attitude, because I felt like she was talking to me like I was some young parent, that didn't know any better. So, I just said, "Well, you know what, here is the paperwork."

While Ms. Ashton checked the forms, Patricia's husband came into the office, saw her expression, and asked what was wrong. Patricia explained: "I said, 'You know what, you need to talk to her, because, I think if I say any more, there might be a confrontation.' I said, 'Because I didn't like the way she talked to me just now.'" By the September their son was supposed to begin kindergarten, Patricia and her husband still did not know if he had been accepted at Grant. When they finally heard from the principal that there was a spot for him, they were also told they would have to repeat the application process for the first grade.[38]

Kim had to struggle to get her three children into Grant as well. Her story began at her neighborhood school in South Philadelphia, where her son received special education services. Dissatisfied with the quality of these services, she requested that he be transferred to one of the high-performing Center City schools. Her first request was denied, and her children remained in the neighborhood school while she "fought for a year to get them out." After speaking several times at public school district meetings, she finally persuaded the district to allow her children to transfer: "Vallas offered us Grant. I was happy with Grant."[39]

While Kim and Patricia were both successful in enrolling their children at Grant, it is important to note that many parents like them were not as fortunate. As I explained in chapter 3, each year hundreds of children applied for admissions to the Big Three schools and only a small number were admitted. It is difficult to determine whether connections, personal appeals, or sheer luck explained their success when so many others had failed. However, Kim and Patricia also applied to Grant before the priority admissions policy went into effect and before many spots at the school were filled by within-catchment students; it is very unlikely they, or other parents in a similar situation, would have been successful had they gone through the process a year later. In addition, Kim and Patricia's victory came at some cost. In their first encounters with the school, they were put in the position of someone who was *not* entitled to be there, someone who had had to "work the system" to gain access to a school that was not supposed to be available to them.

Even before the CCSI, Grant Elementary was home to a powerful discourse around social class that positioned middle- and upper-middle-class families as supportive of education, committed to high academic achievement, and likely to be positively involved in schools. The flip side of this discourse was the implicit and explicit positioning of low-income and working-class families as the source of dysfunction and academic failure. Such perceptions are, of course, rooted in contemporary understandings of race and class in the United States that position middle-class families as functional and virtuous and low-income families as distressed and, in many cases, pathological.[40] For this reason, the differential status attributed to social class groups at Grant could represent an important, and underexplored, dynamic in economically integrated urban schools more broadly. The CCSI, an effort to market schools to downtown professional families, legitimized and strengthened this discourse.

This chapter has shown that the marketing of Grant strove to create a new, elite identity for the school. In the process, the marketing campaign turned downtown families themselves into commodities, sought-after people whose very association could symbolically and materially ensure the success of the schools, downtown, and, indeed, city as a whole. The belief that middle- and upper-middle-class families merited special treatment because they could improve the school exemplifies what Margaret Somers calls a "contractualization" of citizenship.[41] As Somers notes, the increasing dominance of market principles can reshape relationships between individuals and the state, such that a person's right to full citizenship becomes dependent upon what he or she can contribute. Yet unlike the quid pro quo transaction Somers describes (paid labor for the rights of citizenship), the "good" exchanged here was a promise of something to come, based on the financial, cultural, and social capital middle-class families were assumed to offer a resource-poor system.

Within Grant's educational market, students were part of the product as well, with their presence and behaviors at the school helping to shape its desirability. Low-income and minority students, particularly those who did not adhere to the middle-class parents' expectations for appropriate behavior, became a liability. In contrast, the middle- and upper-middle-class children of neighborhood parents were put forth as the ideal.

I have argued here that the marketing of an urban public school—and particularly the intersection between a marketing campaign and existing hierarchies of race, class, and geography—exacerbated inequalities at Grant. In this case, the marketing project did not simply treat some customers (parents) as more valuable than others. Animated as it was by a sense of urgent need, it also legitimized this differential status as ultimately beneficial for the school and the city. As such, the marketing of Grant coexisted uneasily with, and in some instances undermined, the school's traditional responsibility of treating all students and their families equally. The implications of this tension will be explored at greater length in the next chapter.

CHAPTER SIX

"This School Can Be Way Better!"

Transforming Grant Elementary

It's not like this is a private school, where their money is cash and mine is from the government! —Sabrina, African American parent at Grant Elementary

When Catherine, a white Cobble Square mother, enrolled her child at Grant, she committed to spending a great deal of time, energy, and resources on the school. When Patricia, an African American transfer mother (also introduced in chapter 5), enrolled her child, she too planned to do everything she could to help Grant. Both Catherine and Patricia are intelligent, caring, and dedicated parents, but just as these two women experienced the choice process very differently, so too did they differ in their experiences as involved parents at the school. These differences were more than simply a matter of individual preference or personality. Rather, the emphasis within the school and district on attracting middle-class families—and the use of marketing strategies, preferences in admissions, and improved customer service to accomplish this task—intensified dynamics around race, class, and geography and affected parents' status and efficacy at the school.

A large body of research attests to the benefits of economic integration, showing that the presence of a significant number of middle-class families in a school can, in part because of the involvement of middle-class parents, lead to greater learning for all students.[1] At the same time, a growing popular literature describes dramatic transformations to individual urban schools brought about by cadres of energetic and committed middle-class parents.[2] Yet these stories of the benefits of middle-class involvement, so often told by members of the middle class themselves—researchers, journalists, or triumphant parents—are incomplete. They rarely include the voices or experiences of the families who were already there, who neither sought nor contributed to this transformation. Here I argue that events at Grant support the claim that an increased middle-class (and, in this case, upper-middle-class) presence brings resources to the school. However, my research also reveals other dynamics overlooked in tales of urban school "renaissance." First, many poor and working-class parents at Grant had their own ideas about improving the school, ideas that sometimes conflicted with those of the more advantaged parents. Second, when economic integration is brought about by recruiting more affluent parents to the school and giving them special leverage and access, the benefits of their presence can come at the expense of status and power for other groups.[3]

To provide a more complete story of race, class, and urban school change, I first explore parents' activities at Grant, examining the ways different groups of parents were involved and the agendas they pursued. I show that parental involvement was by no means limited to the middle and upper-middle classes. However, parents' views of the school's needs and of the value of different sorts of involvement were heavily patterned by class, with working-class parents focused on supporting the school and middle- and upper-middle-class parents interested in transforming it. Then I turn to parents' differential status at the school, status that was rooted in race and class but also in the particulars of the CCSI, and how that affected parents' ability to achieve their goals.

On the one hand, the CCSI had a positive impact on Grant because it created conditions under which upper-middle-class neighborhood parents could bring significant additional resources to the school, resources that benefited all the students. The additional power and access professional parents derived from their status as the "customers" the district "ought to be wooing," and the ways the school district and the Center City District (CCD) strove to cater to them, made these parents particularly effective in their efforts to improve the school.[4] Aware of their special status, they did not hesitate to use it as leverage.

Middle-class parents' sense of themselves as valued customers was especially apparent in their frequent references to the possibility of leaving the school. According to economist Albert Hirschman, the "exit option" is a strategy commonly used by customers in the marketplace: they choose to exit by not buying an unsatisfactory product. Hirschman contrasts this with "voice," a practice more typical of the public sector, whereby dissatisfied individuals or groups try to change a particular organization to make it more to their liking. He further notes that the "presence of the exit option can sharply reduce the probability that the voice option will be taken up widely and effectively."[5] At Grant, middle-class parents often used "voice," working as activists to change the school. However, they did so with the threat of exit in the background (making it clear that if they were not satisfied, they would remove their children from Grant).

On the other hand, the conditions that empowered professional parents disempowered the parents of transfer students, many of whom were working class and African American. As a result, these families' full membership within the school community and ability to advocate for their own children was compromised. When they were dissatisfied, they could not effectively wield the threat of exit. Their leaving would not inflict the "revenue loss" that the exit of middle-class families would.[6] Moreover, unlike the middle class, these families had few alternatives.

From Bake Sales to a Cybrary: Parental Involvement at Grant

Parents, especially mothers, were a strong and constant presence at Grant Elementary. They were in classrooms, in the lunchroom, meeting with the principal, leading tours, and holding meetings and informal conversations in hallways, empty classrooms, and the schoolyard. Unquestionably, their presence and activities had a major impact on the school. Though parents from all class and racial groups were heavily involved, the types of activity parents pursued tended to vary by social class.

Parents' efforts fell into the following general categories: core academic programs; physical environment; discipline; parent relations and communication; partnerships; staffing; volunteering with students; fundraising; marketing, public relations and recruiting; providing supplies to students and teachers; and supporting students.[7] Because I am interested in the links between involvement and school change, I also divide parents' activities into two broader realms: those that were generally *supportive* of the school, its staff, and pre-existing programs (such as fundraising and volunteering) and those that were more *activist* in orientation (such as advocating for a new principal or starting a new program). For the purposes of this analysis, I call an activity supportive if the parents involved were working with or at the behest of school staff on something the staff believed to be necessary. In contrast, I use the activist label to describe activities that originated with parents' own ideas about what the school needed.

In many cases this distinction had less to do with the nature of the activity than the context in which it occurred. For example, when parents tried to improve the school's snow-removal efforts in the week following a major snowstorm, that could be seen as a supportive activity, because they were assisting with something the school was already doing. However, I call it activist because my fieldnotes describe numerous conflicts between parents and administrators about the school's snow removal, with parents arguing that it was inadequate and calling city and school district officials to complain. Similarly, when a number of Cobble Square parents began answering phones in the office (after the school eliminated a secretary), they did this less out of an interest in supporting the administration than from their concern that it would "look bad" if the office phones were not answered. In terms of understanding parental involvement at Grant, the difference between something that is supportive and something that is activist matters because it speaks to parents' assertion of power within the school. Supportive activities leave the traditional balance of power (i.e., that educators are the "experts" and determine what needs to be done and how) intact, whereas activist efforts challenge this, positioning parents as the ones to set the agenda.

Parents were involved in so many different ways at Grant that an exhaustive discussion here would be tedious (appendix B provides a complete list). I will, instead, give some examples of the types of activities I witnessed, the different parents who were involved, and their agendas. Rather than referring to parental involvement in a general sense, my goal here is to show its complexity and diversity. Being specific about the various types of activities reveals how much they varied by class.

Professional parents (mostly from Cobble Square) led all of the efforts in the area of core academic programs, which included replacing an outdated library with a cybrary and implementing an intensive reading program. When I began my research, the school had no librarian, and the library was shabby and rarely used. After cleaning out the books and repainting the walls and tables, parents convinced the school district to make Grant a pilot in its cybrary program and raised nearly $50,000 to fund the changes. The district (despite its chronic fiscal shortfalls and myriad other obligations) paid the other $150,000.[8] A year later, the cybrary was opened with much fanfare, including coverage from the local media. The old, shabby space was transformed by parents and district staff into a bright, airy room with colorful décor and well-stocked shelves. Outdated books and card catalogues had vanished, replaced by a wealth of high-tech equipment (including laptops, interactive video conferencing and production devices, and "Smartboards"), as well as new books and periodicals.

Middle- and upper-middle-class parents were also responsible for the new playground (a project that included convincing the district to allocate funds, negotiating with neighbors about the construction, and working with district staff on design issues). For this project, a new play structure (largely designed for children in the primary grades) was installed in the formerly empty school yard; improvements were also made to the yard's surface. In addition, middle- and upper-middle-class parents took the lead in expressing concerns to the school and school district about discipline and bullying problems, asking that the administration be more responsive to the parents of bullying victims and pushing for greater parent information about how discipline problems were being handled at the school. However, other activities that fall within the discipline category—such as volunteering to supervise student lunches—attracted a more broad-based group of parents.

Efforts around parent relations also attracted both middle-class Cobble Square parents and working-class transfer parents, many of whom participated in the school's Back-to-School night and staffed an information desk for parents in the school lobby. However, a Cobble Square mother took the lead in asking the school to change its "communication folders," the school's primary vehicle for home-school communications. One working-class parent cultivated relationships with local businesses (such as the florist who donated flowers for different events and the local grocery store), but the majority of partnership work was done by middle- and upper-middle-class parents. These included developing relationships with a nearby bookstore (through a fundraising program that allocated a portion of sales to the school) and creating formal connections with local civic associations.

Marketing, public relations, and recruiting activities were unquestionably and exclusively the province of middle- and upper-middle-class parents. These efforts, as discussed in the previous chapter, were numerous, time-consuming, and varied from the informal to formal. Middle- and upper-middle-class parents also led the most activist efforts around staffing, including replacing the principal, convincing the district to allocate an additional kindergarten teacher to reduce class size, saving a teacher's job when it was threatened, and registering complaints with the district CEO about other teachers and administrators perceived to be incompetent.

Whereas middle-class parents dominated the first seven areas I have discussed (e.g., core academic programs; physical environment; discipline; parental involvement; partnerships; marketing, public relations, and recruiting; and staffing), working-class and low-income parents were far more involved in the final four realms. For example, while PTO parents of all social classes helped out with fundraising activities, the majority of these efforts were coordinated by one working-class mother of transfer students, who organized the annual book sale and sales of wrapping paper and candy. However, the "big ticket" fundraiser, for the cybrary, was planned by upper-middle-class parents. Similarly, many PTO parents volunteered in the classroom, but volunteering with students was a much greater focus for working-class African American parents. The entire PTO participated in funding and purchasing supplies for the school (such as basketball uniforms, copier equipment, and so on). Other forms of student support, such as holding parties for honor roll students, coordinating the sale of low-cost computers, and giving money to the student council, involved a range of parents. But, again, working-class parents were more focused on these activities than were the middle-class parents.

Such patterns are important. They demonstrate that the neighborhood, professional parents' views of—and agenda for—the school were quite different from those of working-class parents. Essentially, whereas working-class parents were generally satisfied with the school, middle- and upper-middle-class parents believed it fell far short of its potential. They were actively striving to recreate both the image Grant projected and the reality of what it offered their children.

Middle- and Upper-Middle-Class Parents: A Transformative Agenda

Professional parents, particularly white parents, were much more likely to be involved in efforts I have labeled activist. Among other things, they wanted a new principal, smaller class sizes, stricter discipline, and a new library. And, as I discussed in chapter 5, they believed that the more professional families there were at the school, the more likely it was that these changes would happen.

In their study of gentrification in London, Garry Robson and Tim Butler describe middle-class parents who, as a way of dealing with what they believe is an inadequate local school, work together to transform the school or to "colonize primary education by 're-inventing' a school." The dynamics they describe—in which a group of parents focused on one school and "transformed its ethos into one of a middle-class school even if their children remained a statistical minority in a school with a socially deprived minority"— resonate with the Cobble Square parents' efforts.[9] These parents strove to create a school that would appeal to other parents like them, parents with the option to select an independent, charter, or other public school, or to move to the suburbs. Their point of comparison when they spoke of Grant was not the other schools in the district but other high-performing public, private, and charter schools. For example, when I spoke with Catherine, an educator who worked part-time, in her Cobble Square home, she referred explicitly to the competition Grant faced from other, higher-achieving schools: "And I do know a bunch of people, last year and now again this year, where Grant is like, last on their list." Because Grant often fared poorly in comparison to those schools (in terms of academic performance, programs, and amenities), Cobble Square parents felt significant changes were in order.

When I asked these parents what they liked least or what goals they had for the school, they were quick to rattle off a list of several items, from enrichment programs to enhancements to the building. Thus, in our interview Catherine smiled wryly, pointed to the computer sitting on a small table in the corner of her dining room, and said she kept a running list. Catherine's list included "marketing, embracing the local resources, and addressing bullying," in addition to the literacy program she helped implement. Overall, while middle- and upper-middle-class parents did work on some supportive tasks (including supervising school lunches and helping with fundraisers), these parents tended to focus the bulk of their energies on tasks designed to alter the school's staffing, programming, facilities, and student population.

Working-Class Parents: A Supportive Agenda

In contrast, the working-class parents saw Grant as a high-status school with a strong academic program and a positive climate. As discussed earlier, transfer parents in particular tended to compare the school to their low-performing neighborhood school and to feel confident about the school's academic programs. When I asked one African American parent from a low-income neighborhood what she liked least about the school or hoped to change, she responded, "Nothing really. I haven't come across anything so far." Janet, a lower-middle-class African American mother (who lived in a small apartment in Cobble Square and was one of the few African American parents from the neighborhood) shared the transfer parents' positive perspectives. She chose to live in the neighborhood and send her children to the school because she had "heard it was a good school, and . . . that that's one of the few schools that is still one of the better schools, as far as the elementary levels." Janet did not work outside of the home and was deeply involved in her two young children's schooling. Later in the interview, she spoke critically of the divisions around race and class she had experienced at the school. Yet, when I asked her about changes she would like to see at Grant, she mused, "Hmmm. Never really thought about it that much." This is not to say that all poor or working-class parents were always satisfied with the school; that would certainly not be the case. One working-class African American mother spoke very critically to me of Ms. Ashton, the principal (whom she believed unfairly singled out her children when they were late to school), and several expressed concerns about the climate and social divisions within the school. Nevertheless, these parents did not offer the same comprehensive critique that middle-class parents did.

Instead, working-class parents focused more on activities around supporting the school and its administration, including volunteering in the classroom, organizing special events and prizes for high-achieving students (particularly in the upper grades), and helping with school performances and sports events. In our interview, Patricia smiled when she discussed volunteering in her son's kindergarten and pointed out a thank-you sign from the class that hung prominently on her living room wall:

> I'm just here for my son, take him to school, make sure everything is going smoothly, and if they need me, if I can volunteer, you know, I definitely volunteer in the class, and I like working with all the kids. They gave me that [points to wall] for helping them out with the 100 Book Challenge.

Of all the activities I have labeled activist in my categorization, not one was led or coordinated by a low-income or working-class parent. In fact, my data include few examples of any of these parents even being involved in the more activist efforts.

This difference in agendas could be tied to a diminished sense of entitlement or agency among the working-class parents, an unwillingness to challenge or question professional educators, or to a fear of rocking the boat and losing their child's coveted transfer spot (a point I return to later in this chapter). However, several of these parents were leaders within the PTO and had no trouble taking charge of fundraising initiatives or organizing student activities, and, as I have said, they were uniformly positive about the school's educational programming. As a result, it appears that the variation in parental activity was due largely to a different set of expectations for the school and a different understanding of the school's strengths, needs, and how parents could be most useful. This implies that class affects not just what parents are *able* to do but what they think is *necessary*, a finding that would certainly not surprise proponents of economic integration, who argue that one reason middle-class schools generally produce better educational outcomes is that middle-class parents have such elevated expectations.

Whereas the middle- and upper-middle-class parents believed their efforts were having a positive impact on the school, working-class parents were more skeptical. To these parents, the middle-class parents' actions were evidence of an unseemly interest in publicity and politics and a disregard for what their children were actually doing in school. Janet, quoted earlier, is an African American mother who lived in a modest apartment near Grant but did not see herself as one of the "neighborhood" parents. Here she speaks derisively of the upper-middle-class Cobble Square parents' involvement:

> I've been in the school fundraiser with the parents who aren't in the news, and I've been around the parents who, every time you turn around, their name is on the front page of a newsletter. And the parents who are outside that loop, they say, "You know, I really don't care about that, I'm really worried about what's going on with my kid in the classroom, and I'm here to help the teachers in that effort." And I see that. And I can even see that in my daughter's own classroom. There's two parents in particular who are very active in the PTO, could care less about what's going on in the classroom with their kid.

Janet's distinction here between being in "that loop" and volunteering in the classroom is similar in some ways to the one I have drawn between activist and supportive activities. Parents who were working through the PTO to make various substantive changes to Grant did not, in Janet's eyes, truly care about what was happening in the classroom. When I met with

Sabrina, a health-care worker who lived in a low-income part of West Philadelphia, she made a similar observation:

> They want to be up there to cut the ribbon, but they're not putting any work into anything. And it's like a hidden agenda. I think that a lot of people are there for political reasons. I think that whatever the steps are in politics, the Grant PTO, that must be one of them. You know what I mean? Because it's such a prestigious school.

Sabrina's comment reveals both her positive view of Grant and her sense that certain parents were overly interested in the attention they derived from their involvement.

These parents' skepticism was rooted in a sense that Grant was *already* a good school and that major changes were simply not necessary. For example, Janet observed that Grant's status as "one of the better schools" in Philadelphia was the reason she and her husband remained in the Grant area, despite the difficulties they had in affording it: "Because I wanted to move. . . . But, when I looked at the different areas, I looked at their schools, and I said, well, let's just hang out here for a little while longer." This perspective underscores the class tensions that dogged parental involvement at Grant: not only did working-class parents not share their more affluent counterparts' agenda, they viewed the middle-class parents' activities as evidence of a motivation that was puzzling at best.

To many working-class parents, the middle-class parents who were putting so much energy into changing the school were doing it for their own (rather than the students' or school's) benefit. Here is Kim, a working-class African American mother, talking about the Cobble Square parents: "[They were] more interested in what was going on in the school as opposed to what was going on in the classroom. They would do one thing in the classroom to make it kind of look good, but then they were busy-bodying around the school." When she spoke of involvement in the classroom, she meant helping students with their academic work, not trying to improve pedagogy or curriculum. Parents who did focus on issues of curriculum—who were interested in "what was going on in the school" as opposed to the classroom—were, in Kim's terms, "busy-bodying around the school."

Parents like Kim, Patricia, and Janet did not necessarily believe the school was perfect—and they were happy to devote large amounts of time and energy to improving Grant and helping the students there—but the sorts of changes they wanted to see were around the edges. For example, Kim was motivated by an interest in maintaining the high academic standards already in place:

> It's the quality and just making sure that the academics are on level, that the kids are being challenged, that the expectations of the kids are high. So the kids can achieve. That problem [low expectations] you don't have too much of at Grant, because the teachers are fantastic. They're really good. They give the kids a lot of exposure to try to make the kids very well rounded.

To the extent that Kim and others who shared her perspectives pursued a different vision for Grant, it was one in which the school essentially continued to function as it had, only somewhat more effectively.

This should not be taken as a dismissal of the working-class parents' efforts, which were quite valuable to the school. In fact, in addition to the fundraising and volunteering activities I have described, working-class parents made another important contribution, which went unrecognized by teachers and was certainly unappreciated by the neighborhood parents: they were often the voice of equity at the school, pushing back against practices that disadvantaged low-income or low-achieving children. Kim was particularly forceful in this role, although she was often urged on by other working-class mothers, who nodded and chimed in while she spoke in meetings and encouraged her in private conversations. For example, at a PTO meeting in the school library, several Cobble Square parents complained to two visiting district officials about students with academic and behavioral issues who had transferred into Grant under No Child Left Behind's (NCLB) provisions for students from failing schools.[10] The new Center City Academic Region superintendent expressed her sympathy for the parents' concerns, saying she intended to take action on such issues. Kim immediately objected, remarking angrily, "You bring these kids in—and don't get me wrong, I think they should come. But when they're not supported, they can't keep up. They feel stupid and act up." When the district official responded, in an impatient tone, "All kids have to be supported. We have to teach respect," Kim frowned, dissatisfied with this shifting of the focus from academic needs to behavioral problems. She protested, "We can't dismiss the fact that though they haven't been identified [as needing special services] they still need extra support. Kids feel uncomfortable. The kids who have been here tease them and make them feel bad." Several African American parents at the meeting nodded and murmured agreement as she spoke, while a number of white middle- and upper-middle-class parents exchanged frustrated looks. The administrator responded by suggesting an orientation for new families, and then changed the subject.

Kim (and other working-class African American parents) also insisted upon more inclusive processes for electing officers or nominating members of key committees. In these cases, the professional parents tended to want to "go ahead with the vote now," arguing that only the people who showed up at meetings really cared about the outcome, and there was no reason to delay the process by soliciting wider input. In response, Kim often pointed to the underrepresentation of African American and Asian American parents at the meeting and maintained that it would be wrong to hold an election or make other important decisions without a wider representation: "It's not fair to have the meeting without letting people know!" As we will see in the next section, Kim and other working-class parents also frequently opposed PTO efforts that directed resources disproportionately toward the grades heavily populated by Cobble Square children. In a sense, Kim's activism (strengthened by the support of other parents who agreed with her) represented a check on the power of the middle-class parents. It guaranteed broader input into decisionmaking and pushed the PTO to take stances or channel resources in ways that benefited a wider swath of the population, rather than just the participants' own children. The role working-class parents can play in helping to ensure equity—and the need for it—has been completely overlooked in the literature documenting the many contributions middle-class parents can make to a school.

It is clear that parents of all social classes were very involved at Grant and had a major impact on the school. This involvement was important, because though the school did have a reputation within the district as one of the most desirable elementary schools, it was by no means a high-achieving school by many standards. Grant's test scores were low compared to Fairview and Hopkins, the other two high-performing schools in Center City. In 2005–6, only 35 percent of the fifth-graders scored advanced or proficient in math on the state tests and 60 percent did so in reading, whereas 79 percent of fifth-graders at Fairview scored advanced or proficient in math and 69 percent did so in reading. Grant's staff, though experienced, was frustrated with the leadership of the (eventually ousted) principal, and the facilities were outdated.

Assessing the Impact of Middle-Class Involvement

During my time at Grant, Cobble Square parents were instrumental in making significant improvements to the school. These included attaining a new playground, persuading the district to lower kindergarten class size by allocating an additional teacher, increasing security and traffic enforcement around the school, implementing a new reading program (including training staff and raising and donating funds for books), replacing an ineffective principal, and creating a new cybrary. All of these accomplishments occurred within the constraints of a heavily bureaucratic school system with limited resources and involved an enormous amount of time, energy, and political and organizational skill on the part of a cadre of dedicated parents.

Grant was a K–8 school, but the majority of the Cobble Square children were in kindergarten, first, and second grades.[11] When it came to choosing priorities and allocating resources, many working-class parents at Grant criticized the neighborhood parents for focusing on programs and innovations that would benefit younger students. This was a recurring tension within the PTO, as parents argued over whether or not students were benefiting equally from parent activities.

At a PTO meeting in the spring of 2004, for example, a discussion about a volunteer program targeting kindergarten through sixth graders immediately became tense because of this issue. At this meeting, which was held in the school's small kitchen (because the library was being used for a book sale), ten parents sat around a table and in nearby armchairs. After the group reviewed last-minute plans for the upcoming opera concert, Sharon, a Cobble Square mother, described her conversation with Ms. Ashton about the volunteer program. She explained that schools needed to pay a stipend to the volunteers (retired professionals) who would come and read with the children. When she proposed that the PTO pay several thousand dollars for the program, a number of parents of older students objected:

KIM: We have to make sure we're supporting all the grades. This is only for K–6. *Once again*, we're not affecting the upper grades.
SHARON [speaking with exaggerated patience]: Seventh and eighth get the Amazon thing [another PTO initiative].
KIM: My concern is that resources go to the entire school—

SHARON: K–6 is *most* of the school—
KIM: But not *all* of the school!
[The conversation became tense, with both parents speaking forcefully.]
ANNA [white, middle-class parent]: Can we tap into alums who are successful?
SHARON: That's not going to address Kim's concern.
BRENDA [African American transfer mother]: That's not only Kim's concern!

The group went on to debate (with some intensity) whether or not the PTO's activities disproportionately benefited the younger grades. To Kim and Brenda, Cobble Square parents were only interested in helping *their* children and cared much less about the school as a whole. There was certainly justification for that sentiment. For example, the reading program introduced by a Cobble Square mother began in kindergarten and added only one grade each year, meaning the upper-grade students would not be affected for quite some time. Similarly, the playground was seen by some parents as a boon for younger children and the neighborhood but as irrelevant to their own adolescent children.

However, other improvements did seem likely to impact the entire Grant community. As discussed in chapter five, the principal ousted by the PTO in the spring of 2005, Ms. Ashton, was a negative presence in the school. She often obstructed parents' efforts (for instance, when a local artist volunteered to repaint some tables in the library with colorful motifs, she insisted they be painted exactly the same as they were before), and she was unpopular with the teachers, who saw her as unsupportive and insulting. Ms. Fordham, the new principal, had a better rapport with both teachers and parents; her assignment to the school significantly improved teacher morale. The cybrary was also an important resource for all grades at the school and, arguably, benefited the older students even more than the younger ones. In addition, the partnerships upper-middle-class parents established brought funds and materials to the school, and the improvements they made to the physical appearance of the school similarly benefited all students.

Educators and administrators tended to speak positively about the accomplishments of professional parents (and the PTO in general). While teachers were particularly appreciative of those parent activities I have labeled supportive, which were not the real province of the professional parents, they also pointed to the cybrary and playground as examples of important parental contributions. One kindergarten teacher, who had been in danger of losing her position at the school when enrollment decreased, was quite moved by how much a group of middle- and upper-middle-class parents did to save her job, including contacting high-level district officials and the head of the local teachers union: "It's because of those parents that I'm still here. . . . It's because they really, they really carried on. And, you know, I was very grateful, very grateful. I couldn't believe how they carried on." Other teachers referred positively to the many supports the PTO provided the school, including materials and supplies: "They provide us with cartridges for our copiers. That's hard to come by." And, of course, teachers were much happier with the new principal.

My conclusion, after spending two years with parents at Grant, is that the middle- and upper-middle-class parents made many positive changes to the school. They were certainly not the only involved parents at Grant; a number of the people who gave a great deal of time to the school were working-class parents of transfer students. However, professional parents brought to their involvement a pool of resources and a vision for change that enabled them to be particularly effective (and, as we will see in the next section, the focus on attracting neighborhood families at the school further enhanced their power). Their goals for Grant were ambitious, and the transformation they envisioned was by no means over at the close of my research. As Rhonda, an African American transfer mother exclaimed, talking about Cobble Square parents, "People from the community get things done!" In this way, the story of Grant is similar to that of other urban schools that experienced increased resources and academic improvements as a result of an influx of professional parents.[12] It lends support to claims by proponents of economic integration about the value of middle-class participation in schools.

Nonetheless, the impact of the Cobble Square parents' involvement appears to have been limited to the school. While middle- and upper-middle-class parents can be instrumental in pushing for greater funding for city schools, there is no evidence in this case that the benefits of the Grant parents' activities spread beyond the school. If anything, from a system-wide perspective, the parents likely diverted resources from other schools to Grant. For example, while the parents' ability to convince the district to make Grant a pilot in the cybrary program or to build a new play-structure in the schoolyard certainly represented victories for the school, each of these victories presumably came at a cost to other schools that, in the absence of the Grant parents' advocacy, might have been targeted for such improvements themselves.

When the "Most Valued Customers" Want Change

The literature on social class and parental intervention has documented the many ways in which middle-class parents activate their social and cultural capital to secure their children's advantage in school. Whereas this literature examines *individual* parents advocating for their *individual* children, my focus here is somewhat different.[13] I am interested in the means through which parents at Grant—both individually and collectively— activated their various forms of capital to make improvements to the school as a whole. The approach I take also adds to our understanding of these processes by showing how they are affected by the particular contexts in which parents operate, contexts that are shaped by many factors, including, in this case, the CCSI. The CCSI altered the "fields" (i.e., Grant and the school district) in which parents operated, giving Cobble Square parents greater power by virtue of their status as downtown parents.[14]

Even in the absence of the CCSI, professional parents at Grant would likely have had ambitious agendas and would have met with some success in achieving their goals. As Wells and Serna point out, middle- and upper-income families have increased power already with respect to the public schools—because of their social status and the extent to which a school's prestige depends on their presence.[15] However, the CCSI *institutionalized* this special value, such that parents, administrators, and teachers spoke explicitly about the importance of attracting neighborhood parents. Because the success of the CCSI (a high-profile initiative) and the reputation of Grant depended on the number of neighborhood parents it could attract and retain, the presence of these parents gained particular importance. Thus, it is likely that activist parents at Grant were able to accomplish even more in this context than they would have otherwise.

The CCSI reshaped family-school relations along market lines, giving middle- and upper-middle-class parents a currency that continued to matter long after their original "purchase" (choice of school) had passed. The CCD and school district's interest in catering to these parents and the willingness of top district officials to recognize and respond to their concerns also created additional mechanisms through which parents could advance their agendas. Although professional parents' activity on behalf of the school suggested deep concern, this engagement was always informed by the knowledge that, if they became dissatisfied, they could use the exit option available to all customers. They did not hesitate to use this possibility as an ultimatum in their dealings with school and district administrators.

Middle- and upper-middle-class parents who had been recruited to the school continued to be aware of their special status once they had enrolled their children. For example, one Cobble Square mother referred often to the school district's ongoing emphasis on keeping affluent, involved parents like her happy. At a PTO meeting early on in my research, the group congratulated her for her success in getting the police to enforce speed limits in the streets around the school. When the meeting ended, I walked out with this mother and asked her, as we strolled down the long third-floor hallway, to tell me more about how she was able to get results so quickly. She attributed her success to the contacts she had with the district and the city ("that's just the way the world works—it's who you know") and, particularly, to the superintendent, Paul Vallas, who "loves Grant because there are educated white women promoting the school!" Thus not only did educators, administrators, and other parents view Center City parents as valued customers, they communicated this belief to the parents by being particularly responsive to their demands.

Because downtown parents were the customers to whom the school and the CCD were seeking to appeal, their approval became a metric by which the school's improvement was measured. For example, when the principal and the PTO discussed the possibility of implementing a Montessori curriculum, one of the parents immediately observed, "Speaking from a neighborhood perspective, people would eat this up!" Essentially, to some parents and the CCD, neighborhood parents took on a sort of mythic status as the final arbiters of the school's quality: it was only a "good" school if it was good enough for these parents to send their children there. Grant's parents were not alone here, of course. As Holme put it in her study of affluent parents' school choice decisions, "other parents' choices" (more specifically, other *high-status* parents' choices) have a major impact on how middle- and upper-class parents measure school quality.[16] Thus Lisa, an upper-middle-class African American parent said, discussing the exodus of white students from the upper grades, "Why are the white kids leaving? . . . This is a neighborhood school. There is a reason people from the neighborhood aren't sending their kids here." To Lisa, the problem was not simply that white students were leaving. The fact that they were leaving implied some *deeper* dysfunction within the school that needed to be addressed.

Working the System

The ways in which the CCSI altered the rules and channels governing parental involvement were particularly clear when Cobble Square parents
attempted to use their status and institutional leverage to influence the
school or school district. A struggle around class size that occurred in the
first months of the CCSI provides a good example of this dynamic. In
late summer 2004, Sharon, a white Cobble Square mother who did not
work outside of the home but was heavily involved in local civic and phil-
anthropic organizations, learned that the two kindergarten classrooms—
which included several heavily recruited Cobble Square children—would
each contain thirty children, an unusually high number for kindergarten.
(The previous year each kindergarten had about twenty students.) In taking action on this issue, she used her status as a neighborhood mother, her
awareness of the CCSI, and her privileged access to key decisionmakers
to promote her cause. Our interview on the subject, which took place in
Sharon's large and sunny kitchen, is worth quoting at length, because Sharon was so candid about the ways she worked within and outside of the
school system to accomplish her goals.

> It ended up that my daughter had thirty-one kids in her kindergarten and one
> teacher. And I was like a maniac. And I was like—the kindergarten teacher
> called me on my vacation, and was like, "Sharon, do you know there are thirty-
> one kids in Sophie's class?" And I was like, "Are you kidding me?" I went nuts.
> I was literally on my summer vacation calling the school district, calling the
> CCD. I was like going insane.

Because she did not believe the principal at that time, Ms. Ashton, would
be particularly proactive, Sharon took matters into her own hands, contacting the school district and the CCD multiple times, and even suggesting that excessive class sizes at Grant would doom the initiative before it
even started.

SHARON: I [kept] making calls to the right people and emphasizing, I continue to
emphasize over and over, like, "You guys are on the cusp of making this school
where you want it to go. You're going to get, you know, five more [name of active neighborhood mother] next year and two more [another active neighborhood mother] and two more [another active neighborhood mother], but you're

not going to get it if they walk in the building and see thirty kids. In fact, I'm taking my kid and going elsewhere, like face the facts."

M: Did you say that?

SHARON: Oh yeah. There's no way I'm keeping my kid in this school with thirty kids in the class!

Sharon's phone calls and threats generated an immediate response from both the CCD and the school district.

They said, "We really are going to work on this. This is an absolute problem. It's unacceptable." So I think that's what happened. I think that they realized that if they want to do this Center City Schools thing and get more of the parents who are already making a difference at Grant—but if they got ten more, wouldn't that be amazing? And wouldn't that make their job so much easier?

According to Sharon, Cobble Square parents, staff at the CCD and school district officials agreed that kindergarten was key.

That's when they come, and that's when you lose them. Because if they walk in and go, "Oh this is great, let's try it." Or if they walk in and go, "Oh, I wouldn't put my kid here on a bet." And thirty kids—they don't even get in the front door. . . . So I think that's how it happened. I think that they really want this to work. And they know that this would have just suicided the project before it even got off the ground.

I asked Sharon to clarify what she meant by "the project," and she explained she was referring to

The Center City Schools [Initiative] and really trying to cultivate the relationship with neighborhood families and keep people in the city. And the fact that Center City District is on it and the school district. Like, you know, there's a lot of critical mass—the people on the CCD board are really high-powered people. And they want this to work. I mean like I said to [CCD staffer responsible for the CCSI] a million times, I'm like, "Are you people crazy? You'd better dust off your resume." She just got this job in August. . . . [A]nd she said that, she's like, "This is my mission. Like, this is it. This is going to kill my whole job before it even starts." So I think she fought really hard and, you know, the right people knew about it.

Sharon's efforts paid off: within a month or so, the district provided Grant with a third kindergarten teacher, dramatically reducing class size. Of course, Sharon's high levels of cultural and social capital played a role here too: she already knew the "right people," felt comfortable making demands of those in power, and knew how to "work the system." But it was the relationship between parents like Sharon and the CCSI that was really consequential. The CCSI institutionalized Sharon's elevated value and provided her with special lines of communication with CCD and district leaders (including a CCD staffer whose job depended upon keeping parents happy). Sharon's increased access and status, and the weight these gave to her threat to exit the school, became additional and critical weapons in her arsenal.

Similar dynamics were at work in efforts to secure a new playground and library for Grant. In both cases, parents used all of their resources—social, cultural, and symbolic—to overcome major obstacles. When Cobble Square parents began to work with the school district to install a large play-structure at Grant, the school's immediate neighbors (none of whom had children at the school) protested, calling the district and local politicians to complain that the playground would become a "hangout" for unsupervised children or the homeless, leading to disorder and crime in the neighborhood. In response, neighborhood parents drew upon their political connections in the city and their relationships with high-level administrators within the district. District CEO Vallas himself facilitated a meeting with concerned neighbors and strategized with one of the Cobble Square mothers by phone and over email about how best to handle this opposition. When the neighbors finally backed down and the project began to move forward, he invited the planning team (Sharon, other PTO leaders, and district facilities staffers) to use his office and even joined in during the meeting—all to symbolize his support for the project. The parents succeeded in having the playground built within a relatively short time in part because, as Vallas and other district staff said quite clearly, the school needed a better play space to attract and retain neighborhood families.

While neighborhood parents' symbolic status enabled them to achieve their goals more easily, it also constructed a discursive link between the interests of the school itself and those of a specific group of parents. At Grant during this period, the value of upper-middle-class parents was such that the success of the school itself was seen by many to be dependent on keeping them happy. As a result, parents invoking their status as neighborhood parents could (consciously or not) use the claim that they were looking out for the best interests of the school to give greater urgency to their concerns and to obscure the extent to which they were also pursuing their own interests. Thus, the parent who did not want her child in a large kindergarten was able to reframe this individualistic concern to argue not just that the other students in her child's class but that the *entire school* would suffer if her request were not granted. In fact, the CCSI's positioning of professional parents as key to Philadelphia's future meant that, by extension, the *entire city* would be harmed by an exodus of dissatisfied Center City parents.

In the instances I have described here, parents' symbolic status and privileged access worked to the advantage of students in general. The kindergarteners gained from smaller class sizes, all the children in the school benefited from having a well-resourced library, and all but the oldest students enjoyed the new playground. However, as I show in the next section, these processes had a harsher side, diminishing the status of another group within the school.

Marginalized Families

In chapter 5 I argued that transfer students were stigmatized by their symbolic construction as *the problem* at the school, as the ones who did not fit with the identity Cobble Square parents (and the CCD) were promoting for Grant. These students were overwhelmingly African American and came from failing schools in low-income neighborhoods outside of Center City. Here I examine how the parents of transfer students understood and were affected by the marketing of Grant and the Cobble Square parents' efforts to change the school.[17] In interviews and casual conversations, these parents spoke in a surprisingly direct fashion about issues of race and class and their own sense of belonging at Grant.

As critical scholar Pauline Lipman notes, policies shape not only official actions but also the ways people in local settings understand their resources, power, and the range of options available to them.[18] At Grant, the CCSI and related efforts forced transfer parents to struggle with their status as the less-desired constituency at the school. For them, the context generated the reverse of the Cobble Square parents' elevated symbolic status: transfer parents became *less* entitled to full membership within

Grant's community and, as a result, were constrained in their ability to advocate for their children or promote their vision for the school.

"We Won't Get All This Riff-Raff"

In chapter 5 I described a meeting at Grant at which a Cobble Square mother spoke proudly of the school's relationship with the neighborhood and the fact that a number of new neighborhood families were enrolling at the school. At this meeting, one of my first at Grant, I introduced myself to the audience (which consisted of parents, teachers, the district CEO, and a handful of central office administrators) as a researcher interested in studying parental involvement at Grant.[19] I explained that Grant was an important school to study because it had such an active parent group and that I was particularly interested in understanding issues of race and class and "how they affected parents' goals and the work of their organization." When the meeting ended and I began to leave, making my way down the aisle of the auditorium, I was stopped by an African American woman who introduced herself as Sabrina. She smiled but spoke with a quiet urgency, telling me she was so glad I was looking at race and class because she thinks they are really important at Grant. She went on to say that she brings her children in from another part of the city, so "when Sharon talks about how great it is to bring in families from the neighborhood, she's not talking about my kids." And that bothered her.

Sabrina is a working-class single mother, with a ready smile and warm demeanor, who was very involved in Grant's PTO. Over a year later, I interviewed Sabrina in her small living room in West Philadelphia. The issue of valuing neighborhood families more than others was still fresh in her mind, and she spoke adamantly, leaning forward and putting her hands on her knees:

> Every meeting we go to they're talking about, "And two more families coming in. They're neighborhoods." That's kind of like a prejudice to me. You know what I mean? . . . What's so important about this person from the neighborhood coming here? It's not like this is a private school, where their money is cash and mine is from the government! You know what I mean? There's no difference!

She felt that the Cobble Square parents' emphasis on "the neighborhoods" undermined her own standing at the school. It also made her question her involvement in the PTO and wonder if the school really valued her son:

I can see the behaviors and things like that playing a part, but they're just so adamant about this neighborhood. . . . When they say that to me, it's kind of like I'm supporting this school that's not even supporting my kid, because he's not from the neighborhood. You understand?

Sabrina's comment illuminates what I have argued is a key dynamic around the CCSI: that the educational market it helped to create in Center City positioned parents differently based upon the resources they could contribute to the school rather than their entitlement to the school's services. While Sabrina was right in noting that neighborhood parents did not pay "cash," they did *pay* for their children's enrollment with forms of capital that the school valued and that parents like Sabrina did not possess.

The extent to which parents like Sabrina felt excluded from Grant's new identity was clear in the tension that emerged around the marketing of Grant and the fact that, if these efforts were successful, there would be fewer spots in the school for students from other parts of the city. In interviews and conversations, several transfer parents expressed their belief that the marketing campaign was in fact a deliberate effort to reduce the number of working-class, African American students at Grant. As one mother said in an interview, with a wry look on her face, "Because they think, 'if we keep it to the neighborhood, we won't get all this riff-raff,' you know?" Kim, one of the most vocal critics of the Cobble Square contingent, complained to me over the phone about what she saw as a not-so-secret agenda: "They want to take it to a point where it's a neighborhood school and excludes people who are outside!" Because of the demographic differences between the students from "the neighborhood" and the students from outside, many parents believed that Grant as a "neighborhood school" really meant Grant as a middle- and upper-middle-class school with few working-class and African American students. Thus, whereas neighborhood parents' own sense of value and efficacy was affirmed by the CCSI, the policy's implicit message for the largely working-class and African American transfer parents was that they and their children were not wanted.

"Why Is That Kid Still Here?"

In fact, at least some downtown parents did try to make Grant less accessible to students from outside of Center City. In an interview, an administrator explained to me that some neighborhood parents had pushed for the school to remove students they saw as excessively challenging:[20]

ADMINISTRATOR: I think that some of the families in the neighborhood are concerned about some of the students who come here from NCLB. I do. And I
think that they—and this is public education, I come back to it. It's public education. And we have the right to educate all—but I've heard comments like,
why is that kid still here?

MC: So it's around discipline?

ADMINISTRATOR: It's around behavioral issues. . . . But I think they have taken it
beyond me. . . . I think they have shared that.

MC: You mean that they have gone above you to the district to say—

ADMINISTRATOR: That they would like those kids not to be here.

In addition to identifying certain students as unfit for the school, some
parents also encouraged the principal to limit the number of spots available to students transferring under NCLB. Janet, the African American
mother living in Cobble Square quoted earlier, was sympathetic to the
transfer students, glad that they were able to escape their low-performing
schools. In our interview she told me in frustration of a conversation
she had had with a white Cobble Square mother. This conversation
makes clear the extent to which "transfer" was seen as synonymous with
"black":

> My daughter is the only black child in her class who has not transferred into the
> school. In her class, all the black children in her classroom were transferred in.
> But, you know, they're getting an advantage by not being stuck, if their school
> isn't as good where they are. And they sent a letter home [saying], if you were
> transferred in this past year, you have to fill out paperwork and be transferred
> in for a second year. A parent, neighborhood parent, said, "Oh, did you see
> that newsletter? Yeah, that way we won't get stuck with all those kids next
> year!"

The requirement that transfer students reapply was widely seen as a way
of redirecting transfer students, particularly those who were behavior
problems or challenging in other ways, back to their catchment area
schools. Because so many transfer students were African American, Janet
was disturbed by this mother's remark: "I was like, 'Whoa!' I took that personally, as if she didn't want all the black kids there. That's the way I took
it." While few conversations around transfer students' spots at the school
were as explicit as this one, the race and class implications were clear to
many parents: reducing the number of transfers would inevitably mean that

many students from low-income and minority areas would lose access to Grant.

This dynamic—in which some Cobble Square parents hoped to decrease the number of transfer students—must be understood within its context. Grant, like all public schools, was operating within the high-stakes NCLB environment, in which a school's reputation and future lay in its ability to make Adequate Yearly Progress (AYP) on the annual standardized tests. Not only could failure to make AYP send a school into a series of corrective measures, but it also (and more important for a school like Grant whose scores usually hovered just around the AYP cutoff mark) could be devastating to its reputation with prospective parents. Grant did not make AYP in 2005, a fact that was of great concern to many parents, especially because AYP status was widely reported in Philadelphia's newspapers and the topic of much conversation among prospective parents. One Cobble Square mother told me, in evident frustration, "Parents don't care that it was really, really close and that we overscored in math and only missed reading by a few points." All prospective parents thought about, she complained, was "whether or not a school made AYP." Given the well-established link between social class and standardized test scores, many quite reasonably believed that an influx of low-income students would negatively impact the school's test scores and, hence, its AYP status and reputation.[21]

In addition, after having made AYP in the NCLB program's first year, Grant became a receiving school for students whose home schools were labeled failing under NCLB. When Grant did not make AYP in 2005, many parents and teachers attributed this at least in part to the students who had transferred to the school under NCLB. These parents and teachers believed that the "choice children," who were often several years behind the other students, had depressed Grant's test scores—a logical assumption given their academic records. Thus, the parents who tried to convince the principal to limit the number of choice children at Grant were responding to a very real fear that another influx of NCLB students would prevent the school from making the all-important AYP cut. (In fact, the mother quoted earlier bemoaning parents' fixation on AYP status also observed that the one benefit of not making the cut in 2005 was that at least the school "did not have to take any more NCLB kids.") This is just one example of the difficult, often-unaddressed, tensions that emerge when underresourced institutions struggle to meet the needs of very different constituencies.

Diminished Status, Diminished Entitlement

The district's policies on transfers (especially the new policy giving Center City families priority) and the ways officials discussed the process served to institutionalize the diminished status of transfer families. During a visit to Grant's PTO, at another meeting held in the school's auditorium, district CEO Paul Vallas suggested to the several dozen parents there that they require a commitment of parental support and involvement from all parents hoping to transfer their children into the school. He continued, underscoring the contrast between within-catchment-area students (who had the right to attend Grant) and transfer students (who did not), "That would be my criteria. I can't do anything about within-catchment-area students. We can do something about transfers." A few days later, at a special PTO meeting called to discuss the selection of a new principal and other changes that were taking place at Grant as a result of the CCSI, the regional superintendent spoke several times about moving transfer students who were behavior problems out of the school: "This is another responsibility we have as a region—when there are violations that occur, we have to draw the line. I would say maybe we need to offer the children another opportunity [in a different school]." A Cobble Square mother later praised this attitude, noting to me that these students were "guests" at the school and should be easily removed. Transfer families thus functioned as the group *not entitled* to be at the school, and their tenuous status was affirmed both by district policy and by discourse within the school.

Transfer parents' references to their status, particularly their reports of being careful about how they behaved at the school, imply that they felt their right to be at Grant was limited in this context. In general, these parents expressed a certain amount of hesitation when it came to asserting themselves or advocating for their children, a hesitation they attributed to the fact that they did not live within the catchment area. One parent said she and another mother refrained from criticizing the principal because they felt that their children's ability to remain in the school was dependent on the principal's goodwill: "We weren't neighborhood parents, so we kind of had to keep our mouths shut." Another mother similarly said that if she had any problems with the school, she would address them if they were important enough but would "feel like I have to watch, because I'm not in the area." Kim told me that she believed that transfer parents were generally prevented from speaking up because of their fears for their children's spots. She contrasted her own assertiveness with the fearfulness of other transfer parents:

> And plus, you know, you're not from the area so you're always treading lightly that they'll get rid of you, because you're not coming in from the area, you're not a neighborhood person, you don't *have* to be here. They could find a way to get you out. Like Ms. Ashton would love to find a way to get me out. But I know better. She's slick though. . . . So that's why you tend to tread lightly. And people just don't want to make waves when they don't have to. A lot of times I think they think it's a blessing and a privilege to be here, where I think I have the right to be here.

Kim, an experienced advocate for her children who worked closely with the school district on certain issues and had a strong sense of her own entitlement, did not allow her status as a transfer parent to prevent her from "making waves" when she felt she needed to. However, she was a notable exception in this respect, and even she spoke of her status as more tenuous than that of the neighborhood parents.

"Public School Is Public School"

This distinction between parents, like other dynamics of race and class at Grant, did not go uncontested. In attempting to counter these status differences, some parents and educators pointed to a more universal vision, one rooted in *all* students' right to a quality education. For example, Brenda, an African American transfer parent, was discouraged by what she saw as differential treatment of transfer families: "Like I said, public school is public school. Now whether I live here or there, I shouldn't be made to feel any different than any of the parents." Similarly, the administrator (quoted earlier) who felt pressured to push out chronically misbehaving transfer students objected because of the school's status as a *public* institution and its responsibility to *all* students. After describing the parents' efforts, she concluded that she had resisted them "Because we educate all; we have to care about all—for all of them."

This resistance to the demands of middle- and upper-middle-class parents appeared to be most effective around discipline issues, where Cobble Square parents' efforts to use their status to garner special information ran up against opposition from other parents and the district. For example, at a PTO meeting in 2005 about ten parents sat in the library, listening respectfully as the school police officer and the administrator responsible for "school climate" described the school's new doorbell system, a plan to give students prizes for good behavior, and a peer mediation program. After a few minutes, however, Catherine, a Cobble Square mother, interrupted. Her tone was impatient as she turned the conversation to problems with bullying:

CATHERINE: You are aware that there are bullying issues? I think the school's greatest challenge is to let parents know as much as you can how things are being handled. Otherwise, you're going to lose people. You've already lost some and others are on the fence.

ADMINISTRATOR: We can't give information about other kids because of confidentiality.

CATHERINE: You need to figure this out. You need to go to people who are higher than you because you're going to lose people.

Kim, a transfer mother, objected angrily to Catherine's request for more information about bullying incidents (and, presumably, her veiled threats that the school would "lose people"), saying "No school gives you that sort of information!" Catherine responded, her voice calm but her face twisted in frustration, "I'm aware of that. I'm a certified principal. But don't tell me we're doing all we can." Frustrated with the administrator's innocuous response of "I hear you," Catherine then turned to the other parents in the room and said urgently, "If your child is being bullied, please tell the PTO. You need to have an advocate. As a neighborhood parent, people have come to me about this issue."

Here Catherine referred directly to her status as a neighborhood parent (and a professional) and to the possibility of losing "people" (i.e., other neighborhood parents) to add urgency and legitimacy to her concerns. Yet school administrators never satisfied Catherine's request for information; to do so would have involved breaching district procedures on discipline. In this instance, it appears that the discipline system, with its orientation around the rights of the offender (rights which are separate from any particular geographic designation) and federal law protecting student and parent privacy, was impervious to the parents' efforts—even parents making such a concerted effort to leverage their status. Clearly the empowerment of neighborhood parents (and disempowerment of others) was not all-encompassing. Nevertheless, it had a major impact, as I have shown, on how parents perceived and acted upon their position within the school.

This chapter examined parental involvement at Grant and the ways in which the CCSI and the marketing of Grant affected parents' status and efficacy. Though parents of all social classes were involved at the school, their goals and activities varied by class, with middle- and upper-middle-class parents invested in transforming the school and poor and working-class parents focusing on supporting the school as it was. Whereas all public school parents are nominally "equal" in their relations with schools, the reality in this setting was that efforts to market Grant to middle-class families gave those families additional power and leverage.

Because middle- and upper-middle-class parents had the option to take their children out of the school at any time, it was not enough simply to "sell" the school to them. To the extent that educators and administrators were invested in maintaining the status and resources such parents brought to the school, they had to continue to satisfy professional families long after enrollment decisions were made. In addition, the new emphasis under the CCSI on showing the school district as especially responsive to Center City families led to the creation of a dual system of rules and channels for providing feedback, gaining access, and impacting the school district as an organization. The link the initiative drew between the presence of professional families in the schools and the future of the city heightened this dynamic, giving those families even greater status and power. In contrast, the workings of the market provided little incentive for educators and administrators to ensure that low-income and working-class transfer families were satisfied with their experiences at Grant. In addition, institutional policies and practices related to the CCSI undercut their right to be at the school. Thus, while this chapter documents the many ways an increased middle-class presence can benefit an urban school, it also shows that these benefits can come at some cost to other groups within the school. In doing so, it highlights a key tension that existed at Grant between some Cobble Square parents' desire to create a school that served a more middle- and upper-middle-class population and the mandates and responsibilities of a public school.

Given the growing policy interest in economic integration as a reform strategy and renewed interest among groups of middle-class parents in transforming urban public schools, it is important to realize that these are complicated projects experienced differently by different groups. The process through which integration is achieved matters. Unfortunately, the perspectives and experiences of poor and working-class families affected by these processes have barely been explored. Yet if the crisis in urban public education is about more than just marketing—if it is rooted in the inability of urban schools to serve lower-income students well—these are the very families who should not be cut out of newly revitalized schools and precisely the voices that should not be ignored. As we have seen here, their perspectives call into question some of the key assumptions underlying these strategies and argue for a much more nuanced approach.

CHAPTER SEVEN

The "Segregated Schools Initiative"?

Lasting Consequences of a Short-Lived Project

I'm offering basically to a white middle-class population things that we have not offered to families of color who are poor, but since we want these people to stay here, we're going to offer this, but too bad for you other folks!—Central office administrator, School District of Philadelphia

The Center City Schools Fair, held on a Saturday in October 2005, was a much-publicized event jointly sponsored by the Center City District (CCD) and the School District of Philadelphia and held in the city's convention center. Before the fair, there had been significant media coverage of the Center City Schools Initiative (CCSI), and the CCD's efforts to publicize the initiative had created a "buzz" among Center City parents. As a result, the event was well attended. Hundreds of parents, students, administrators, and school staff filled the large exhibition hall in which it was held, where balloons, colorful signs, and student performances created a festive air. Paul Levy, the president of the CCD, was there, as was district CEO Paul Vallas, disguised slightly in a baseball cap and windbreaker.

Approximately forty schools—public, private, charter, and parochial—from the broader Center City area were represented, with each school responsible for decorating and staffing its own display area. The CCD had planned the fair, and it was clear that a great deal of thought had gone into making it a success. The schools were distributed in the hall according to their location within Center City (each aisle between the displays was a main street), which allowed parents to simulate a stroll across Center City as they explored the range of schools available to their children. At every table, parents and school staff chatted with visitors, distributing information about the school, highlighting its attributes, and calling attention to displays of student work. Some of the tables were designed to make a particular statement about the school's identity, with, for example, pairs of serious-looking students playing chess at the display for Masterman, the district's top academic magnet.

Grant's table was staffed by Ms. Fordham, the new principal, and several Cobble Square mothers, including Sharon, Sara, and Catherine. Kim, the African American mother of transfer students, who was critical of the campaign to attract "neighborhood" families to Grant, was there as well, but only briefly. The table was busy, with prospective parents coming and going, talking with current parents and the principal and admiring the pictures of students and their work. As Ms. Fordham, who was wearing a tailored leather jacket and elegant gold jewelry, greeted parents, it was easy to see why the CCD had wanted her for the job: her warmth and accessibility, as well as her understated elegance, seemed perfectly suited to the task of reassuring prospective Center City parents that Grant would be a "safe" choice for their children.

Coming into the fair, parents were greeted by a long CCD table, where cheerful staff passed out information and gave parents directions. Among the information distributed was an overview of the new transfer policy, explaining to Center City parents that their children would have priority over students from other parts of the city in admissions to all Center City elementary schools. As I walked through the fair, chatting with people I knew either through my fieldwork or from my own neighborhood, I encountered a great deal of confusion about this policy. One acquaintance, a mother who hoped to enroll her four-year-old in one of the Big Three high-performing downtown schools in the fall, expressed frustration about the lack of clarity she had received on this process from the district. Catherine, a parent from Grant, said she had heard the new policy was *already* in effect. Curious, I went to the school district's Center City Academic Region table and spoke to two district staff members there, asking directly whether or not a child from Center City would be accepted before one from, say, North Philadelphia. They would not give me a straight answer, insisting that admissions would be on a "case-by-case basis," as it had in the past. When I asked what the criteria would be, they simply repeated,

"Case by case." Frustrated, I pointed to the CCD table, located only a few yards away, and said, "But this doesn't fit with what they're saying right over there!"

"I know that," one staffer responded.

"It's pretty touchy, isn't it?" I asked.

"Yes!" they both exclaimed and then suggested I talk with the new regional superintendent for an official answer. A few minutes later, when I ran into the CCD administrator responsible for the fair and asked her whether or not the new transfer policy was in place, she responded confidently that the issue would be resolved shortly.

The district's message and that of the CCD were different for a good reason: there was a strong feeling within the district that the initiative was unjust. District employees worried that the transfer policy would give Center City families increased access to some of the district's highest-achieving elementary schools. In fact, the CCSI was so unpopular within the halls of the school district's central office that it was nicknamed the "Segregated Schools Initiative."

In this chapter, I take a step back from Grant. Returning to the idea, discussed in chapter 1, that market, state, and society are "multiply embedded" within one another, I examine how the intersection between the CCD, the district, and local culture shaped and reshaped the CCSI.[1] Most important, this intersection led to an expansion in the number of schools the initiative targeted. A closer examination of the CCSI in its final form, however, shows that though it was modified in response to concerns about unduly advantaging Center City families and schools, the equity imposed by the district was a veneer that obscured continued patterns of privilege.

In 2008, only three years after the excitement of the Center City Schools Fair, the political equation shifted. The partnership between the CCD and the School District of Philadelphia ended, and Center City families no longer received priority in admissions. This transition, which is explained in more detail below, did not, however, put an end to the initiative's impact, both locally and nationally. The racial balance at the schools targeted by the marketing campaign continued to evolve, as more Center City families enrolled their children and the proportion of students who were white grew. Understanding how this happened necessitates delving more deeply into the details of the initiative and the demographic characteristics of its targeted population. These specifics matter because not only did the initiative impact schools in Philadelphia, but it also continued to serve as a model for other cities and to be cited by urban scholars and policymakers in the years that followed. For these reasons, even though the partnership between the school district and the CCD was short-lived, it had long-term consequences, in Philadelphia and more broadly.

"I Really Haven't Talked to Anybody that Is Supportive of It": District Staffers and the CCSI

Despite the apparent consensus among Paul Vallas, Paul Levy, and other high-level actors about the myriad benefits of using market strategies to induce professional families into the public schools, the views of many within the district were far more negative. In fact, while it is a useful short-hand to refer to "the district" as though it were a monolithic entity act-ing and reacting in a coherent manner, doing so obscures the fact that a school district is made up of individuals operating within an organizational culture in which certain values and practices are more acceptable than others. Enthusiastic press releases and Vallas's vows of support notwith-standing, most central office staffers, particularly middle managers, were quite negative about the CCSI. Much of the criticism of the CCSI from local civic leaders (discussed in chapter 4) focused on the transfer policy. In contrast, within-district concerns also encompassed other aspects of the initiative. This could be because they were aware, in a way that people outside of the district were not, of how the creation of a new academic region, the shuffling of administrators, and the special attention high-level officials were devoting to Center City schools meant channeling scarce dis-trict resources toward already successful schools. District staffers tended to point to disparities between Center City and the rest of the city as the problem, and their criticism reflected a clear sense that the majority of the district's constituency was far less advantaged than the residents of Center City.

Opposition to the CCSI was such that when I asked a district admin-istrator to describe the factions within the district around the initiative, she said, "I don't think there are any factions, because I really don't think there are that many people who are in favor of it. . . . I haven't really talked to anybody who is supportive of it." To some extent, this administrator suggested, within-district skepticism was rooted in tension between down-town and the "neighborhoods." This conflict has long been an issue in

Philadelphia, because much of the city's redevelopment energy went into the downtown, leaving the rest of the city distinctly unrevitalized. She continued: "Lots of district people . . . long-time district people who live in the neighborhoods, are pissed off that their communities aren't being taken care of in the same way. So they feel like, my North Philadelphia community isn't getting this!" The downtown versus neighborhoods tension was about much more than a matter of neighborhood identification. Given the overlap between social status and geography in Philadelphia, the tension represented a dual critique—of race and class privilege in the city and of development policy that directed resources toward more advantaged communities. According to my interviewee, one source of frustration for staffers was that the Center City population was "upper-middle class," whereas the "real middle class" (including many district employees) lived in other parts of the city. The rhetorical slippage around the term "middle class," which helped make the initiative more broadly appealing (see chapter 4), apparently was not as effective within the walls of the school district central office.

Staff members who expressed criticism or skepticism about the CCSI almost always tied it to issues of fairness. One administrator explained that the district's message—which she described as "I'm offering basically to a white middle-class population things that we have not offered to families of color who are poor, but since we want these people to stay here, we're going to offer this, but too bad for you other folks"—was troubling to her. Another district employee (and long-time activist), who believed that true equity would require putting the "best principals in the worst schools," complained that the district was "going overboard in attracting the middle class" by giving such priority to Center City. To these staffers, the CCSI was problematic because it interfered with the district's responsibility to provide all students with equal educational options.

Concerns about equity were not entirely limited to mid-level staffers. One member of the School Reform Commission (SRC), the state-installed body responsible for overseeing the district, also expressed concerns about the initiative's implications for equity, particularly the changes to the transfer policy giving Center City families priority in admissions to Center City elementary schools.[2] As a result, though district staffers followed CEO Vallas's directions in moving the initiative forward, skepticism about the CCSI manifested in a number of formal and informal ways and, as I explain below, helped shape the initiative's trajectory.

It Only "Sounds High Rent": Modifications to the Initiative

Between 2004 and 2006, as people within and outside of the School District of Philadelphia criticized the CCSI for being inequitable, the initiative was modified behind the scenes in several ways.[3] The first alteration addressed the definition of the new Center City Academic Region, the subset of schools identified at the CCD's request and on which the initiative focused. The particular boundaries of the new region were important because they determined which schools received the additional attention and which neighborhoods were privileged under the new transfer policy.

The terminology is confusing here, so let me be clear. There are three different geographic areas under consideration. The first is "Center City," the downtown area of Philadelphia, an area that, as my discussion in chapter 2 showed, is fairly affluent. It includes several high-status neighborhoods, Philadelphia's trendiest shopping and dining strips, and the major business district for the city.[4] However, the CCD had recently expanded its definition of "Center City" to include the gentrifying neighborhoods adjacent to the downtown and was interested in fueling revitalization in the entire area, creating what it called the "Expanded Center City" area. The third geographic area is that covered by the school district's new administrative unit, the "Center City Academic Region." The Center City Academic Region, created as a part of the CCSI, combined the dozen or so schools within Center City and its surrounding neighborhoods into one geographic area. It encompassed the "Expanded Center City" area, as well as a handful of surrounding low-income neighborhoods. It may be helpful to think of these three areas as concentric circles, with Center City as the smallest, the Expanded Center City as the next circle, and the Center City Academic Region as the largest. As the circles grow, the affluence of their residents becomes less concentrated—thus, "Center City" refers to the city's most prosperous area, "Expanded Center City" encompasses some gentrifying areas, and the "Center City Academic Region" further includes a number of low-income neighborhoods.

In 2004, when the CCD first proposed the CCSI, it incorporated the traditional definition of Center City and focused on the Big Three schools serving the downtown. As I have discussed, these schools had histories of mostly strong academic achievement and were known across the city to be relatively high performing and safe (see chapter 3). Once the partnership with the district began to take shape, however, the list of targeted schools and neighborhoods grew. District administrators, local politicians, and other officials involved in the early days of the initiative insisted that the region be drawn more broadly and that the population served by the region more closely resemble that of the district as a whole. An official with the mayor's office noted, "I think it was important to have the mix of schools. . . . So it wasn't just about a few darlings. It was about having schools that had all sorts of populations and results." An administrator with the CCD confirmed this, also describing the involvement of two City Council representatives in defining the region and adding, "and then a state representative convinced the school district to shove in two very low-performing schools." According to a district administrator, "Equity is, and has always been a huge piece of it for the district" and "there is some issue around how the CCD defines Center City and how the district defines Center City." As a result, the administrator continued, "We struggled with what the region would look like around these equity concerns. We didn't want it to match the Center City [area]." In other words, it was important to district officials that the region reach beyond the boundaries of what was traditionally known as Center City.

Reflecting on this process, a CCD administrator similarly told me that people at the district and in city government pushed for a more inclusive region. He concluded that, in the end, this broader definition made sense:

> I was frankly a bit more conservative [in terms of which schools should be included]. Anyhow, it seems to me a very good compromise, because there are schools in transitional neighborhoods, in which you've got a lot of lower-income and working-class families eager for change.

The final list of schools in the new region, released in 2005, included the Big Three as well as a number of low-performing schools that served predominantly low-income and minority students. Map 7.1 shows the difference between the smaller—and more heavily white—catchment areas of the Big Three schools (the darker, cross-hatched areas) and the full set of neighborhoods encompassed by the Center City Academic Region, many of which had a higher percentage of non-white residents. This map also shows that while the new region covered Center City and its immediate environs, it also extended slightly beyond the "expanded" Center City area.

By defining the region in this way, the district and the CCD hoped to minimize both the appearance and reality of inequity. Both organizations

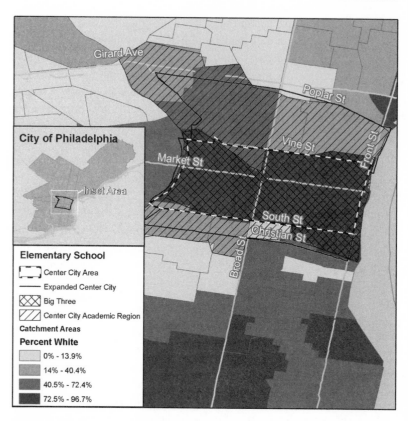

MAP 7.1. Elementary school catchment areas, percent white. Source: US Census, 2000.

repeatedly claimed that, because it had been drawn so broadly, the new region was demographically very similar to the school district as a whole. For example, when the school district sent parents a letter about the new region, it spoke directly to the concern that the Center City Academic Region would be more advantaged than other regions. Asserting "The Center City Region socioeconomic composition is a virtual snapshot of the District, predominantly minority and predominantly poor," the letter explained that whereas 65 percent of the students in district schools were African American, in the new region, 72 percent were African American. Similarly, the district was nearly 14 percent white and 67 percent low-income, while the corresponding figures for the new region were 13 percent and 70 percent, respectively.[5] In my conversations with one CCD administrator, I frequently raised the issue of equity with regards to the initiative. In response, she pointed to numbers like these to argue, "there's an enormous misperception about what the Center City Region looks like" and "the demographics are exactly the same as the district as a whole." In the section that follows, I will evaluate these claims about the region's demographics more carefully. For the moment, it is sufficient to say that the district was accurate in claiming that the student population in the Center City Academic Region resembled that of the rest of the district.

The second modification had to do with the controversial transfer policy, the source of so much confusion at the Center City Schools fair. As I noted earlier, a CCD staffer I spoke with about this confusion was confident that it would be easily resolved. However, instead of the quick implementation she anticipated, the process took months. CCD leaders, district administrators, and members of the SRC met several times in late 2005 and early 2006. When the transfer policy finally came up for a vote in February 2006, it was different from the one originally proposed by the CCD. The new version included specific language giving priority to students transferring under NCLB and ensuring that "physical integration and racial and educational equity" were maintained, while still admitting children from the Center City Academic Region before children from other parts of the city.[6] It was not clear whether these changes were symbolic or substantive or how they would affect the actual implementation of the policy; what was clear was that the district and SRC were aware of, and responding to, concerns about the equity implications of the transfer policy. In addition, rather than applying the policy only to the Center City Academic Region (as originally suggested by the CCD), the district decided that, as a matter of equity, all regions should follow the same procedure and planned to make the policy district-wide over the next several years.[7]

Even with these changes, the two SRC commissioners appointed by the mayor were not satisfied, continuing to express concerns about equity. Explaining her "no" vote to a reporter, Commissioner Sandra Dungee Glenn argued that as long as educational opportunities across the district varied so widely, any changes to the transfer policy were premature:

> I get so many calls in my office from parents who are struggling and sometimes almost in tears about trying to get access to schools that they believe are better. That's stressful. . . . The real answer is to make all of our schools quality schools . . . and, until we reach that goal, try to keep the doors as open as possible across the district.[8]

Dungee Glenn proposed an amendment that would require the district to provide equal options in all regions over a four-year period. When it was turned down by the three state-appointed commissioners, Dungee Glenn and the other city-appointed commissioner voted against the new transfer policy. The resulting 3-2 vote was rare for a commission that had generally voted unanimously and tried to keep disagreements behind closed doors.[9]

District and CCD administrators also pointed to the initiative's status as a pilot program—which could be replicated in other regions in the city—as a way the initiative was shaped in response to equity concerns. According to an administrator who worked closely with CEO Vallas, district leadership was eager to see organizations create the same sorts of partnerships in other Philadelphia neighborhoods: "I mean, there's just generally an overall, ongoing concern about how do we make this equitable and about how do we use this good model and replicate it in other areas throughout the city." The hope was that groups across the city could work to create strong partnerships with schools and with other local organizations that would bring more advantaged constituencies and additional resources to their neighborhood schools. In public meetings and conversations with local media, district officials repeatedly stressed this as an option available to all neighborhoods.[10] Similarly, an administrator with the new Center City Academic Region, in discussing her efforts to recruit partners for Center City schools, said they were no different from something "somebody else can do in another part of the city," and an administrator with the CCD spoke frequently about her work with community and business organizations in other regions to replicate the initiative. As a pilot program, these administrators argued, rather than simply carving out a privileged set of schools, the CCSI had the potential to lay the groundwork for a network of similar partnerships, which would benefit schools and neighborhoods across the city.

To some extent the more inclusive region, the revised transfer policy, and the positioning of the initiative as a pilot were about damage control: district leaders realized that in a city where the condition of many schools was so deplorable, the prospect of giving additional resources to already advantaged students and schools was politically untenable. However, these modifications were also the result of efforts within the school district and on the part of local elected officials to maintain a commitment to equality of educational opportunity. There is no doubt that they were made at least partly because of genuine concerns about equity. Whether the changes achieved their goals is another issue entirely.

Assessing the CCSI's Consequences

Despite these modifications, the initiative continued to have serious implications for the distribution of resources and opportunities across the district. In this section, I will explore these implications, focusing on three main questions. First, what were the differences between the population targeted by the CCSI and that of the rest of the city? Second, to what extent did the initiative really target all schools in the broadly drawn region and to what extent did it focus on those schools already known to be good options? Third, was the strategy of making it a pilot viable?

Different Populations?

The decision to draw the boundaries of the Center City Academic Region more widely resulted in a region that covered a much more diverse set of neighborhoods. A comparison of the children in neighborhoods served by the Center City Academic Region with the children living within Center City itself (i.e., in the neighborhoods served by the Big Three schools that were originally targeted by the CCD) makes this clear (see table 7.1). Here I use census data on the number of children living in these neighborhoods who were five years old and younger in 2000 to provide a rough representation of the population of children in the early elementary years in 2005, 2006, and 2007.[11]

These data show that a far greater proportion of the children who lived in Center City were white and nonpoor than in the areas served by the Center City Academic Region. Whereas only 8 percent of very young children in Center City were African American in 2000, 46 percent of children living in the Center City Academic Region were. Similarly, only 14 percent of Center City children were classified as low-income, compared to 42 percent in the Center City Academic Region. By defining the region in this way, the school district dramatically reduced (but did not eliminate) the disparities between the pool of students in the region and those of the city as a whole.

TABLE 7.1. **Pool of potential students: Ethnic composition and poverty of children in Center City Philadelphia, the Center City Academic Region, and Philadelphia, 2000**

	Center City[a]	Center City Academic Region[b]	Philadelphia
Race–ethnic group			
White	.71	.38	.33
African American	.09	.47	.51
Other	.20	.15	.16
Poverty status[c]			
Low-income	.13	.47	.54
Not low-income	.87	.53	.46

[a]For this analysis, I included tracts 1–12 and 366.
[b]For this analysis, I included tracts 1–19, 22–25, 29, 125–136, 139, 141–142, 145, 150, and 366.
[c]Low-income refers to all children whose household incomes were below 185% of the poverty level in 1999. This corresponds to the school district's definition of students who are eligible for free or reduced lunch as low-income.
Source: U.S. Census 2000.

While demographic data may alleviate some concerns about the equity implications, it also raises new questions. Earlier I discussed the district's claim that *student* demographics in the new Center City Academic Region were quite similar to those in the school district as a whole. Though this argument that the new region was a "snapshot" of the district was technically true, it overlooked the fact that an important goal of the CCSI was bringing *more* people from Center City into the schools, particularly people who might otherwise have chosen independent schools or moved to the suburbs. The pool of children living in the inclusively drawn Center City Academic Region may not have been demographically very different from the pool of all Philadelphia children, but it was quite different from the *existing* student population in the public schools. This is because large numbers of middle- and upper-class families leave the city when it comes time for their children to start school or send their children to private schools, whereas low-income families do not have the same options. An understanding of the distinction between the *actual* student population and the *potential* pool of students begins with a comparison of census and school district data (see table 7.2).

As these data show, even using the Center City Academic Region (which was expanded to be more diverse than Center City proper), a far greater percentage of young children living in the area were white than actually attended the schools, and far fewer young children in Center City were low-income than in the schools. The region's student population may in 2005 have been a snapshot of the district, but by deliberately recruiting more middle- and upper-middle-class families to the region the CCSI was effectively ensuring that this resemblance was only temporary. In other words, if the initiative were successful, *fewer* children from outside of the region would be able to transfer into Grant and other Center City schools and over the course of a few years the demographics of the region's schools, particularly the ones deemed most viable by middle- and upper-class parents, would change.

In the decade since the 2000 census, the Center City area has become even more highly educated, and incomes there have risen at a rate that far outpaces the rest of the city. In the area covered by the Center City Academic Region, the white population increased, while its African American population decreased. At the same time, there has been a dramatic increase in the number of children born in Center City and in the number of young families remaining in the downtown area. During the 2005–9 period, the percentage of children ages 0–5 in the Center City Academic Region who were white rose from 38 percent in 2000 to 57 percent. Similarly, the percentage of children in this area who were black fell from 47 percent to 24 percent. The percentage of children who were low-income also

TABLE 7.2. **Philadelphia students, potential and actual: Ethnic composition and poverty of resident children versus children attending school in the Center City Academic Region and Philadelphia**

	Children aged 0–5, 2000		Student Population, 2005–6	
	Center City Academic Region[a]	Philadelphia[b]	Center City Academic Region[b]	School District of Philadelphia
Race–ethnic group				
White	.38	.33	.13	.14
African American	.47	.51	.72	.65
Other	.15	.16	.15	.21
Poverty status[c]				
Low-income	.47	.54	.71	.67
Not low-income	.53	.46	.29	.33

[a]For this analysis, I used tracts 1–12 and 366.
[b]For this analysis, I used tracts 1–19, 22–25, 29, 125–136, 139, 141–142, 145, 150, and 366.
[c]Low-income refers to all children whose household incomes were below 185% of the poverty level in 1999. This corresponds to the school district's definition of students who are eligible for free or reduced lunch as low-income.
Sources: US Census, 2000; School District of Philadelphia.

fell: from 47 percent to 32 percent.[12] This suggests that the population of middle- and upper-middle-class families ready to use the Center City public schools will continue to grow in the years to come.[13]

Such a shift would be significant. As I have explained, before the initiative nearly half of all students in Center City elementary schools came from other parts of the city.[14] The majority of students who transferred into Center City schools were from failing schools in low-income parts of the city outside of the downtown. According to school district data, in 2005–6, before the new transfer policy went into effect (and before the marketing campaign had impacted parents' school choices), 72 percent of students who transferred into Center City schools from other regions were African American, 8 percent were Latino, and 6 percent were Asian. Thirty-one percent of all transfers came from the "EMO region" (a group of schools whose performance was so consistently dismal they had been turned over to private educational management organizations), 21 percent came from the South region (an adjacent area with a large number of low-performing schools), and another 10 percent were from the "CEO region" (another group of schools targeted for intensive intervention).[15] What these statistics mean is that hundreds of students transferred to Center City schools each year to avoid schools that were—by all sorts of indicators—inadequate. They lend support to School Reform Commissioner Dungee Glenn's assertion (quoted earlier) that these schools provided an important alternative for parents desperate to avoid sending their children to low-performing neighborhood schools.

The preceding analysis suggests that the CCSI, even with the modifications made due to equity concerns, would exacerbate stratification within the district by helping to create a group of schools whose student population was significantly more advantaged than the population of the district as a whole. It would do this by recruiting white and middle-class families to these schools, and it would cut off an important escape option for a group of largely African American students eager to leave racially isolated and low-performing neighborhood schools. Later in this chapter, I will show that this is exactly what happened, resulting in changes in the student population at key schools.

Differential Treatment?

Even after the new region had been drawn to include a range of schools, the CCD's focus continued to be on marketing and making improvements to Grant, Fairview, and Hopkins, the three highest-performing elementary schools in Center City. The CCD assumed that professional parents would be most attracted to schools with reputations for high achievement and strong parental involvement, since these were seen as indicators of "good" schools that—because parents were active—could become even better. According to an administrator with the CCD, the Big Three were targeted because "they were the most viable and have the most active PTOs. That made it easier." Thus, when a group of architects volunteered to draw up plans for physical improvements to schools in the region, they only toured and drew plans for the Big Three. The CCD's outreach to Toll Brothers, a local developer, also reflected this strategy. During this period, Toll Brothers constructed a gated community of luxury townhouses and condominiums in a gentrifying neighborhood on the fringes of Center City. Describing an effort to interest Toll Brothers in forming a partnership with (and donating resources to) a local elementary school, a CCSI administrator explained that this partnership would *not* be with the low-performing school in the new development's neighborhood, because the parents living in the development were unlikely to send their children there. Instead, the developer could work with one of the Big Three schools that served an adjacent community, a school parents in the new development would be much more likely to see as an option for their children. The CCD was being strategic about where to invest its energies and resources, choosing schools that were most likely to appeal to middle-class parents and were, therefore, "better bets."[16]

Not only were the more desirable schools the target of the CCSI's marketing campaign, they were also the prime beneficiaries of the CCD's and school district's efforts to forge partnerships between individual schools and local organizations. As of 2011, each of the Big Three elementary schools had multiple relationships with high-status cultural and educational institutions, as do a number of the schools on the gentrifying edges of the downtown. In contrast, a few of the schools that were included in the Center City Academic Region to satisfy equity concerns (but serve predominantly low-income and African American populations) work with local churches and service organizations like the Eagle Eye Van or the Women's Christian Association. These partners certainly provide important services, such as vision screening and after-school tutoring. But they do not offer the sort of academic enrichment or exciting cultural experiences that organizations like Center City's Arden Theater provide for students at one of the Big Three schools: tickets for performances and "instructional materials for each production to enhance the children's enjoyment and understanding."[17]

"The Approach We're Taking Is a Center City Approach"

In discussing the ways the initiative evolved in response to equity concerns, I described earlier its positioning as a pilot for other regions in the city to follow. Thus, when Vallas spoke publicly about the CCSI, he not only congratulated Paul Levy for his vision but also argued that the "Center City approach" would actually be followed in all regions of the city.[18] What this rhetoric around replication ignored, however, were the vast disparities in the sorts of resources available in different regions in the city. When district and CCSI staff spoke of the initiative as a pilot, they frequently gave examples of neighborhoods that could implement similar projects. The areas they identified—East Falls, Northwest Philadelphia, Northeast Philadelphia, and University City—all had sizable middle- and/or upper-middle-class populations or significant institutional resources. For example, University City has a relatively small middle- and upper-middle-class community but is home to two major universities, the University of Pennsylvania and Drexel University, and a business improvement district modeled after the CCD.

In the most depressed parts of the city, organizations with anything close to the resources, connections, and political savvy of the CCD simply did not exist. Vallas himself admitted as much when he compared the district's work in Center City with its work in other regions: "The advantages of Center City are actually Paul Levy. Not every region is as organized or has individuals that are as aggressive about advocacy for the region as Paul is." Of course, Paul Levy's efficacy as an advocate for Center City was due only partly to his own personal qualities; he was able to promote partnerships, generate resources, and push for change also because his organization was uniquely positioned within the city and had a wealth of resources and connections on which to draw. Other parts of the city lacked a Paul Levy, the sort of organization he headed, and the status and wealth of Center City. In fact, there were large swaths of the city that were bereft of resource-rich organizations like the Franklin Institute, the Philadelphia Museum of Art, universities, and the CCD.[19] While schools within these regions could cultivate relationships with local organizations, their pool of potential partners was far more limited and consisted of cash-strapped grassroots and community organizations instead of cultural institutions or BIDs.

The CCSI itself helped secure Center City's advantage in this respect. Though other schools across the district could also seek out institutional partners, it was more likely that Center City school and regional staff would be effective in this endeavor, because, as one district administrator told me, the initiative raised the profile of the downtown schools:

> Center City District is pretty high on the radar screen and making sure the schools in Center City are successful is pretty high on the radar screen. As opposed to, say, Tilden [a middle school in a poor neighborhood]. Nobody is really that focused on what's going on at Tilden, until there's a major incident. . . . Anyway, I think that even if it's just sort of raised the profile of the Center City schools. . . . And of course, business partners or university partners, this is more appealing to them than going to one of these schools that are doing so poorly that it's like starting from scratch. It's really taking mediocre and making it great. Which is much easier than taking a complete disaster and making it great.

This official also explained that Center City schools had been given "priority in partnership development" by the district and a staff dedicated to the success of these efforts. As the administrator of a local nonprofit organization, who had expressed support for the initiative because it recognized the connection between education and the local economy, mused in discussing the new emphasis on partnerships, "if you were to sort of duplicate that way of thinking in other regions, there are some regions—here's the problem with that strategy—there are some regions that it doesn't work." For a variety of reasons, then, schools in resource-rich communities within the city were more likely to benefit from the cultivation of external relationships than schools in struggling communities. The notion of a neighborhood school and the prospect of bringing community resources into a school have great appeal to parents, educators, city leaders, and community members. However, given the vast differences in neighborhoods, increasing the connections between a school and its immediate surroundings actually exacerbates inequality. It can channel resources toward schools in advantaged areas—making them more attractive to middle-class families looking for enrichment for their children—while lessening the resources available to schools in low-income neighborhoods.

Longer-Term Consequences

In 2007, facing an unexpectedly large budget gap, Vallas resigned as CEO of the school district, and the CCSI lost its greatest champion within the school system. The new superintendent, Arlene Ackerman, who assumed control in 2008, did not display the same interest in retaining the middle class. Instead, her agenda involved shifting resources toward the city's lowest-performing schools, largely through her signature initiative, "Renaissance Schools," which targeted chronically underperforming schools for major overhauls. Though never formally revoked, the CCSI received no further resources or attention during Ackerman's tenure. When Ackerman embarked on a reorganization of the district's administrative structure, the Center City Academic Region was collapsed into another academic region. (In 2010, she dissolved the region system entirely.) However, the "preferred admissions policy" remained in effect for at least the 2008–9 school year, and the changes to the schools' demographics begun under the initiative continued. As CCD president Paul Levy explained in a 2008 article, while "the leadership of the school district has changed . . . the momentum continues."[20] Indeed, though the formal partnership with the district lasted only a few years, district data on student enrollment show that it had a significant, and lasting, impact. Here I focus just on the Big Three Center City schools, the ones downtown professional families generally saw as the most viable options for their children and the ones most often featured in CCD materials, and use the data to make two comparisons.

First, I compare the 2005–6 and 2009–10 enrollment patterns of students in these schools. Because the marketing of schools began in the winter and spring of 2005 (after applications for the 2005–6 school year had been filed), data for that year provide a baseline measure. By 2009–10, the transfer policy had been (quietly) revoked, but the CCD was still promoting schools. Figure 7.1 shows the number and percentage of students in these three schools who lived within the catchment, transferred from other parts of Center City, and transferred from regions other than Center City for those school years.

These data suggest that enrollment patterns changed in important ways. First, and surprisingly, the change in transfer policy giving priority to Center City families—presumably because it was only in effect for a few years—did not significantly impact the schools. While several district administrators confirmed that the majority of Center City students ap-

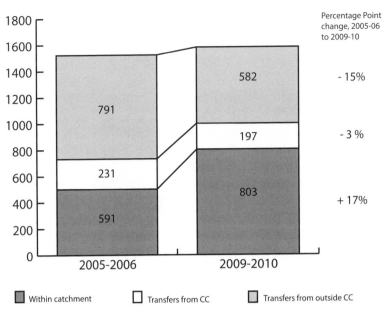

FIGURE 7.1. Within-catchment versus transfer students. Source: School District of Philadelphia data; author's calculations.

plying for transfers for 2007 received their first choices, and *no* students from outside of Center City attained admissions to the Big Three through the normal transfer process, the policy did not appear to have had the long-term impact of increasing within–Center City transfers. This is likely because, as an administrator at Grant explained, the schools had become so popular to students within their catchments that they enrolled very few students from outside of them, Center City region or not. On the other hand, the effort to market the schools to families within their catchment areas has been quite consequential. In a four-year period, the number of within-catchment students increased by 302, and the number of children from outside of Center City decreased by 209.

Because the CCSI targeted families whose children were just entering schools, it had its greatest impact on the early grades. Focusing again on the Big Three, a comparison of first-graders in 2005–6 with first-graders in 2009–10 provides a more fine-grained analysis of the initiative's impact (see fig. 7.2). In 2005–6, when the CCSI's marketing campaign had not yet affected enrollment, approximately 50 percent of first-graders came from within the schools' catchment areas. By 2009–10, this number had

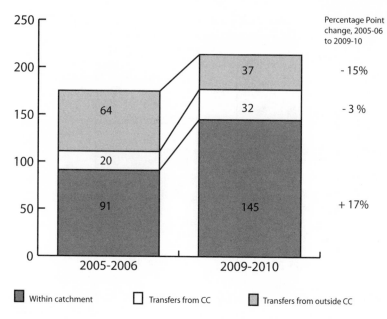

FIGURE 7.2. Within-catchment versus transfer students. Source: School District of Philadelphia data; author's calculations.

jumped to 67 percent. The percentage of students transferring into the schools from outside of Center City dropped accordingly, from 37 percent to 17 percent. In other words, the four years following the unveiling of the CCSI witnessed a significant increase in the number of families from key neighborhoods who decided to enroll their children in their local public schools.

Presumably some of this increase was due to the recession that, beginning in 2008, may have made private school less of an option for many middle- and upper-middle-class families. It is difficult to untangle the interest in these schools that resulted from the CCSI from that resulting from the economic downturn, both of which created a larger sense among Center City parents that more and more "parents like them" were using the public schools. Because isolating out the causal variables is impossible here, I can only say that it is likely the CCSI played a role in setting such patterns into motion. The CCD itself celebrated this change in a 2008 newsletter:

As a result of this communications campaign, registration for kindergarten at three of the Center City public elementary schools was impressive, with 70 percent of the September 2008 kindergarten classes at [the Big Three schools] coming from their immediate surrounding neighborhood.[21]

"I Do Worry about the Racial Implications of Something Like This"

To the CCD, this shift was something to celebrate: it meant that the initiative had been successful in convincing more downtown professional families to choose their local schools. However, since the number of students in all three schools grew by only 58 at the same time that the number of within-catchment students grew by over 300, significant displacement occurred.[22] The schools did not simply grow to accommodate the new interest among neighborhood students. Rather, fewer spots were available to students from outside of the catchments, particularly from outside of Center City.

It should come as no surprise that the pattern the CCSI set in place—of recruiting children from within the catchment area and replacing minority students from outside of Center City with white students from the immediate neighborhood—affected the demographic composition of the schools. Fairview, the most desirable Center City school in recent years, is a case in point. In 2003–4 (before the initiative went into effect), the school was 46 percent African American and 45 percent white. By 2006–7, the school was 39 percent African American, and by 2010–11 the percentage had fallen even lower, to 25 percent. At the same time, the percentage of white students increased from 45 percent in 2003–4 to 61 percent in 2010–11. The percentage of African American students decreased at all three of the high-performing schools (the Big Three) during this period (by nearly half at Fairview and Grant), and the percentage of white students increased. These changes were particularly apparent in the early grades, the grades targeted by the marketing campaign. Looking across the three schools, the number of white students in grades K-2 increased by 30 percent, while the number of black students decreased by 29 percent.[23] Similar patterns have occurred in other cities, wherein an influx of white, middle-class families into certain urban elementary schools led to sudden, often dramatic, shifts in the racial composition of those schools.[24]

While it is clear that enrollment patterns at these schools changed, the implications for educational improvement are less apparent. Another way to understand the data discussed here is that more Center City families have begun using their neighborhood schools, which means that families who might have otherwise left for the suburbs (particularly if the economic downturn made private school out of the question) were able to remain in the city, support their public schools, and contribute to the local economy. Many parents and civic leaders located in the downtown area would likely agree with the CCD that this is cause for celebration. However, the displacement described here represents an important, and often overlooked, consequence of increasing the number of professional families enrolling their children in the local public schools.

This issue of displacement is not much discussed in articles and reports that trumpet the new interest in urban public schools among the middle class and suggest it could lead to wider school improvement. Yet the schools that middle-class parents view as acceptable options for their children are, in many cases, the same ones that poor and working-class parents see as vital escape routes from the often-dysfunctional schools in their neighborhoods. Because there are relatively few quality options available to students in cities like Philadelphia, patterns of displacement reveal the limitations of this approach to improving urban schools.

In considering the impact of the CCSI, it is important to keep in mind that, like many large urban systems, Philadelphia's schools have long faced enormous challenges, from financial shortfalls, a dysfunctional organizational culture and mismanagement at the district level, to violence and low student achievement at the schools.[25] In the years and decades before the CCSI, Philadelphia's schools had failed innumerable low-income and minority students. By arguing that the CCSI restricted opportunities for some low-income students, I do not intend to suggest that, in the absence of such an initiative, all students would have been well served. However, the CCSI did create new patterns of inequality and disenfranchisement, both generating improvements at targeted Center City schools and, at the same time, limiting access for those students from outside of Center City whose families would have sought out these schools.

It is essential to understand the many consequences of the CCSI, including the ways it affected racial demographics at key schools, because news of the project has reverberated in urban policy circles, with the initiative spoken of as a model for other cities to emulate.[26] Leaders in other cities, including Boston and Baltimore, have studied Philadelphia's experience in their efforts to develop similar initiatives.[27] Thus, another legacy of the CCSI is its own standing as an "experiment" worth copying—an innovative effort to market urban schools to middle-class families and to institutionalize that goal in school and district policy.

Consequences at Grant

In 2010, four years after the close of my research, I visited Grant to tie up a few loose ends. In walking around the school and talking with an administrator, I learned that the school was in many ways quite a different place, with the events I had observed during my research setting into motion patterns that continued to shape the school. Most important, it had become a popular choice among Cobble Square families. The administrator noted that Grant was truly a neighborhood school, with Cobble Square families increasingly enrolling their children for kindergarten:

> And each year, it's funny. Last year the kindergarten parents at the open house said, "I think we're the largest classroom of kindergarten kids from the neighborhood now." Now this year, they're like, "But we're now the largest." And it's like, well, they're all here.[28]

She reported feeling no more pressure to recruit "neighborhood" parents because the word was so clearly out in the community already.

This administrator further acknowledged the tensions that had existed during my time at the school between neighborhood and transfer parents and observed that the CCSI had the unfortunate effect of highlighting differences along race and class lines: "It heightened the tensions between the haves and have-nots, [making it] feel like without the haves my school's not going to be successful. Well, now, that's really terrible to say that!" Thus, in her time at the school, she had been witness to the conflicts and marginalizations that arose when attracting a critical mass of middle- and upper-class families became *the* strategy for educational improvement.

One consequence of Grant's popularity is that the issues around transfer students have become essentially irrelevant. This administrator reported that the school no longer accepts *any* children from outside of its immediate catchment zone, whether or not they live in the broader Center City area. As a result, demographics at the school have changed, with the percentage of African American students decreasing significantly. On the one hand, this means that the tensions caused by the marketing campaign have lessened. However, it also shows that precisely what many African American parents (and critics of the CCSI in general) feared has come true: Grant has become less available to African American students. Kim, the parent who was most vocal in her criticism of efforts to market Grant to Center City families, was right.

The Debate Continues

The conflict this marketing campaign brought to the surface—between providing equal educational opportunity to all students and ensuring that middle-class families have options they believe are adequate for their children—also continued to simmer in the city. In the spring of 2010 a local research organization released a report about high school choice in the city. The report showed that students of color were far less likely than white students to attain admissions to their schools of choice. In particular, whites and Asian students who applied to academic magnets were twice as likely as black and Latino students to be enrolled.[29] Shortly thereafter, local newspapers reported that the district was considering altering the admissions process at magnet schools, including Masterman, the city's most prestigious magnet, to give applicants living in underrepresented (i.e.., low-income and minority) neighborhoods an advantage. This was big news, because, as one story noted, "The proposal could upend a decades-old selection system for the magnet schools, long an educational refuge for the city's middle class, where many powerful and influential leaders send their children."[30]

Criticism of the plan was immediate. The head of the PTO at Masterman was furious about the possibility that admissions to the school would be based on anything other than students' grades and tests scores. She argued that changing the process to admit students whose grades and scores would previously have kept them from attending Masterman would diminish the academic rigor of the school. It would also, she insisted, send more middle-class families to the suburbs by making it harder for their children (so many of whom are the high-scorers who get into Masterman under the current system) to gain admission: "If our children were not in these special-selection schools, we would be taking ourselves and our tax dollars out of the city. You have to provide a way for middle-class people to be able to live in the city and not have to pay $25,000 a year in tuition."[31] Like many supporters of the CCSI, this parent argued that though the system may have disadvantaged low-income and minority students, the goal of retaining middle-class families in the city was important enough to trump this concern. And she cited the fiscal contributions families like hers made to the city to justify this tradeoff.

In the face of such opposition, the district almost immediately reported that it had never considered changing the admissions process for magnet schools. This about-face generated another firestorm, with district superintendent Arlene Ackerman denying that she had supported any change to admissions criteria, and blaming members of her staff for moving forward without her knowledge. Though brief, this controversy is a reminder that cities like Philadelphia will continue to struggle with the tensions explored in this book, particularly because there are so few high-quality educational options and the disparities between the "good schools" and the rest of the system are so vast. The quick repudiation of the proposal to alter admissions on the part of Superintendent Ackerman, who had made educational access for low-income students the centerpiece of her administration and could have been expected to favor the proposal, is further testament to the continued power of the fear of middle-class flight. It also reveals that, even in the absence of a formal partnership, the goal of increasing the middle-class presence in public schools continues to shape education policy and often coexists uneasily with policies designed to increase access for low-income students to high-performing schools.

In this chapter, I have examined how the CCSI evolved in response to charges that it was inequitable, and assessed its consequences for students and schools. Despite the collegiality between the CCD and top school district officials discussed in chapter 4—the requests granted and favors returned—response to the initiative among district administrators was more tepid. Many expressed concerns about the initiative because it appeared to channel additional resources and opportunities to an already advantaged part of the city, a strategy that did not sit easily with the equity-oriented culture within the district's central office. As a result, the CCSI was altered in a variety of ways.

However, a closer look shows that the initiative still contributed to the constriction of educational opportunities for students from outside of Center City, large numbers of whom were African American children seeking to escape low-performing neighborhood schools. At the same time, the increase in Center City students and decline in transfer students at these schools means that the additional resources and programming parents like Sharon, Catherine, and Sara brought to Grant—as well as those generated by their counterparts at other "desirable" schools—benefited increasingly advantaged populations. In this way, the patterns set into place by the CCSI are reminiscent of sociologist Mary Pattillo's observation that, in a gentrifying neighborhood, once "mixed-income communities tip upward, then whatever structural reforms had been enacted—better schools, more jobs, cleaner environment—now disproportionately benefit the incoming gentry rather than the outgoing poor residents."[32] This chapter further suggests that by tightening the link between geography and opportunity—with respect to enrollment patterns and the ability of schools to form productive relationships with external institutions—the CCSI furthered the creation of a two-tiered system of educational options and resources across the city's schools.

CHAPTER EIGHT

Citizens, Customers, and City Schools

Six months after I completed my research at Grant, I happened to be walking past the school just before dismissal. A few parents were standing outside in the schoolyard. Among them, I saw Sharon, the Cobble Square mother and active PTO member introduced in chapter 2. I waved and crossed the street. Sharon greeted me with her usual rushed friendliness, and we stood talking near two large, swinging gates that were open to the sidewalk and the street beyond. I did not notice at the time but, standing open, the gates created a perfect entry for cars to pull into the schoolyard, which would shortly be filled with children leaving school. As Sharon and I chatted, the school's custodian approached us and, in a tone that managed to combine both hostility and excessive courtesy, asked us to step out of the way so he could close the two gates. After he moved away, Sharon whispered to me, "He hates me so much!"

"Why?" I asked, anticipating another of Sharon's stories about her battles with school district staff.

"They always leave those gates open at dismissal time, and parents drive their cars right into the yard when kids are getting out of school. Last week I saw a little girl literally pulled out of the way right before a car hit her. It's ridiculous! Of course someone is going to get hit! So now, every time I see the gates open at dismissal time, I call the office and say, 'It's Mrs. Roberts. The gates are open again.' And they send someone out to close them. So he hates me. But I don't care."

Sharon told the story with a grin I knew well. It communicated her frustration with the school staff's inability to meet her expectations and the satisfaction she derived from, once again, making sure they did what needed to be done. Over the course of my research, I had dozens of conversations like this with Sharon and other Cobble Square parents. Time after time, they saw something happening at the school that seemed unsafe or unacceptable to them, and time after time they made phone calls, arranged meetings, or otherwise made sure the problem was fixed. For the reasons discussed in chapters 5 and 6—the district's interest in keeping them satisfied, their social status, their skill at maneuvering through the district bureaucracy, and their sense of entitlement and efficacy—these parents' efforts were almost always successful.

During the years I was conducting my research, newspaper accounts of accidents involving young school children appeared with some frequency. Weighed down with backpacks and art projects, they were struck by careless drivers as they left school or crossed a street. In this context, the value of Sharon's vigilance is undeniable. She had the time, energy, power, and investment in the school that enabled her to hold staff accountable for keeping the children safe.

This event reminded me, as I struggled through mountains of data and growing piles of drafts, why I had found the Center City Schools Initiative such a compelling research topic in the first place. Parents like Sharon have the resources to make schools safer and better for all children. Unquestionably, urban public schools should hold on to families that have the ability to pressure school districts to meet higher standards for safety, academics, enrichment, and school climate. Yet what are the costs of targeting them so explicitly? Can an influx of middle- and upper-middle-class families even begin to address the deeply entrenched problems of urban schools, problems that are rooted in such macrostructural factors as federal policy, racial discrimination, poverty, and the chronic underfunding of education?

This book began with a quotation from an editorial in a local newspaper arguing that if Philadelphians want "white and affluent parents" to use the public schools "some accommodation has to be made." The succeeding chapters examined these accommodations and their consequences. I have shown that though the goals of the CCSI were compelling in many ways, one outcome was the exacerbation of existing inequalities. The task for civic leaders, educators, and policymakers is both to re-engage the middle class in urban public schools without setting into motion the inequities documented here and to be cognizant of the promises and limitations of this strategy for improving cities and schools.

Key Arguments

In this book, I have explained that civic leaders in Philadelphia turned to the CCSI in response to local and national conditions that made an effort to attract and retain middle- and upper-middle-class families in the city's downtown appear both reasonable and pragmatic, even if it meant providing them with greater resources and options than other groups. Philadelphia had only recently begun to emerge from decades of decline, and the possibility of yet another downward spiral remained very real. The city continued to lose population, face competition from the suburbs and other cities, and grapple with crime, a decaying infrastructure, and concentrated poverty. Its schools faced ongoing fiscal shortfalls and struggled to educate a disproportionately low-income population. As a result, many local stakeholders were sympathetic to the initiative, seeing it as an important effort to reverse middle-class flight and bring people with resources back to the city, and viewing any differential treatment as an unfortunate, but necessary, consequence. The CCSI positioned middle- and upper-middle-class families as the constituency on which the city's future depended. Local newspapers, as well as many civic leaders, accepted this positioning, expressing in subtle and not-so-subtle ways that such families were more valuable and more virtuous than others. If the term "citizenship" can be understood as encapsulating complex notions of contribution and entitlement, the initiative and its accompanying discourse distinguished among Philadelphians, making those more able to contribute to the city's economy and its institutions also more fully entitled to their citizenship. The initiative's reliance on market mechanisms also meant that such families became the schools' and city's most valued customers. As tables 8.1 and 8.2 show, the result was a set of privileging mechanisms that operated in both tangible and intangible ways to the advantage of Center City as a whole, its schools, and its residents.

While this book criticizes some aspects of the initiative, it is important to note that the administrators behind the CCSI and the parents who marketed Grant to other professional families all believed, with some

TABLE 8.1. **Advantaging mechanisms — tangible/policy/resources**

Beneficiaries	Mechanisms
Center City	Partnership between Center City District (CCD) and School District of Philadelphia CCD gets privileged access to school district leaders and internal school district data
Center City elementary schools	Funding to market schools and work with Center City parents $250,000 from Pennsylvania Department of Education $350,000 from William Penn Foundation ~$25,000 for parent consultant (hired by School District of Philadelphia) New Center City Academic Region bringing together downtown schools Talented regional superintendent Significant School District of Philadelphia resources devoted to creation of region (~$200,000) Creation of partnerships with numerous downtown institutions Additional staff devoted to schools and parents Center City District staffer helps with partnership development, fundraising, communicating with parents, and other projects School district staff provide additional support and outreach Additional resources for Center City schools ~$100,000 for Grant playground renovation ~$150,000 for Grant library renovation New websites for schools Other improvements to facilities and programming
Center City parents at Grant	Changes to district policy New transfer policy to give Center City children priority Syncing of district admissions timeline with that of local independent schools Privileged channels of communication/leverage Special access to high-level city and district officials CCD staffer serves as liaison between Center City parents and schools Parent consultant solicits and conveys parents' perspectives and goals to high-level officials

justification, that they were part of the solution. They saw themselves as doing valuable work for an institution that many had abandoned. Rather than casting judgment upon their intentions, my aim is to show that the solution the CCSI embodied was highly problematic. This is partly because of the specifics of the policy and who benefited (and who did not) from the initiative, but, more broadly, it is due to the way the CCSI constructed both the challenges cities face and the possibilities at their disposal. While couched in the language of the greater good, the CCSI focused narrowly on the needs and interests of one already advantaged group and used the resources of a public institution, the School District of Philadelphia, to achieve its ends. Of course, public schools in the United States have often

TABLE 8.2. **Advantaging mechanisms—intangible/symbolic**

Beneficiaries	Mechanisms
Center City	Ongoing public discourse linking success of downtown revitalization with city as a whole
	Broad use of term "middle class" to refer to a (largely White) professional/upper-middle class population, justifying benefits for Center City

Center City elementary schools	Marketing of Center City schools
	  Increased public attention to Center City schools
	  Increased media coverage of key Center City elementary schools

	Symbolic and institutional distance between Center City schools and "inner-city" district
	  Center City schools are "high on the radar screen" of district leaders while others are not
	  Elevated status for Center City schools within district

Center City parents at Grant	Marketing of school targets middle- and upper-middle-class parents
	  Strong messages about who is valued (Center City/middle- and upper-middle-class families); implicit messages about who is less valued (poor/working-class families from outside of downtown)
	  Improved "customer service" for middle- and upper-middle-class families in Center City
	  Principals expected to attract/retain Center City parents to their schools
	  Discourse around importance of attracting/retaining Center City families positions the good of the school and city as dependent upon such parents' satisfaction

	Intersections between the CCSI and institutional rules/policies/practices
	  Positioning of "neighborhood" families versus "transfer" families suggests that only Center City families have the "right" to be at the school
	  Center City parents are empowered in making claims/demands on the school and district; "transfer" parents are disempowered
	  District officials' investment in attracting Center City families and in presenting the district as particularly responsive them further empowers middle/upper-middle-class families

	Reshaping of parent-school relations along market lines
	  Emphasis on exchange (i.e., parents' ability to generate resources for the school in exchange for full membership) elevates middle- and upper-middle-class parents' status; only middle-/upper-middle-class families have "currency"
	  "Exit option," when threatened by Center City parents, becomes source of leverage

failed in their mission of treating all students equally. However, these differences have generally persisted *in spite of* a larger ideology emphasizing equality of opportunity. One of the more striking aspects of the events I studied in Philadelphia was a shift in this equation, such that the ideology *justified* the inequality.

Lessons from Other Cities

Boston's Y/BPS Program

Many school districts across the country are—either through explicitly designed programs and policies or through more subtle practices—trying to convince middle- and upper-middle-class families to enroll in public schools and remain in the city. Boston's experiences are particularly informative. There, as in Philadelphia, civic and educational leaders embarked on a deliberate effort to market the public schools to parents who might have otherwise avoided them. Boston's effort, launched in 2003 and known as Y/BPS (i.e., Why Boston Public Schools?), was a public-private partnership, a collaboration between the mayor's office, the Greater Boston YMCA, and the Boston Public Schools.[1] Curious about the similarities and differences between Y/BPS and the CCSI, I traveled to Boston during the spring and summer of 2009 and conducted over a dozen interviews with educators, administrators and parents involved with Y/BPS (see appendix A). That research yielded some useful points of comparison.

In contrast to Philadelphia, whose status in the postindustrial economy remains tenuous, Boston's is fairly solid. The city is home to a large number of colleges and universities and has a robust economy focused on education, health services, and technology. Indeed, Boston has one of the most highly educated workforces in the country. Yet Boston's 2000 poverty rate (19.5%), though lower than Philadelphia's (22.9%), represented an increase over 1990. This increase, combined with growth in the number of high-income households (and notoriously expensive real estate), suggests a polarization by income similar to that found in Philadelphia.[2] Both cities have majority-minority school districts with large numbers of low-income students, though Boston's system is smaller than Philadelphia's.[3] Compared to Philadelphia, Boston schools have a better track record of steady and sustained improvement, including winning the 2006 Broad Prize for best urban school district in the country.[4]

Funded by the Boston Foundation and other private funders, the Y/BPS program was developed to encourage families to consider Boston Public Schools, help parents "become more informed consumers" of Boston schools, and help schools reach out to and communicate with prospective parents.[5] Though ostensibly designed for "all" families, the project targeted middle- and upper-middle-class families and was often presented in that way, both in newspaper coverage and by those involved with it.[6] As with the CCSI, proponents of Y/BPS assumed that schools would benefit from an influx of middle-class families. The program used social networking, information sessions, websites, newsletters, and listservs to make information about public schools available to families and help families negotiate the application process. Like the CCSI, Y/BPS also provided staffers to liaison between prospective parents and schools, answer parents' questions, and guide them through the enrollment process. Also like the CCSI, the additional information provided by Y/BPS benefited an already relatively advantaged population. Attendees at Y/BPS information sessions, which were held in parents' homes, were largely white and middle- and upper-middle-class.

Another similarity between the CCSI and Y/BPS was that both led to an increase in middle-class families using the schools and displacement of other families. This dynamic was more dramatic in Boston than in Philadelphia.[7] In some cases, schools lost their Title I funding because the percentage of low-income students decreased so dramatically. Other research shows that during this period a number of Boston schools also experienced significant decreases in the percentage of African American students and corresponding increases in the percentage of white students. As we have seen, demographic changes also occurred in some Philadelphia schools, but they were not as extensive.[8]

A key difference, however, lies in the willingness of educators and Y/BPS coordinators to address dynamics of privilege and exclusion within the targeted schools. Rather than focusing on a few high-achieving schools, Y/BPS coordinators deliberately strove to increase the pool of schools middle-class families would consider. While this was associated with displacement in some schools, it also tended to spread the benefits of middle-class involvement more widely. Y/BPS coordinators spoke of eleven or twelve schools, as opposed to the three to five the CCSI targeted. In addition, administrators involved with Y/BPS were deliberate about dealing with equity issues. Describing the founding of the initiative, one Y/BPS insider explained that they wanted to make it as inclusive as possible: "From the very beginning we hired staff of color as well as white staff. We housed it in the Y [as opposed to a city agency or private organization] because the Y's considered fairly neutral." Aware of the possibility that non-middle-class parents could be marginalized at schools experiencing an influx of more affluent families, Y/BPS coordinators reported working with principals and parents to help them manage the process in an equitable way—a possibility that simply never came up in Philadelphia.[9]

Due to limitations in the data (i.e., the reliance on interviews only), I cannot claim that Y/BPS was more successful or more equitable than the CCSI. However, the Boston case does suggest that alternative strategies for managing an influx of middle-class families may ameliorate some of the troubling dynamics associated with a policy like the CCSI. In particular, it implies that school employees can adhere to their mission of educating all children equally, even in the context of growing economic diversity. But it also indicates that, in Boston as in Philadelphia, efforts to engage a more advantaged population with a public institution may inevitably lead to new inequalities, including the displacement of low-income students, and that these outcomes must be managed carefully. More research into the ways other cities are addressing the issue of equity in similar circumstances would be helpful.

Wake County

Marketing is not the only way to create racially and economically diverse public schools. Other cities have used a variety of strategies, from magnet schools to redistricting to elaborate systems of "controlled choice." Perhaps the most famous example of a system-wide effort to bring about economic integration of schools comes from North Carolina.[10] Wake County, which includes Raleigh and its outlying suburbs, has long been a national leader in school integration. Leaders there merged the city and suburban school systems in 1976 and then, in the 1980s, created a system of highly desirable magnet schools scattered throughout the county. These schools were designed to attract white students to the city and black students to the suburbs. In 2000, in the face of growing judicial hostility to race-based desegregation plans, the Wake County schools became the largest system in the country to integrate its schools by social class rather than race.[11] As sociologist Gerald Grant argues in a book explaining "why there are no bad schools in Raleigh," the outcome was a system of economically diverse, high-achieving schools.

Wake County is the second-largest school system in North Carolina. It served over 140,000 students in 2010, of which 32 percent were eligible for free- or reduced-price lunch, 50 percent were white, 25 percent were African American, 15 percent were Hispanic, and 6 percent were Asian.[12] According to journalist Emily Bazelon, who profiled Wake County in a 2008 article in the *New York Times*, "Wake County adopted class-based integration with the hard-nosed goal of raising test scores. The strategy was simple: no poor schools, no bad schools." Under the 2000 plan, families in Wake County could choose between neighborhood and magnet schools. In making final enrollment decisions, the board took income, rather than race, into account, making sure that no school had more than 40 percent low-income students and no more than 25 percent performing below grade level.[13] During this period, Wake County also implemented ambitious reforms focusing on teacher professional development and data-driven instruction.

The results were impressive. Student achievement in Wake rose steadily after the new plan went into effect, and the system came close to meeting its goal of having 95 percent of all students passing state exams—even though the percentage of students living in poverty actually increased. The county's innovative approach to integration and the remarkable outcomes brought national attention.[14]

Wake County's success with integration was due in large part to the fact that the county encompasses *both* city and suburbs. This fact is hugely significant for efforts to create desegregated schools—either by race or by income. The 1974 Supreme Court decision in *Milliken v. Bradley*, which rejected a plan to create a "metropolitan" school district integrating the largely African American Detroit system with the white suburban systems surrounding it, established a barrier for desegregation plans that cross county lines. Yet in older cities in the Northeast and the Midwest, city, school district, and county lines are typically coterminous (the same). Given the demographic shifts of the last half century, which left city populations disproportionately poor and minority and suburban populations middle class and white, within-county desegregation plans in the Northeast and Midwest are often essentially meaningless. Bazelon noted as much in her profile of Wake County. In contrast to systems like Wake County, where there is a significant middle-class population from which to pull students, she observed, in Philadelphia, Detroit, New York, and Chicago, "simple demographics indicate that they can't really integrate their schools at all, either by race or class."[15]

In 2009 critics of Wake's student assignment system elected a new school board, one that was hostile to the economic integration plan and particularly critical of the time students were spending traveling to and from school. The board voted in early 2010 to dismantle the plan and assign students to schools based solely on their place of residence. The story did not end there, however. Wake bore the brunt of national criticism for retreating from a successful model, and business, civic, and educational leaders fought against the impending resegregation. By early 2011 Wake was considering a new strategy for maintaining its school diversity and high academic outcomes: integrating schools by student achievement.[16]

Like Boston's Y/BPS program, Wake County's system of economically integrated schools holds lessons for cities like Philadelphia. In particular, it highlights what is possible when political will and a shared emphasis on equity generate an ambitious reform plan. In Wake County the school system, rather than the preferences of individual parents, played a lead role in creating integrated schools. Not only did the system set up an educational market, it actively managed that market. When he was interviewed for a story about Wake's success in 2005, then-superintendent Bill McNeal linked this management to the system's responsibility for ensuring equity and excellence: "I believe in choice as much as anyone. . . . However, I can't let choice erode our ability to provide quality programs and quality teaching."[17] Wake County also reminds us that, despite the celebratory rhetoric about a middle-class return to urban public schools, true and equitable integration may not be possible as long as cities and suburbs continue to function as separate systems.

Can Schools Create a Better City?

The Chicago sociologist Robert Park called cities "man's most successful attempt to remake the world he lives in." Quoting Park decades later, urban geographer David Harvey argues that the "freedom to make and remake our cities and ourselves is . . . one of the most precious yet most neglected of our human rights." He asks the next generation of scholars and activists to think more expansively about cities' future and, particularly, to take on the all-important question of "what kind of city" they want to create. Harvey criticizes the dominance of market-oriented thinking in the United States and around the world. He insists that, powerful as this ideology has become, its dominance is not inevitable.[18] Similarly, I would argue that the particular vision the CCSI helped foster of Philadelphia's future, and its implications for patterns of class, race, and geography, are not inevitable.

The CCSI did, however, make a valuable contribution to the ways people think and talk about the future of cities: it brought public education into the conversation about urban redevelopment, highlighting the importance of education in twenty-first century American cities. Much of the literature on urban change tends to ignore education or, when it does address public schools, treats them as yet another casualty of urban decay and middle-class flight.[19] Likewise, urban development policy and education policy have tended to operate independently of each other, ignoring the huge impact schools have on the life of the city, on people's choices of residence, and on neighborhoods themselves.[20] As cities redefine themselves in the postindustrial economy, it is critical that policymakers and researchers pay attention to the myriad interconnections between urban spatial, social, economic, *and* educational processes.

As a strategy for linking urban development and education, the CCSI resonated with the growing tendency in the United States to view education as a private good, a commodity that facilitates social mobility or, in the case of the middle and upper classes, a means through which children maintain their class advantage. This tendency represents a divergence from earlier visions for public education, which focused on more collective purposes, such as fostering democratic citizenship and economic productivity, and solving social problems such as crime and poverty.[21] Though often cloaked in the rhetoric of a public good—with references to the ways it would fuel Philadelphia's revitalization—the CCSI was largely a function of a more individualistic understanding of public education.

The mechanisms the CCSI employed to lure professional families into the public schools (marketing, customer service, the creation of symbolic and institutional boundaries between Center City schools and the rest of the school district) were all rooted in, and reinforced, the assumption that education is a commodity that parents pursue solely as a matter of their children's best interests. The most troubling consequences of the initiative, such as limiting access for students from outside of Center City and reinscribing power relations at the school level, can be traced back to these mechanisms and the assumption that upper-middle-class parents will send their children to public schools only when they can be assured of superior treatment, special services, and a higher-quality product. Any effort to enlist schools in creating cities that are at once more prosperous and more equitable must begin by challenging the assumption that a parent's interest in education is limited to what schooling can do to promote the material well-being of his or her own children and articulating a broader vision of schooling as a public good. A more equitable approach to enlisting schools in urban development will also require a deeper understanding of the relationship between education and gentrification and of the possibilities and limitations of middle-class engagement in urban public schools.

Gentrification of Schools?

My research did not address gentrification per se. Grant's neighborhood, and much of Center City, had gentrified decades before the CCSI
was launched, though the process was in full swing along Center City's
"expanding boundaries." Still, similarities between the gentrification of
residential neighborhoods and the investment of middle-class families
in urban public schools are worth exploring here, especially because the
contrasts between the two suggest policy solutions uniquely suited to
education. Gentrification is generally understood as the process through
which middle- and upper-class people move into a largely low-income and
working-class neighborhood and renovate or restore existing homes in
such a way that the neighborhood becomes more desirable to other members of the middle class and to the businesses that cater to them. The results
include a change in neighborhood character, increased property values,
and displacement of previous residents. As sociologist Japonica Brown-
Saracino notes in *The Gentrification Debates*, there is a vast, complex literature on gentrification. Oddly, given the longstanding connections between
residence and education, scholars of gentrification have rarely addressed
education.[22]

Scholars have documented the displacement of residents who, after
the arrival of gentrifiers, can no longer afford rising rents or real estate
taxes.[23] Research has also uncovered tensions between new and old residents around neighborhood norms and practices, as the two groups often
have different ideas of acceptable behavior.[24] These tensions are exacerbated when long-time community members believe that businesses and
local politicians are more concerned about the needs of the gentrifiers
than they are about other residents. Yet it is also sometimes the case that
gentrification leads to an improvement in services to the neighborhood
and that low-income residents benefit from their contact with more affluent neighbors.[25]

The processes I have described in this book—of middle- and upper-
middle-class families investing in and transforming urban public
schools—are in many ways similar to those associated with gentrification:
displacement and tensions on the one hand, and more attention and better services on the other. But there are differences, too. Unlike neighborhoods, schools have a commitment, as public institutions, to equity. And
schools have as one of their missions promoting social mobility on the part
of students, mobility that could be fostered by the increased resources

generated by more affluent constituencies. Indeed, there is a profound difference between living down the block from someone whose class status is different from your own and sharing the *institution* responsible for shaping your child's life with that same person. One implies the relationships, often quite casual, that come from residential proximity; the other implies a truly shared investment and the intertwining of daily activities and hopes for the future.

So, is it useful to think of what happened at Grant, or what is happening at many schools in Boston, as the gentrification of schools? Yes, if doing so helps us better understand the relationship between school and neighborhood change. But the comparison is also limiting, particularly as it obscures the reality that when low-income children attend school with more affluent peers, the benefits of middle-class parents' activities on behalf of the school often reach those children: shared membership can mean shared enrichment. While scholars and activists often condemn gentrification as a process that harms low-income residents and erases the unique character of urban neighborhoods, with respect to schools the analysis is necessarily more complicated. A more productive way to understand the issues addressed here, I would argue, is to focus on the public nature of schools and the tensions that emerge around notions of citizenship and entitlement when a public institution is put to such strategic use. For this reason, many of the policy suggestions I offer below are informed by a concern for the *public* role schools play.

Middle-Class Families: Saviors or Strivers?

There are important differences between the CCSI as a strategy to promote urban revitalization and the decision of middle- and upper-middle-class parents to send their children to urban public schools. As an urban strategy, the initiative was problematic because it positioned these families as saviors both of the city and its schools, a positioning that gave them disproportionate power and privileges. But middle-class parents are like all parents in their responsibility to their children and their interest in providing them with a quality education. And urban middle-class parents—also like all parents—are justified in demanding better schools for their children and in working to create these schools.

The problems emerge when middle- and upper-middle-class families' interests collide with those of other families and when the middle class is seen as both a vital *and* an inherently benevolent presence. When this happens—when what is good for the middle class is assumed to be good for all—it is possible for families to, consciously or not, cloak their efforts to secure advantages for their own children within the rhetoric of the greater good. This makes it difficult for other families, educators, and administrators to object or advance alternative agendas.

The promotion of one's own child's interests is "normal." It is what parents do. Because our society is so segregated by race and class, however, people do not often pursue their children's interests within the contexts of shared institutions or spaces. In fact, the divisions in our society are such that we share few institutions with people from different groups. When middle- and upper-middle-class parents move to the suburbs or send their children to private school, the impact on other children is abstract. Middle-class flight hurts cities, and the fact that so many families with resources opt out of public schools is one reason urban public schools have struggled. But these consequences, while arguably more profound than the inequities described in this book, are less immediately obvious to the individuals involved. The question of the distribution of resources, for example—of who gets what—does not emerge in any concrete way when families move to the suburbs. In urban schools with growing middle- and upper-middle-class populations, however, the situation is different: institutions are shared and resources are insufficient. In this context, when one person pursues his or her own child's interests, the consequences for other children are often very clear. Sometimes the results are positive, as when the new families create a beautiful new library or bring in enrichment programs. Sometimes they are negative, as when other children are displaced or devalued because they do not fit within the middle-class parents' agenda for the school. These schools thus bring to the surface key tensions in education and in our society between notions of individual and collective good and require active engagement on the part of school and district administrators to ensure equity.

Policy Implications

My hope is that the analysis presented here will inform how urban and education policymakers think about the relationship between education and urban revitalization, and help guide those interested in increasing the economic diversity of schools but wary of perpetuating inequalities. On a basic level, many of the most troubling dynamics related to the CCSI are a function of scarcity—a scarcity of resources for school improvement, a scarcity of opportunities in the city, and a scarcity of middle-class families willing to send their children to urban public schools. Given this, the most powerful reform strategies would begin by addressing this scarcity. In Philadelphia and many other large cities, that would mean developing a regional approach to educational and social policy. As long as schools in Philadelphia are separate from those in the suburbs, they will (barring massive demographic shifts) continue to serve a disproportionately disadvantaged population. Urban middle-class families will always be in short supply. As the Wake County case makes clear, the obvious way to create and sustain more racially and economically balanced schools on a large scale, and thus avoid the inequities found in Philadelphia, is to integrate the city and the suburbs.

While promising examples of regional approaches to economic development and education exist, that possibility has not come up in relation to Philadelphia's ongoing education crises.[26] For city-suburban integration in the Philadelphia metropolitan area to succeed, residents of affluent suburbs would have to see their fates as intertwined with those of Philadelphia's poor and their responsibilities as extending to the city in a way that currently seems unlikely.[27] The fact that regional integration is not at this moment politically feasible should not, however, prevent proponents from raising this as a solution. Perhaps our unthinking acceptance of the separation of city and suburbs is part of the problem.

Similarly, Philadelphians have become so accustomed to the unjust school funding system in Pennsylvania that the issue often goes unmentioned; it is a "fact of life" that the schools and citizens must contend with, rather than one of many possible arrangements. A poorly funded school system serves no one well, and a lack of resources is an obstacle both to implementing major reforms and to making the schools a more viable option for middle- and upper-middle-class parents. Because Philadelphians take the funding situation for granted, they embrace solutions that, like the CCSI, turn to outside individuals and entities to bring improvements to the schools. Though references to funding equity also seem absent from the national conversation about education "reform," the issues discussed in this book remind us that the underfunding of public schools is not a problem restricted to the urban poor. Like regional approaches to education, school funding is another topic that could usefully be put back on the table.

That said, it is also necessary to consider strategies that, short of regional and state-level policy changes, could also address the problems identified in this book. First, with cities becoming increasingly polarized between prosperous and impoverished areas, education policy should be mobilized to counteract, not further, that polarization. When developing new schools or creating new choice policies, school district leaders should ensure that options are distributed equitably across the city and are available to all students. Policies that increase the schools' reliance on the resources in their immediate neighborhoods, thus tightening the links between school location and the level of resources available to students, should be regarded with skepticism.

Second, it is clear from my findings at Grant that many parents of transfer students felt both devalued and threatened by efforts to attract more neighborhood families to the schools. Because of the race and class differences between the two groups of families, this marginalization exacerbated race- and class-related inequalities. District and school administrators have a responsibility to take a more proactive stance and to use their power as representatives of a public institution to ensure that all families in a school are on equal footing. In the highly charged context of an urban public school, where differently positioned families come together around their children's education, it is unreasonable to expect parents, whatever their class status, to safeguard equity. As urban schools—particularly those in affluent downtown areas—become increasingly economically diverse, fulfilling the school's responsibility to serve all families equally should be taken seriously by school administrators. This should also involve creating greater transparency around choice and transfer processes and ensuring that families know their rights and that admissions decisions are made in a systematic and equitable manner.

Third, efforts to recruit middle- and upper-middle-class families into the public schools should not simply be based on identifying and marketing an elite group of schools, and they should not focus on only one section of the city. Such marketing is problematic both because it fails to make real improvements to schools and because, as I have shown, it constructs some parents as more valuable customers than others.

Rather than appealing solely to parents' interests in the ways schools can benefit their own children, urban school districts could engage parents as citizens in the process of making substantive improvements to the public schools. My research has shown that professional families have a wealth of resources to offer schools and are eager to be involved in making them better. The neighborhood parents at Grant viewed themselves as part of the solution and were proud of the work they had done on behalf of the school. While such parents were able to bring more resources to Grant, they often needed to overcome bureaucratic obstacles to do so. The district's approach to civic engagement provided minimal opportunities for parents to be involved in agenda-setting or crafting policy.[28] I suggest that parents are more likely to send their children to public schools, and remain invested in these schools, if they believe they can play a significant role in improving them.

Given the statistics on Center City's recent growth, it seems likely that in the years to come there will be a pool of educated, relatively affluent parents who would at least consider the public schools—a pattern that will be repeated in Boston, Chicago, Baltimore, and elsewhere. Many of these parents are committed to living in the city and want their children in racially and economically diverse environments. This suggests that we may be at a "golden moment" in urban history, a time when those parents who in another era may have left for the homogeneity of the suburbs can be re-engaged in the public schools. Parents reminded me many times that "people in Center City want this to work." For various ideological, logistical, and financial reasons, they wanted to be able to use their local public schools. Districts could capitalize on this desire and engage parents around a broader mission of educational change—rather than around an agenda designed primarily to secure advantages for their children. Of course, such efforts should involve deliberate outreach to low-income families to ensure their voices are also heard and valued. Parents in these settings could also work with teachers and administrators to ensure that their involvement occurs in an inclusive manner and that no group is seen as having a greater "right" to the school than any other.

At the same time, it is essential not to become so fixated on the ways in which greater race and class integration could benefit schools that we are blinded to the barriers to educational improvement caused by chronic poverty and the underfunding of urban schools. Of course we want more middle- and upper-middle-class families invested in cities and in schools. However, in the absence of increased school funding, it is unlikely that the presence of middle- and upper-middle-class families alone can address the real failure of urban schools, which is their inability to serve low-income students well.[29]

In September 2011, seven years after the *Growing Smarter* report that launched the CCSI, the CCD released a new report, *Population Growth Downtown*, using 2010 census data to describe a decade of dramatic growth in Center City. Since 2000, the larger Center City area (the core downtown and the gentrifying neighborhoods to the north and south) grew by nearly 17,000, a 10 percent increase and the largest population growth of any part of the city. Many of these new residents were children, resulting in a "proliferation of baby strollers on sidewalks, in parks and playgrounds, as well as the dramatic growth in pre-school programs throughout Center City."[30] Like the 2004 publication, *Population Growth Downtown* argues that Philadelphia must hold onto these young families and that schools could play a critical role in making that happen. And, as in 2004, the CCD argues that the presence of new district leadership (following yet another tumultuous departure of a Philadelphia superintendent) provides an important opportunity.[31]

Yet there are some key differences between the two documents. First, whereas *Growing Smarter* focused only on attracting and retaining professionals, the more recent report identifies "two equally important tasks": improving student achievement in all public schools *and* keeping professionals in the city by providing them with good educational options. It then points to the roles Center City parents have played in improving certain schools and the benefits their efforts brought to other students. It suggests that the school district should work with these parents to revitalize more neighborhood schools, focusing more on such families' activism on behalf of schools than on the need to market to them. While the report requests that the district return to the "Vallas-era policy" that notified parents whether or not their children had been admitted to a school before the deadline for submitting private school deposits, it makes no mention of special priority for Center City families in admissions or any other regard. On the contrary, the CCD suggests that to "guard against wholesale 'gentrification' of downtown schools" the district could reserve 30 percent of the spots in each grade for children from outside of Center City. This represents a striking change in policy and resembles the provisions for low-income units in new housing developments often suggested by urban planners as a means of ensuring equity in the context of economic growth. The outcomes of this latest overture to the district remain to be seen. It may be, however, that the CCD itself is reaching toward a more nuanced, and promising, approach to engaging professional families in schools.

City schools need parents like Sharon. But when Sharon is treated as more important or more necessary than other parents, the dynamics between families and schools are changed in a troubling way. The distinction between "citizens" and "customers" is helpful here. Whereas citizens have certain rights and are entitled to certain services by virtue of their membership within a polity, customers' rights are limited to participation in the market, and customers are entitled to nothing beyond the fruits of that participation. Though the reality may fall short, by traditional definition all citizens are entitled to equal treatment under the law.[32] Customers, by contrast, may be treated differently or valued differently depending on the goods they have to exchange. The CCSI disrupted the traditional understanding of parents and students as citizens who, by virtue of their citizenship, are entitled to a school's services. It changed institutional policies and practices and helped recast families as customers and commodities who have varying levels of resources to offer and are widely different in their value. In doing so, it raises important questions. Who are schools for? Can the state or school district's obligation to provide equal services to all be outweighed by other considerations? Have we created a city in which some people are so much more important than others that they are also more entitled to government services?

The significance of this distinction between citizen and customer encompasses more than issues of entitlement. It also raises questions about responsibility. As consumers, parents have no responsibility for the schools other than what they "pay" for their services. In contrast, the term "citizen" implies a reciprocal relationship. Yes, citizens receive a host of benefits from their government, but they also have an obligation to the state and to one another. The positioning of professional families as the customers to whom cities must appeal assumes those families have no obligation to cities or to city residents. Their task is simply to *choose* whether or not to remain in a city or whether or not to patronize its schools. If they choose to remain, they "pay" for the services they receive with their various forms of capital and with the value their very presence adds. If dissatisfied, they may simply exit. Their participation in the life of a city need not include joining in any broader project of creating schools that are more effective and equitable or building a city that meets everyone's needs. In fact, the notion of such a project is at odds with this way of understanding the relationship between individuals and the state.

Differentiating between parents as citizens and parents as customers is theoretically useful because it illuminates the ways these positions produce particular identities and practices with respect to schools. In practice, however, the sharp analytical distinction between citizen and customer blurs. Parents are both customers and citizens, though their beliefs and actions can index one or the other role with greater frequency or intensity.

This is a reality the CCD itself recognizes. Despite its central role in re-shaping families' relationships with schools, the organization, in its lat-est report, extols parents' activism on behalf of city schools, their use of "voice" rather than "exit" to meet their children's needs and those of other children.[33] This is an important development.

Like districts across the country, Philadelphia's schools will continue to negotiate tensions between market principles and public responsibili-ties, between economic and social goals for education, and between in-dividual and collective goods. In the process, families will sometimes be cast as citizens and sometimes as customers. To the extent that a focus on parents (and city-dwellers more broadly) as customers takes precedence, important notions of social responsibility, equality and collective good are lost, replaced by a fixation on individual interests and desires. At the same time, a reassertion of the ideals and strategies of citizenship on the part of civic, educational, and community leaders, and parents themselves could help interrupt these trends.

Achieving an appropriate balance between the two roles is essential be-cause greater divestment from public education on the part of the middle and upper-middle class would be harmful to city and schools. The goal of this book is certainly not to dissuade cities (or families) from taking on this challenge. However, like all projects that involve differences of race and class and the sharing of resources, the work of creating more diverse urban public schools is complicated and must be handled with care. The prevailing wisdom about this issue is far too simplistic. Schools are more than urban amenities. Treating them as such undermines their promise as public institutions equally responsible to all citizens. It is my hope that this book will not discourage vigorous and broad-based involvement in public education but will rather contribute to the creation of more inclusive and functional city schools—and cities themselves.

Research Methodology

Like most ethnographic studies, this project took a different path from the one I had originally envisioned. Here, I describe how the study evolved, review the research design, and explain my approach to collecting and analyzing data. I also explain how I managed my relationships in the field and dealt with issues of confidentiality.

First Stages

As a graduate student interested in civic engagement in urban education, and influenced by work on how class structures parental involvement in schooling, I intended to do my dissertation research at two Philadelphia public schools—one with a largely middle-class parent-teacher organization (PTO) and one with a largely working-class PTO.[1] I planned to study how parents worked to improve their school, the class-related resources they brought to the task, and their impact. In early 2004, as I was planning my research, an article on Grant Elementary appeared in a local newspaper. The story mentioned the school's location in Cobble Square and the efforts of neighborhood middle- and upper-middle class parents to recruit similar families to Grant (see chapter 5).

Interested in learning more, I found contact information for Sara, the PTO president, through the school's website. I emailed her, explaining that I was a doctoral student at the University of Pennsylvania interested in doing research on parent organizations. We arranged to meet at Sara's Center City law office and went to a nearby café to discuss my study. At her encouragement, I attended a PTO meeting at Grant a few days later. There were a dozen parents at the meeting (all women), including Sara, Kim, Sharon, and others who later featured prominently in my study. The meeting was organized and businesslike, and the group was obviously ambitious in its plans for the school.

Over the next few weeks, I was in touch with Sara frequently about my research and was looking forward to returning to the school. However, I still had to secure formal access to the school, which required permission from the principal and the School District of Philadelphia. My initial attempt to introduce myself to Ms. Ashton one day after school was discouraging. When I began to explain my research, Ms. Ashton interrupted coolly, saying, with a small frown, that I should "go through the district." I said I would and offered her an envelope containing my CV and a description of the project. She took it with marked reluctance. I thanked her and left, imagining my carefully crafted letter would soon end up in the trash.

The next day, after a quick exchange with the school district research office, I learned that securing approval for my study required only the principal's permission (because I was interested in parents, not students). I called Sara to let her know and to discuss my unpromising encounter with Ms. Ashton. Sara assured me that she would talk to the principal. When I visited Grant two days later, I met a changed Ms. Ashton. I approached her in the hallway to ask, nervously, if I could talk with her about my research, and she seemed surprised by the question, exclaiming, "I already said I was fine with it!" (to Sara, presumably). Ms. Ashton then went on, with a smile, to say she was impressed that I was conducting ethnographic research, because it is such a time-consuming process. This dramatic shift in the principal's attitude was early data for me about the power professional parents like Sara wielded at the school.

After that, I began visiting Grant regularly, attending PTO meetings, volunteering at book sales and other school events, and developing friendships with several parents, exchanging phone calls and emails, and talking comfortably with them before and after meetings. I quickly came to feel a part of the PTO. Meanwhile, my efforts to identify a low-income parents' group had yielded two potential sites. Observations of PTO meetings at these schools, however, made me question their utility for my study. Both

PTOs were focused on organizing special activities for students and families, such as a father-daughter dance. Although clearly important to the parents, these activities did not address the issues of school improvement my research aimed to investigate.

In discussing options with my dissertation advisor, I mentioned how interested parents at Grant were in marketing the school to other middle-class families and described what I had been hearing about the CCSI. We both agreed that this was a potentially important topic. As a result, I decided to drop the comparative part of my study and focus more directly on the CCSI.

New Design

Shifting my research focus enlarged the parameters of the study and dramatically altered my research design. The CCSI targeted Grant, but it also targeted other Center City schools. In addition, the specific context in which the initiative developed—the city of Philadelphia, with its history of postindustrial decline, its thriving downtown and deteriorating neighborhoods—was important. The CCSI was likely to be controversial, if only because it seemed to be giving more resources to an already advantaged part of the city. Thus, my design needed to examine the interrelationships between the initiative, the elementary school, the school district, and the city.

I used a nested or "embedded" case-study design, rather than the traditional "holistic" design in which researchers have only one unit of analysis.[2] This enabled me to paint a more contextualized picture of city politics around growth and education and to show how these dynamics were experienced on the ground. My research took place on three levels, allowing me to explore the reasons civic and educational leaders in Philadelphia turned to the CCSI, local support for and push-back against the initiative, and consequences for the distributions of resources, opportunities, and power. Because I was working on multiple levels, I drew from a number of data sources. Table A.1 summarizes my subquestions and the data collected.

The third level of my study was in many ways the most extensive. To understand how the CCSI affected Grant, I conducted a multiyear ethnography of the school's PTO. I chose to keep my focus on parents for

TABLE A.1. **Research questions and data**

	Research Question(s)	Data/Sources
CCSI as policy	1. What strategies does a coalition of business leaders and education officials use to reposition schools as urban amenities? 2. How does the local social, political, and economic context shape the development, evolution, and implementation of this policy? 3. What assumptions about the "problems" and "solutions" inform these efforts? 4. What are the implications for educational equity, understood as the distribution of resources and opportunities within the school district?	1. Secondary sources on U.S. and Philadelphia urban history and redevelopment trends 2. U.S. Census data 3. Newspaper coverage (primarily *The Philadelphia Inquirer, The Philadelphia Daily News,* and *The Philadelphia Public School Notebook*) 4. Interviews (9) with CCD and district leaders 5. CCD and school district documents related to the CCSI 6. School District of Philadelphia data 7. Pennsylvania and U.S. Department of Education data on school and district demographics 8. Reports on school reform in Philadelphia 9. Observations (5) of public meetings and events
Philadelphia's Civic Field	1. How do local actors perceive the initiative and the assumptions that underlie it? 2. To what extent do civic, educational, business, and political leaders support or contest the initiative and its goals?	1. Interviews (30) with local civic actors 2. Local newspapers 3. Local blog: www.Phillyblog.com 4. CCD and school district documents
Individual school (Grant Elementary)	1. How does the policy impact a local school and groups that are—by virtue of race, class, and area of residence—differently positioned within the school? 2. What are the implications for educational equity, understood as the distribution of resources and power within the school?	1. Participant-observations at 21 PTO meetings (approx. 1.5 hours each) over 24 months 2. Participant-observations at 10 other meetings (planning special events, selecting a new principal, etc., 1–2 hours each) 3. Participant-observations at 9 special events (school carnival, fundraisers, etc., 3–8 hours each) 4. Volunteering in kindergarten classroom (5 hours) 5. Informal conversations, telephone calls and email exchanges with parents, teachers, and administrators (~40) 6. Interviews (19) with parents, teachers, and administrators 7. Newspaper coverage of Grant 8. Grant and district documents 9. District, state, and federal data on student achievement and enrollment

several reasons. First, the CCSI explicitly targeted parents. Second, at the elementary school level, it is parents (not students) who make the majority of school choice decisions. Third, as I note in chapter 1, a great deal of research has documented the importance of parental involvement and the ways class and race shape parents' relationships with schools. In particular, the literature on economic integration emphasizes the assets middle-class parents bring to public schools. I did, however, document how the CCSI's consequences for parents in turn impacted their children. For example, I used interview and observation data to see how changes to parents' status at the school affected their ability to advocate for their children. And I used school district data to document changes in schools' enrollment patterns and racial composition.

Data Collection

Observations

The bulk of the observations for this study were conducted at Grant. However, I also observed public meetings and events related to the CCSI. These included the Center City Schools Fair, meetings of local education advocates, and a meeting of the Building Industry Association, an organization of local real estate developers and construction firms, where Paul Levy (president of the CCD) and Paul Vallas (CEO of Philadelphia's schools) spoke about the CCSI.

Between spring 2004 and spring 2006, I attended all PTO meetings at Grant, including regular monthly meetings and those held for particular reasons, such as selecting a new principal, planning special events, and designing the new playground. I also attended admissions open houses, fundraisers, performances, and other events. To make a contribution to the school (in exchange for the parents' and educators' help with my research), I put in dozens of hours of volunteer time. I helped with book sales, the school carnival, and other fundraisers; picked up supplies for special events (including large vats of water ice—a Philadelphia specialty—for the school carnival); and created a database with contact information for PTO members. During this time, I had numerous casual conversations with PTO parents—as we walked to and from meetings, arranged books at the book fair, sold tickets at the carnival, or set up sign-in sheets for Back-to-School night. I also had many telephone and email exchanges with parents, both to talk about PTO business (e.g., what prizes they should order for the carnival) and to debrief after particularly eventful PTO meetings. One mother even invited me to her daughter's birthday party.

As I have shown, there were serious disagreements within the PTO. In particular, parents differed about how important it was to market the school to "neighborhood" families. To prevent my becoming so invested in a particular agenda that it would bias my analysis, I confined my volunteer activities to those about which all PTO members agreed (such as helping with the book sales or planning the carnival) and avoided those related strictly to marketing. I also made sure to vary where I sat during meetings, so that I never seemed to be allied with one faction or another, and even monitored my own eye contact to avoid exchanging glances with particular parents during tense moments. It was essential that I not be seen as taking sides during conflicts within the PTO, and I strove to maintain the stance of an "objective" researcher.[3] I believe this stance was particularly helpful when members of both factions talked with me individually about PTO conflicts. It subtly altered the normal rules of conversation in a way that encouraged them to share their views while relieving me of the obligation of chiming in with my own.

I took copious notes in a small notebook whenever it was appropriate and practical. In fall 2004, when no one volunteered for the position of PTO secretary, the group decided that I should take the minutes at each meeting. ("Maia's always writing down everything anyway," one parent observed.) After each meeting, I typed up my notes and sent the PTO president an abridged version for her records.[4] In instances where it would have been inappropriate to be writing so openly (e.g., at an open house or book sale), I jotted down key points or direct quotes. Then, generally later on the same day, I typed up my notes. I wrote notes right after casual conversations, took notes during phone calls, and saved emails.

Interviews

I used interviews throughout my research. (A list of all interviews conducted appears in appendix C.) All were audio-recorded and transcribed. For the examination of the CCSI as policy, I conducted nine interviews with school district and CCD administrators responsible for the initiative. Each interview lasted 45–60 minutes. All interviews asked about the origins and development of the initiative, its goals and consequences, and issues related to equity, such as how schools were chosen for attention and marketing, whom the initiative would benefit, and whether or not interviewees believed the initiative would harm anyone.

For my research on Philadelphia's civic field, I used data from interviews with thirty individuals. Eight of these were conducted explicitly for this project. Each of these respondents was selected because he or she had expressed a particular interest in the CCSI or represented an important viewpoint on the initiative (e.g., media, advocacy, education, etc.).

Throughout much of the time I was collecting and analyzing my data, I was also a member of a research team at Research for Action (RFA), a Philadelphia-based, not-for-profit organization conducting research on school reform. The additional twenty-two interviews with local actors were part of RFA's study of civic engagement in Philadelphia's school reform. (I conducted three and the rest were conducted by other members of the research team.) These interviews covered school reform, local politics, engagement with schools, and the CCSI.

For the interview component of my ethnography of Grant's PTO, I also interviewed fourteen parents, four teachers, and one administrator. I used "purposeful sampling" to select parents who fit particular criteria, such as race, class, level of involvement, and area of residence.[5] To enlarge the pool of parent interviewees beyond the PTO, I used "snowball sampling," asking respondents to identify other parents who did not attend PTO meetings but might have interesting perspectives. This yielded four additional parents who were not active within the PTO. My parent sample included five whites (all middle to upper-middle class), seven African Americans (three middle class and four working class), and two Asians (one middle class and one working class).[6] My selection of teachers was also purposeful: I deliberately included new and experienced teachers, African American and white teachers, and upper-grade and lower-grade teachers.

Parent interviews generally lasted an hour, and some were longer. Because I had a previous relationship with many parents (due to my participation in the PTO), these interviews were informal and friendly, moving easily between responses to my questions and more casual conversation. I used a protocol but altered it for each interview in response to the respondent's remarks and to follow up on particular issues, such as an argument that occurred at a PTO meeting or a parent's comment to me in the hallway. For example, when I saw one working-class African American parent reacting angrily to the "neighborhood" parents' plan to proceed quickly with the principal selection process, I used the interview to ask her about it.

The teacher interviews lasted approximately thirty minutes each. In these, I explored the teachers' perspectives on the school, students, parents, and the impact of the CCSI. Finally, I interviewed a Grant administrator twice, once toward the end of my data collection, and once four years later, to follow up on the CCSI's long-term consequences. Each interview lasted approximately one hour.

Student and Census Data

I used school district data to examine enrollment patterns and the demographic composition of Center City schools and to track how the patterns changed over time. When necessary, I also drew upon demographic data from the U.S. Department of Education. (For example, in chapter 3 I used federal data on the demographics of the schools from which various Grant parents transferred their children.) In her study of middle-class enrollment in Boston public schools, sociologist Shelley Kimelberg showed that an infusion of middle-class families could lead to a significant decrease in the percentage of students receiving free- and reduced-price lunch (FRPL) at that school. I had hoped to use school district data to investigate similar outcomes in Philadelphia. However, the way the district calculates its FRPL percentages makes such tracking impossible.[7]

I used census and real estate data to document the class and racial composition of the Center City area.[8] Matching school catchment areas with census tracts, and focusing on children ages 0–4 in 2000, allowed me to develop a snapshot of potential students living in the areas targeted by the CCSI.[9] I contrasted these data with the demographics of students in Philadelphia's schools (in Center City and in the district as a whole) to show differences between the two populations.

Analysis

My analysis drew on the qualitative and quantitative data described here, as well as on CCD and school district documents, secondary source material about the city and its schools, and local media coverage. I used qualitative data-analysis software (Hyperresearch) to categorize data and compare it within and across categories.[10]

Analysis of the Grant data began with a round of inductive coding. Using a grounded theory strategy, I recoded as categories emerged and combined codes under broader concepts, moving from descriptive to analytical categories.[11] To examine how differently positioned parents experienced and understood both the CCSI and dynamics within the school, I divided parents into groups, looking for patterns and variations within and across groups. As I moved between inductive and more theoretical coding, I created diagrams of codes, showing their relations to one another, the literature, and my emerging theories. To assess parents' contributions to the school, I compiled a list of all activities in which parents were involved. I then broke my list into themes and created a table (a modified version appears in appendix B) displaying the activity, its category, who was involved, why parents pursued this activity, who benefited, who (if any) was harmed, and whether the activity was successful.

To describe the ways Philadelphia's political field shaped the initiative's development, I wove together multiple sources—interviews, CCD and school district documents, newspaper coverage, and fieldnotes taken at meetings and public events. This allowed me to compare differing accounts, contrast information available publicly with that held by people "in the know," and document the links between particular events and policy changes. This approach was especially valuable for analyzing controversial issues, such as the proposed change to the district's transfer policy (see chapter 7).

Assuring Internal Validity

Validity in qualitative research can be threatened in three areas: description, interpretation, and theory.[12] To address possible validity threats to my descriptive work, I made sure all interviews were recorded and transcribed. I typed fieldnotes on the day they had been taken or, occasionally, within a few days of the event. At Grant, my position as official PTO notetaker provided another check.

I used triangulation across various data sources as a way to check the validity of my interpretations.[13] I recorded a particular event in my notes, including my interpretation of how different parents understood that event, and then used interviews with parents both to check the validity of that interpretation and to explore their responses. In many instances, I was able to attain multiple descriptions, from different perspectives, of the same event—a rich form of data that was invaluable in helping me to explicate the CCSI's impact on Grant. Because I conducted my interviews over an eighteen-month period, I refined my protocols to address emerging theories and check facts and conclusions. Finally, I used "quasi-statistics," or the development of numerical results from qualitative data that allows researchers to "test and support claims" and "assess the amount of evidence" in the data.[14] I found this method useful, for example, for testing my theories about class differences in the types of activities parents were involved in at Grant.

Member checking was another helpful strategy. Because I remained in contact with several parents after my formal research was completed, I used emails and face-to-face conversations to assess the validity of my emerging conclusions. In addition, a highly placed school district official, who worked closely with the CCSI, read a draft of several key chapters. She confirmed that, with the exception of a few minor errors (which I then fixed), my portrayal of the CCSI's origin and evolution was accurate.

I addressed other threats to theoretical validity by collecting discrepant data and developing alternatives to my conclusions. Here, my work with RFA was important. Since the CCSI was a case study in RFA's larger exploration of civic engagement in Philadelphia, the research team's conversations about the initiative helped me revise my preliminary theories and assumptions. I also presented my work-in-progress at academic conferences. These presentations—and the discussions that followed—further developed my thinking and helped me identify the ways my position as a member of the professional middle class shaped my analyses.

Confidentiality

For the most part, when sociologists publish studies of schools and communities, they disguise the names of all respondents, schools, and cities in which they are located.[15] I took a different approach. Because my research examined the CCSI within a particular social, political, and economic context, disguising Philadelphia would have undercut much of the power of the analysis. For example, it would have been difficult to write compellingly about the ways ongoing fears of middle-class flight shaped education policy without a discussion of the city's depopulation over the past half century. As a result, I chose to name the city but—out of an interest in protecting the confidentiality of my participants—disguise the identities of particular schools and all respondents. This is not a perfect solution. Sometimes I provide less information about Grant or another school than

I would have liked, because giving more details or locating a school on a map would have revealed the schools' identities. Similarly, when I include potentially controversial quotations from Grant parents, I withhold information, such as the speaker's position within the PTO, which could make him or her identifiable.

These limitations are offset in at least one significant way. As Mitchell Duneier has noted, a researcher who identifies his or her research site has an incentive to establish "a higher standard of evidence" because others could visit the site and check the findings.[16] In my case, the knowledge that readers could not only compare my descriptions to the "real" city, but also that people actually affected by the CCSI—including people who appear in the book—could read my work, gave me additional reason to be sure my data and interpretations were accurate.

Boston

After the completion of my Philadelphia data collection and analysis, I grew increasingly curious about whether or not the patterns I had documented were replicated in other settings. In 2009 I conducted an abbreviated interview study of Boston's Y/BPS initiative, an effort to market a number of Boston public schools to families who might otherwise avoid the public system (see chapter 8). The goals of my Boston study were twofold: first, to understand the initiative; and, second, to examine any equity issues that emerged and how they were understood and discussed.

I began with newspaper coverage of Y/BPS, using that coverage to identify potential interviewees, including parents, the developers of the initiative, and school personnel. Melina O'Grady, a Boston-based educational consultant who was familiar with the initiative, served as a research consultant. We conducted interviews with fourteen local stakeholders selected to represent a variety of views and constituencies (see appendix C). Twelve of the fourteen were conducted jointly; Melina conducted the final two on her own, using protocols I developed. Melina's familiarity with the targeted neighborhoods and the Boston school selection process was invaluable. She asked important follow-up questions and helped clarify points that were confusing to me as an outsider.

Using *Atlas.ti*, a graduate research assistant coded the Boston data. I contextualized the findings using secondary source materials on Boston's history, current social and economic context, and experiences with school reform. Given the abbreviated nature of this study, I could not track the consequences of Boston's marketing campaign the same way I did in Philadelphia. As a result, I do not make broad claims about the differences between Y/BPS and the CCSI. I do, however, compare how those involved with the two efforts talked about issues of race and class as they related to the marketing of schools.

Divided Loyalties

If I could have written about the CCSI as an unmitigated success, as an initiative that brought resources to Philadelphia's schools, slowed suburban flight, and had a uniformly positive impact on families, this book would have been completed years ago. By the same token, this book would have been easier to write if I had been wholly critical. It would have been easy to condemn the CCD's singular focus on retaining "knowledge workers," for example, as a lack of concern for Philadelphia's poor but for my awareness that this focus was rooted in Philadelphia's history of middle-class flight and economic decline. Similarly, a portrayal of the Cobble Square parents' interest in attracting more "neighborhood families" to Grant as an instance of simple classism would have been compelling were it not for the research literature on the benefits of economically integrated schools and my own data on the contribution such parents made to the school.

These dilemmas were particularly meaningful when it came to my ethnography of Grant, where I often found myself rooting for both "sides" at the same time. I understood why the middle- and upper-middle-class parents felt they were benefiting Grant by sending their children there and why they felt frustrated when their efforts were viewed with skepticism by other parents. Because I am a professional white woman, my identification with the parents of color at Grant, and particularly with the low-income, African American transfer mothers, was not as automatic as it was with the Cobble Square mothers. Aware of that, I strove to examine the ways my own positionality affected my interpretations of events at the school. Interspersing interviews throughout the fieldwork process was important in this regard, because my in-depth conversations with African American parents attuned me to their concerns and helped me to see events through their eyes. I understood why these parents often felt angry at what they saw as the more affluent parents' entitlement and lack of sensitivity. The

African American transfer parents' vision of a high-achieving, inclusive school that welcomed families like theirs was threatened by the CCSI. While my ambivalence made the research process more difficult, it also added to the quality of my data and analysis, pushing me toward what I believe is a more complete and accurate portrayal.

Parents' Activities at Grant Elementary

TABLE B.1. **Parents' activities at Grant Elementary**

Activity	Type	Activist or Supportive[a]	Parents Involved
Securing physical education classes	Core Academic	Activist	Mostly MC/ UMC[b]
Refurbishing library	Core Academic	Supportive	Mostly MC/ UMC
Creating cybrary	Core Academic	Activist	MC/UMC only
Establishing new reading program	Core Academic	Activist	MC/UMC
Developing/coordinating music program	Core Academic	Activist	MC/UMC
Trying to remove discipline problems and/or NCLB students	Discipline/ Climate/ Safety	Activist	MC/UMC
Providing supervision before school and during lunches	Discipline/ Climate/ Safety	Supportive	All
Securing traffic lights and improved safety enforcement	Discipline/ Climate/ Safety	Activist	MC/UMC

Activity	Type	Activist or Supportive[a]	Parents Involved
Pressing for greater enforcement of discipline code	Discipline/Climate/Safety	Activist	Mostly MC/UMC
Advocating for and designing new playground	Physical environment	Activist	MC/UMC
Beautification of grounds	Physical environment	Supportive	MC/UMC
Improving snow removal	Physical environment	Activist	MC/UMC
Air conditioners for classrooms	Physical environment	Supportive	All
Repairs to schoolyard	Physical environment	Activist	MC/UMC
Restarting the PTO	Parent Relations	Activist and Supportive	Led by MC/UMC
Staffing parent help desk	Parent Relations	Supportive	All
Staffing/planning back-to-school night	Parent Relations	Supportive	All
Coordinating improved family-school communication	Parent Relations	Activist and Supportive	MC/UMC
Establishing relationships with local civic associations and foundations	Partnerships	Activist	MC/UMC
Establishing relationships with local businesses	Partnerships	Supportive	All
Selling t-shirts	Fundraising	Supportive	All
Soliciting donations for cybrary	Fundraising	Activist	MC/UMC
Organizing cocktail party fundraiser	Fundraising	Activist	MC/UMC
Organizing and performing in opera concert	Fundraising	Supportive	MC/UMC
Applying for grants	Fundraising	Activist	MC/UMC
Organizing pizza and wrapping paper sales	Fundraising	Supportive	Led by WC

Activity	Type	Activist or Supportive[a]	Parents Involved
Organizing "Open House"	Marketing/PR	Activist	MC/UMC
Soliciting coverage of school from local media	Marketing/PR	Activist	MC/UMC
Advertising to preschools	Marketing/PR	Activist	MC/UMC
Hosting party for prospective parents	Marketing/PR	Activist	MC/UMC
Recruiting "neighbor-hood" parents	Marketing/PR	Activist	MC/UMC
Advocating to retain/add a K teacher	Staffing	Activist	MC/UMC
Complaining about vice principal	Staffing	Activist	MC/UMC
Answering phone in office	Staffing	Activist	MC/UMC
Transforming teachers' lounge	Staffing	Supportive	All
Purchasing teacher/staff appreciation gifts	Staffing	Supportive	All
Pressing for removal of principal	Staffing	Activist	Mostly MC/UMC
Helping choose new principal	Staffing	Activist	All
Donating money to student events/awards	Student Support	Supportive	Led by WC
Coordinating spring fair	Student Support	Supportive	All—led by MC/UMC
Holding events for honor roll students	Student Support	Supportive	All
Coordinating school pictures	Student Support	Supportive	All
Coordinating talent show	Student Support	Supportive	All
Purchasing school equipment	Student support	Supportive	All

Activity	Type	Activist or Supportive[a]	Parents Involved
Paying for RIF allocation	Student support	Supportive	All—led by WC
Working in classroom	Volunteering with students	Supportive	Mostly WC
Helping with performances, trips, sports	Volunteering with students	Supportive	Mostly WC

[a]See chapter 5 for a discussion of these terms.

[b]"MC/UMC" here refers to middle- and upper-middle-class parents. Parents in this category had at least a college degree and/or a partner with a college degree. See chapter 1 for more on the distinction between middle and upper-middle class. "WC" refers to working-class or poor parents. Parents in this category did not have a college degree.

List of Formal Interviews by Category or Title

TABLE C.1. **Interviews conducted for study of the CCSI**

Interviewee	Research Level
CCD administrator 1	1
CCD administrator 2 (interviewed four times over two years)	1, 2, 3
CCD board member	1, 2
School district administrator—Center City Region	1, 2
School district administrator—Central Office (interviewed twice over two years)	1, 2, 3
School district administrator—Central Office	2
City official	2
Media	2
Advocacy 1	2
Advocacy 2	2
Advocacy 3	2
Education program specialist	2
General influential	2
Grant parent, transfer—Sabrina	3
Grant parent, transfer—Kim	3
Grant parent, transfer—Lisa	3
Grant parent, transfer—Donna	3
Grant parent, transfer—Patricia	3
Grant parent, transfer—Rhonda	3
Grant parent, transfer—Amy	3
Grant parent, neighborhood—Sharon	3
Grant parent, neighborhood—Sara	3
Grant parent, neighborhood—Catherine	3
Grant parent, neighborhood—Sue Anne	3
Grant parent, neighborhood—Judy	3

TABLE C.1. (*continued*)

Interviewee	Research Level
Grant parent, neighborhood—Janet	3
Grant parent, neighborhood—Ellen	3
Grant administrator	1, 3
Grant teacher, kindergarten	3
Grant teacher, kindergarten	3
Grant teacher, fifth grade	3
Grant teacher, seventh/eighth grade literacy	3

TABLE C.2. **Additional interviews conducted through Research for Action's** *Learning from Philadelphia's School Reform*

Interviewee	Research Level
School district administrator—Central Office	2
School district administrator—Center City Region school (not Grant) 1	2
School district administrator—Center City Region school (not Grant) 2	2
Advocacy 1	2
Advocacy 2	2
Advocacy 3	2
Advocacy 4	2
Community-based organization 1	2
Community-based organization 2	2
Education program specialist 1	2
Education program specialist 2	2
Education program specialist 3	2
Education program specialist 4	2
City official	2
General influential 1	2
General influential 2	2
General influential 3	2
General influential 4	2
General influential 5	2
General influential 6	2
General influential 7	2

TABLE C.3. **Boston interviews**

Interviewee

Y/BPS administrator 1
Y/BPS administrator 2
Y/BPS administrator 3
BPS administrator
BPS leader/advocacy
City administrator/mayor's office
Foundation representative 1
Foundation representative 2
BPS parent 1
BPS parent 2
BPS parent 3
BPS parent 4
BPS parent 5

Notes

Chapter One

1. For a discussion of voluntary choice programs, see Morrison 2004; Counts and Lavergneau 1992. There is a large literature on magnet schools. See, especially, Frankenberg and Seigel-Hawley 2008; McPherson 2011; Rossell 2003. In Baltimore, in particular, charter schools are sought after by middle-class families and viewed as a means of preventing flight to the suburbs (Bowie 2004; Silvestri 2008). For examples from other cities, see Hankins 2007; Hendrie 2004; Santos 2011. On programs that cross city-suburban lines, see Grant 2009; Orfield 2009; Orfield et al. 1998; Wells and Crain 1999.

2. Downtown revitalization and economic integration of schools are discussed later in this chapter. On mixed-income housing, see Fraser and Kick 2007; Joseph, Chaskin, and Webber 2007; Levy, McDade, and Dumlao 2010; and Tach 2009. A related initiative, Moving to Opportunity, which provided low-income families with the opportunity to move out of impoverished neighborhoods, had mixed results (DeLuca and Dayton 2009). These policies often developed in response to 1960s-era initiatives that concentrated poverty in high-rise public housing (Venkatesh and Wilson 2002). See Imbroscio 2008 for a critical discussion of the consensus among policymakers and academics about the value of "dispersing" low-income residents into more affluent communities and Pattillo 2007 for a critique of the "class bias [that] fuels urban renewal's emphasis on attracting the middle-class back to the city" (106).

3. See Babitch et al. 2006; Birch 2006; Buschmann and Coletta 2009; Karpewicz 2010; *Philadelphia Daily News* 2006.

4. For examples, see Carr 2006; Jacobsen 2010; Jan 2006; Lipman 2002, 2004; Perl 2010; Sampson 2009; Shipps, Kahne, and Smylie 1999.

5. Campbell 2008; Edelberg and Kurland 2009; Graham 2010; Grim 2006; Posey 2012; Siefer 2010; Smith 2009; Stillman 2012.

6. See chapter 2 for a discussion of business improvement districts (BIDs).

7. Kotkin 2007.

8. The area referred to as Center City actually reaches beyond the CCD's official service area. See chapter 2.

9. CCD 2004, 2, 4; italics in original.

10. The Center City Schools Initiative (CCSI) was the official name of this project, according to CCD documents, including a 2005 application to a local foundation requesting funding. However, the initiative was also known as the "CCD-District Partnership" or simply "Center City Schools."

11. Buschmann and Coletta 2009. CEOs for Cities "works with its network partners to develop great cities that excel in the areas most critical to urban success: talent, connections, innovation and distinctiveness" (www.ceosforcities.org/about).

12. These included the shift in manufacturing from northern cities to the suburbs, the South, and abroad; an influx of migrants seeking jobs that were in increasingly short supply; and federal policies that encouraged flight to the suburbs and further concentrated poverty. All are discussed at greater length in chapter 2 with respect to Philadelphia. For information on the federal role in promoting suburbanization, see Jackson 1985. For a discussion of urban renewal and racial segregation, see Massey and Denton 1993.

13. For analyses of this approach, see Boyer 1992; Frieden and Sagalyn 1989; Grazian 2003, 2007; Zukin 1995.

14. For more on the association between an educated populace and urban prosperity, see Florida 2002; Gottlieb and Fogarty 2003; Weissbourd and Berry 2003.

15. Florida 2002, xiii.

16. Ibid., 218. University of Chicago sociologist Terry Nichols Clark is another advocate of the "amenities" approach to urban development. He maintains that in today's global era human capital is the greatest driver of economic growth. Affected by concerns about quality of life, mobile companies and individuals seek out such key urban amenities as a vibrant cultural scene, recreational activities, and boutiques and cafés. (Clark, Lloyd, Wong, and Jain 2002, 496)

17. See Newman 2004. According to some commentators, strategies that attract the "creative class" can be *too* successful, creating "childless cities"—cities that have become too expensive or, due to high density, unlivable for families. See Egan 2007; El Nasser 2008; Gragg 2005; Holt 2007.

18. For analyses of gentrification and its outcomes, see Anderson 1990; Brown-Saracino 2010; Smith 1992; Solnit 2000; Zukin 2011.

19. Mollenkopf and Castells 1991.

20. In a 2006 study conducted for the Brookings Institution, George Galster, Jackie Cutsinger, and Jason Booza found that in the 100 largest U.S. metropolitan areas, the number of households at the ends of the income distribution (i.e., the very affluent and the very poor) grew during the past few decades, while the number in the middle declined (Booza, Cutsinger, and Galster 2006).

21. The label implies more separation between various parts of a city than typi-

cally occurs; in reality, there are many social, political, and economic interconnections between affluent and poor areas within cities.

22. See Furdell, Wolman, and Hill 2005; Pattillo 2007; Wilson 1997.

23. Dreier, Mollenkopf, and Swanstrom 2004, 165. See also Fainstein 2010

24. Dreier, Mollenkopf and Swanstrom 2004, 150.

25. See, for example, ibid.; Fainstein 2010; Marcuse et al. 2009; Stone 2005.

26. Stone 2005, 242.

27. Varady and Raffel 1995. See, for example, Hall et al. 2003.

28. The benefits of economic integration are well documented. See Coleman et al. 1966; Grant 2009; Kahlenberg 2001; Kennedy, Jung, and Orland 1986; Rumberger and Palardy 2005.

29. See Diamond and Gomez 2004; Dornbusch and Wood 1989; Hart and Risley 1995; Lareau 2000; Muller 1993; Useem 1992.

30. Kahlenberg 2002. According to Linda Darling-Hammond, teachers are "the most inequitably distributed resource" in U.S. education (2010, 40).

31. See, for example, Brantlinger 2003; Lipman 1998; McGrath and Kuriloff 1999; Posey 2012; Wells and Serna 1996. See also Crosnoe 2009 for a discussion of the correlation for low-income high school students between negative social and academic outcomes and increases in the number of middle- and high-income students in a school.

32. Lipman 2002, 2 (see also Lipman 2004, 2008); Smith and Stovall 2008, 137.

33. In "the world of urban policy," Pattillo explains, "the middle class continues to be lionized for its generative capacities, not only for the material resources its members bring to struggling cities and neighborhoods, but also for their enactment and modeling of proper ways to live as neighbors, in other words, their respectability" (2007, 106).

34. Smith and Lupton 2008.

35. For a discussion of earlier waves of middle-class parental investment in urban public schools, see Cucchiara and Horvat 2009; Sieber 1982. Examples of popular media coverage include Graham 2010; Mieszkowski 2010; Rogers 2009; Smith 2009.

36. Edelberg and Kurland 2009.

37. The literature on market influences in education is vast. For some examples, see Apple 2001; Bartlett et al. 2002; Chubb and Moe 1990; Ravitch 2010; Witte 2001.

38. See, for example, Abowitz 2005; Anderson and Pini 2005; Apple 2001; Covaleskie 2007; Saltman 2000, 2005.

39. For example, Deborah Meier, progressive educator and founder of the renowned Central Park East Schools, has long been an advocate of public school choice. See Meier 2003. See also National Center for Educational Statistics 2010.

40. O'Riain 2000, 191.

41. Address to the Society of American Newspaper Editors, January 17, 1925, Washington, DC.

42. Somers 2008, 2. Somers credits financier George Soros with coining the term.

43. Ibid., 72; Katz 2001, 348.

44. Marshall 1964, 72, 81. See Katz 2001 for an extended discussion of Marshall's writing on citizenship and Somers 2008 for evidence of renewed scholarly interest in Marshall's work.

45. Marshall 1964, 84.

46. The naming of the 2001 federal education legislation as the "No Child Left Behind Act" exemplifies this pattern. On *Brown v. Board of Education* see http://www.nationalcenter.org/brown.html. For a discussion of the promise of social mobility and American ideology, see Hochschild 1996.

47. Crozier et al. 2008; Grossman and Kamani 2011; James et al. 2010; Kimelberg and Billingham 2010; Lipman 2004; Posey 2012; Raveaud and Van Zanten 2007.

48. While I focus on class here, in the United States class and race are intertwined in profound and complex ways, with Whites continuing to have, on average, significantly higher levels of wealth than other minority groups. For recent and dramatic evidence of this pattern, see Taylor et al. 2011. Nonetheless, the numbers of middle-class African Americans, Latinos, and Asians are growing, reshaping traditional conceptions of race and class. Chapter 5 discusses the role key middle-class African American parents played at Grant Elementary.

49. British literature on social class has been more explicit about differences within the broad category of "middle class"; see Butler and Savage 1995. Summarizing findings from a 2008 poll of adult Americans conducted by the Pew Research Organization, labor economist Stephen Rose notes that when asked to "describe what social class they belonged to, nine out of 10 Americans saw themselves as middle class" (http://stats.org/stories/2008/myth_decline_middle_june9_08.html); see also Brantlinger 2003, 9.

50. For example, in a speech in January 2010, President Obama proposed new tax credits for childcare and reduced rates on student loans, arguing that they would benefit middle-class families, a group that believes "if you work hard and live up to your responsibilities, you can get ahead" (Allen 2010).

51. Bourdieu 1985, 1990.

52. The literature on *cultural capital* is large and complex. In a general sense, the term refers to knowledge, skills, and practices that can be activated to secure advantages in particular contexts. Cultural capital may include high-status knowledge (e.g., expertise in classical music), but it also includes academic knowledge, familiarity with subtle social and cultural distinctions, an ability to negotiate within institutions, and educational credentials. It is acquired at home and in schools. According to Bourdieu, what counts as cultural capital is not constant; rather, particular practices are accorded value by the extent to which they correspond with the standards of schools and other institutions (Bourdieu and Passeron 1990). For

more on cultural capital and educational research, see Weininger and Lareau 2003. See also Lareau 2011, appendix B.

53. Anyon 1980; Boschken 2003; Brint 1991; Butler and Savage 1995.

54. Brantlinger 2003, 9. This group has also been labeled the "affluent professional class" (Anyon 1980) or the "new middle class" (Wright 1989).

55. According to Bourdieu (1990), in the process of growing up children learn certain habits, dispositions, and practices from their families. This becomes their habitus, and members of a social class often share the same habitus because their experiences have been similar in many ways. See Swartz 1998 for more on Bourdieu's analysis.

56. In contrast to "upper-middle class," the terms "professional," "knowledge worker," and "creative class" all refer a person's occupational status (rather than social class per se), as class is determined by income, wealth, education, *and* employment. However, "professionals" and "knowledge workers" were used often in discourse around the CCSI and applied to city residents who could also be labeled "upper-middle class." I thus use these terms out of an interest in remaining true to local understandings and usages.

57. I disclose my study's location in Philadelphia because the city's history and current social, economic, and political environment are essential to the story I want to tell. However, I use pseudonyms for Grant and other Center City schools in order to protect the identities of my informants, who confided in me about a situation that was often highly charged. For a discussion of how I have handled confidentiality issues in this book, see appendix A.

58. See Carr 2006.

59. For examples of the power of community organizing for school reform, see Gold, Simon and Brown 2002; Shirley 1997; Warren 2011.

Chapter Two

1. Cobble Square (like Grant and all names of parents) is a pseudonym. "Filthadelphia," "Filthy-delphia," and "Philthadelphia" are nicknames for Philadelphia (see, for example, www.urbandictionary.com). These nicknames highlight the city's problems with litter, pollution, and general urban decay.

2. Citation repressed to protect confidentiality.

3. For more on middle-class parents' activation of cultural capital, see Chin and Phillips 2004; Lareau 2000, 2011; Lareau and Horvat 1999. For the most influential sociological treatise on social capital, see Coleman 1988. The term "social capital" has multiple meanings in sociology, political science, and popular culture (for discussions of these, see Portes 1998 and Lin 2001). Drawing on Bourdieu's formulation (1985), I use "social capital" to refer to the resources individuals and groups are able to access through their social networks. As Horvat, Weininger, and

Lareau have shown, class status affects the size and composition of parents' networks, such that, "for middle-class families, webs of social ties tend to be woven through children's lives and especially through the organized activities they participate in, as well as through informal contacts with educators and other professionals" (2003, 327). Their social capital allows them to be more effective than poor and working-class parents (whose networks are quite different) in securing resources for their children.

4. Pressler 2005

5. *Philadelphia Inquirer*, July 28, 1989.

6. For a discussion of Philadelphia's neighborhoods, see Adams et al. 1991. For more on industrial-era challenges, see Davis and Haller 1998.

7. Madden and Stull 1991.

8. Bissinger 1997, 71.

9. Philadelphia City Planning Commission 2005.

10. Brookings Institution 2003; Booza, Cutsinger, and Galster 2006. Many poverty researchers believe that the official poverty line is set too low, underestimating the number of families living in financial distress. A better estimate, researchers argue, is actually twice the poverty level (Rothstein 2004).

11. The wage tax is a levy on the income of all Philadelphia residents, whether or not they work in the city, and on nonresidents who earn income in Philadelphia. In 1992 University of Pennsylvania economist Robert Inman estimated that increases in local taxes resulted in the loss of tens of thousands of jobs and encouraged businesses and middle- and upper-income families to leave the city. See Bissinger 1997 for a discussion of union contracts and onerous work rules during this period.

12. By 2010 it was down to 306. See Pew Charitable Trusts 2011.

13. See, for example, Curry 1990; Hinds 1990.

14. *Pittsburgh Post-Gazette*, July 10, 1991.

15. Bissinger 1997, 30.

16. http://www.city-journal.org/article01.php?aid=1409.

17. Smith 1979. Gentrification also occurred in other parts of the city, especially around major universities. See Anderson 1990.

18. See Adams et al. 2008.

19. Maroukian 2003.

20. Levy 2001a, 3.

21. For examples of *Inquirer* coverage, see Slobodzian 2005a, 2005b, and 2005c; Holcomb 2005; Tanaka and Von Bergen 2005. See also Pressler 2005 and Nelson 2005.

22. Quotation in header, "Private-Sector Energy Towards the Solution of Public Problems," is from MacDonald 1996a.

23. Mitchell 2001, 115–16.

24. Mitchell 1999.

25. Levy 2001b, 124.

26. See Steele and Symes 2005; Mitchell 2001. Steinke 2006 discusses Philadelphia BIDs that have been less successful than the CCD.

27. Levy 2001b; Lewis 2010; Schaller and Modan 2005.

28. Duneier 1999, 232.

29. Lewis 2010, 187.

30. This policy change reflects broader demographic shifts: by the 1980s, the majority of metropolitan residents lived in suburbs, and the population of the south and of southern cities had grown, tipping "the balance of national power away from the older, industrialized cities" (Judd and Swanstrom 1994, 12). See also DiGaetano and Lawless 1999.

31. In 1985 the U.S. Conference of Mayors released a report documenting the fiscal challenges facing the nation's large cities. *Rebuilding America's Cities* protests the "redirection" of public spending that had been damaging to cities and outlines a range of policy solutions. See also Dreier, Mollenkopf, and Swanstrom 2004 and Katz 2001.

32. See Dreier, Mollenkopf and Swanstrom 2004.

33. In Michigan, for example, and using constant (1991) dollars, a family of four received about $15,000 in AFDC payments and food stamps in 1972 but only $9,260 in 1991, a 39% decline in funding (Danziger and Gottschalk 1995, 34).

34. Richard Rubin, Philadelphia City Council testimony, February 27, 1990.

35. For discussions of BIDs' efficacy in these arenas, see Hoyt 2005; MacDonald 1996; Mitchell 1999; Steinke 2006.

36. MacDonald 1996b.

37. Levy 2001a.

38. Lewis 2010. For example, Philadelphia's CCD announced in 2010 that it received a $15 million federal grant to refurbish a plaza adjacent to City Hall (http://www.centercityphila.org/pressroom/prelease_dilworth1010.php).

39. According to its website, the Central Philadelphia Development Corporation "conducts research and urban planning and advocates for policies that enhance Center City Philadelphia as a competitive location for business and entrepreneurship." Its membership rolls include representatives from architecture, law banking, real estate, and other businesses in Center City (http://www.centercityphila.org/about/CPDC.php).

40. All quotations here are from testimony at Philadelphia City Council Public Hearings, February 27 and October 10, 1990.

41. See, for example, *Inquirer* editorials on July 28 and December 23, 1989; September 22, 1990; and March 26 and December 9, 1991.

42. *Philadelphia Inquirer*, September 22, 1990. According to the original terms, the project could be voided if one-third of all property owners in Center City (i.e., 866 of 2,585) submitted letters of opposition. Only 340 people wrote such letters (*Philadelphia Daily News*, September 20, 1990).

43. CCD 2005.

44. Shea 2006. Thompson's 2011 profile of Levy includes his annual salary and a lengthy discussion of his impact in the downtown and beyond. Levy was selected for the "Philadelphia Award" because "his continuous flow of ideas, leadership and attention to the development and improvement of the Center City landscape . . . have been major factors in transforming Center City." See www.philadelphiaaward .org/levy.html.

45. CCD 2005, 1.

46. Levy 2001a, 6.

47. Levy 2001b, 125, 126. Levy's defense of the broader role of BIDs, published in *Economic Development Quarterly*, was a direct response to Jerry Mitchell's (2001) categorization, in the same journal, of BIDs as chiefly service providers. Florida's work is discussed in chapter 1.

48. Ibid., 130.

49. CCD 2004, 2.

50. www.centercityphila.org.

51. CCD 2005.

52. Cassel 2003. Drawing on its own research, the CCD reported that in 2008 earnings in Center City accounted for over 45% of all private-sector earnings in Philadelphia. When city, federal, and School District of Philadelphia employees were counted, that percentage rose even higher (CCD 2010a).

53. Levy 2003a, 3.

54. Levy 2005.

55. McGovern 2009, 664

56. See Philadelphia City Planning Commission 2005; Birch 2005; CCD 2010b.

57. CCD 2002, 1. The CCD estimated that housing values in the expanded area increased 386% between 1970 and 2000, compared to 98% in the "core" downtown (CCD 2002).

58. Birch 2005.

59. Other areas with high percentages of college-educated adults include Chestnut Hill and Mt. Airy (located on the far northwestern side of Philadelphia) and University City (in West Philadelphia, surrounding the University of Pennsylvania and Drexel University campuses).

60. CCD 2002, 2004, 2011; Slobodzian 2007

61. Data from "Tax Stats," Internal Revenue Service, 2008. http://www.irs.gov /taxstats/.

62. Philadelphia City Planning Commission 2005.

63. Emeno and Heavens, June 25, 2006. The number of Philadelphia residential properties selling for over $1 million (many of which are located downtown) also increased dramatically in recent years, a shift that is not necessarily reflected in the median sale price.

64. Mollenkopf and Castells 1991.

65. Booza, Cutsinger, and Galster 2006.

66. Philadelphia Workforce Investment Board 2007.

67. Ibid., 3.

68. For a discussion of the persistence of poverty in "revitalizing" cities, see Furdell, Wolman, and Hill 2005. For more information on Philadelphia's languishing economy, see Philadelphia Workforce Investment Board 2007. According to the Brookings Institution (2003), segregation between blacks and whites in Philadelphia in 2000 was more extreme than in Cleveland, Detroit, St. Louis, and Boston.

69. See Jackson 1985; Grant 2009.

70. Brookings Institution 2003.

71. For a discussion of the racialized nature of suburban flight, see Frey 1979; Frey and Fielding 1995; Jackson 1985; Kruse 2005. See also Sugrue 1996 for a description of white flight in Detroit. Recently large numbers of households of color also have moved to the suburbs, and suburbs have replaced cities as the "first stop" for many immigrant groups. Older, inner-ring suburbs in particular have become increasingly diverse in terms of income and ethnicity. See Brookings Institution 2010.

72. Kruse 2005.

73. The proportion of high-income households also increased during that period—evidence of the further economic polarization of U.S. cities (Booza, Cutsinger, and Galster 2006).

74. See Beauregard 2003.

75. Adams et al. 1991; Philadelphia City Planning Commission 2005. Quotation in header above is from Bissinger 1997, 272.

76. Adams et al. 1991, 84.

77. For some examples of the ways Philadelphia leaders attempted to deal with middle-class flight, see Bissinger 1997; Gold et al. 2007; Gorenstein 2001a.

78. Boyd and Christman 2003.

79. Rendell 1994.

80. Diaz 1999.

81. Gorenstein 2001b.

82. See Dreier, Mollenkopf, and Swanstrom 2004; Fainstein 2010; Katz 2001.

Chapter Three

1. A few other elementary schools in the city were known among middle-class parents as "good schools." These include Henry in the northwest part of the city, and Powel and Penn-Alexander in West Philadelphia.

2. These data are taken from *Inquirer* coverage of desegregation litigation in Philadelphia.

3. Busing across district boundaries was outlawed by the *Milliken v. Bradley* decision in 1974.

4. The struggle to desegregate Philadelphia's schools began in 1972, when a court ordered the School District of Philadelphia and four other Pennsylvania districts to develop plans for creating racial balance in the schools. The next three decades were marked by repeated court cases as the Pennsylvania Human Relations Commission (the state's civil rights agency) pressed to district to desegregate. In 1977 a state court accepted a district plan for voluntary desegregation (using magnet schools and other choice mechanisms), but the Human Relations Commission argued four years later that the plan had failed. A state court then imposed limited reassignment measures. In the 1990s the goal of desegregation litigation shifted from creating racially balanced schools to increasing educational opportunity within Philadelphia's largely segregated schools. As a result, the district implemented such measures as full-day kindergarten, lowered class size, and increased professional development and parental involvement. Later in the decade, issues of school funding became more prominent, as litigation sought, unsuccessfully, to force the state to provide additional funding to the district. See Morrison 2004 for a history of desegregation in Philadelphia. Court supervision ended in 2009 when Superintendent Arlene Ackerman announced a plan to target Philadelphia's lowest performing schools for dramatic improvement (Mezzacappa 2009).

5. For a discussion of events leading up to the state takeover, see Travers 2003.

6. This contrast is even more striking given the districts' percentages of low income students. In the 2004–5 school year, 69% of Philadelphia school district students qualified for free or reduced-price lunch. In Lower Merion, a nearby suburb, only 5% did (data from National Center for Education Statistics, Institute for Educational Sciences, U.S. Department of Education, http://nces.ed.gov/ccd/).

7. This is a commonly cited quote. See, for example, http://www.pbs.org /elections/archives/essays_shell.html?essay_scottlamar and http://www.fandm .edu/politics/politically-uncorrected-column/2002-politically-uncorrected/it-s -pennsylvania-stupid.

8. For more information on school funding in Pennsylvania, see http://www .paschoolfunding.org/. This dynamic changed when Philadelphia's former mayor, Edward Rendell, was elected governor in 2002. During Rendell's second term (2006–10) funding for poor districts, including Philadelphia, increased significantly. In 2011 newly elected governor Tom Corbett slashed funding for public education.

9. Travers 2003, 4.

10. See Payne 2008 for a discussion of this dynamic.

11. Children Achieving did lead to increases in achievement test scores for Philadelphia students, particularly in the elementary grades, but the absolute scores were still very low (Travers 2003).

12. Ibid.

13. Useem, Christman, and Boyd 2006. Research for Action, a Philadelphia

nonprofit educational research organization, conducted extensive research on the state takeover and its aftermath. See www.researchforaction.org for a full list of publications.

14. Governor Schweiker's other two appointees were Daniel Whelan, a business executive, and James Gallagher, the president of Philadelphia University. Mayor Street appointed Michael Masch, a former budget director for the city, and Sandra Dungee Glenn, a former school board member active in state and local politics.

15. Useem, Christman, and Boyd 2006, 9.

16. For an analysis of Philadelphia's test scores and their variance across providers, see Gill, Zimmer, Christman, and Blanc 2007. For more on the reforms following the state takeover, see Gold, Christman, and Herold 2007 and Useem 2005.

17. Cucchiara, Gold, and Simon 2011. See also Bartlett et al. 2002; Kwong 2000; Whitty and Power 2000.

18. Nevels 2005.

19. Quoted in Gold et al. 2005, 9.

20. See Lipman 2004.

21. E.g., Snyder 2005a.

22. *Metropolis* 2010. This article contrasts Vallas's support for Masterman, a top-rated magnet secondary school that enrolls a disproportionately middle-class student body, with Ackerman's apparent lack of interest in the school.

23. Useem, Christman, and Boyd 2006, 12.

24. In 2000 there were over 200,000 students in district-operated schools; by 2004–5, there were just over 186,000 (data from National Center for Education Statistics, Institute for Educational Sciences, U.S. Department of Education, http://nces.ed.gov/ccd/). Between 2002 and 2006, the number of charter schools increased from 40 to 56.

25. Under the federal No Child Left Behind legislation, districts as well as schools are categorized according to their students' achievement on standardized tests. Those that fail to meet the state's goals do not make "Adequate Yearly Progress" (AYP). The School District of Philadelphia did not achieve AYP status under Vallas (nor has it done so since he left). As of 2011, the district was in "Corrective Action II" (indicating significant failure) for its ninth straight year.

26. Quinn, September 3, 2008.

27. Snyder 2003.

28. E.g., Grant 2009; Kahlenberg 2001. See discussions of this issue in chapters 1 and 5.

29. Institute for the Study of Civic Values 2006. This report acknowledged that increased reporting might account in part for the rise in reported assaults. See also Moran and Snyder 2000; Snyder 2004.

30. Tuition was high for independent schools in Center City. For example, for the 2006–7 school year, tuition at one school began at $14,325 for kindergarten and peaked at $20,995 for twelfth grade.

31. U.S. Census data.

32. For example, Independence Charter School, located in Center City, was such a popular option among downtown parents that the school maintained a long waiting list. Whereas the percentage of low-income students in many charter schools matched or exceeded Philadelphia's overall percentage of 70%, at ICS this number was only 50% in 2005.

33. In 2006 Masterman was rated number 20 in the Delaware Valley by *Philadelphia Magazine* and number 74 in the country by *Newsweek*. Admissions to Masterman begins in the fifth grade. Students must score in at least the 88th percentile on the state standardized, have mostly A's on their transcripts, and good attendance and behavior records. See http://webgui.phila.k12.pa.us/schools/m/masterman/our-faculty—staff/schools/m/masterman/admissions.

34. Of the remaining two schools, one was overwhelmingly white and the other overwhelmingly Latino. For more information, see the *Philadelphia Public School Notebook*'s special issue focusing on segregation in Philadelphia's schools (Summer 2005).

35. Neild 2005.

36. Teacher turnover in general was high in Philadelphia. Research for Action tracked a cohort of new teachers inducted in 1999–2000 and found that by 2003 only 40% were still in the district and fewer than 30% were teaching at the school in which they had begun. See ibid.

37. As of 2011 the Voluntary Transfer Program remains in place, but the district no longer uses the EH-36 form.

38. When these district-supplied statistics were published in the local education newspaper, they were criticized for underestimating how many students were accepted to schools; the numbers represented "first round" admissions and many students were admitted from the waiting list and through informal processes, with social and political connections influencing admissions (Letters to the Editor and editor's reply, *Public School Notebook* [Winter 2003–4]).

39. There also were schools in gentrifying areas around Center City that parents in other parts of the city sought out, seeing them as an improvement over the schools in their own neighborhoods. At Bache-Martin, for example, the elementary school in the Fairmount neighborhood just north of Center City, over half the students were transfers in 2005–6. The percentage of transfers at other schools in the periphery of Center City ranged between 9% and 38%.

40. School District of Philadelphia. Data from National Center for Education Statistics, Institute for Educational Sciences, U.S. Department of Education, http://nces.ed.gov/ccd/.

41. Ibid.

42. Informal communication, former Big Three principal, November 2010. The shadow system is beyond the scope of this research. It is my sense, however, that middle-class families were generally better equipped—through their stores of

social, cultural, and financial capital—to convince a principal that their families would be assets to the school.

43. Donna's children started at Grant in 2004, before the new transfer policy went into effect and before the marketing of Grant had made it more popular with Cobble Square families. As I will show in chapter 7, she likely would not have been as successful a few years later.

Chapter Four

1. These thirty interviews are discussed in appendix A. See appendix C for a complete list of interviews.

2. CCD press release, April 19, 2004. Subhead quotation is from CCD 2004, 6.

3. CCD 2004, 1.

4. CCD 2004, 4 (italics in original).

5. Ibid.

6. The CCD's application to a local philanthropy for funding for the CCSI similarly noted the "eagerness of School Reform Commission Chairman, James Nevels, and School Superintendent, Paul Vallas, to embrace market-oriented improvements that can place public schools on equal footing with independent, parochial, and charter schools" (CCD application to the William Penn Foundation, #2007125, May 24, 2005). The quotation in the header above is from an interview with a CCSI administrator.

7. Stone 1989, 229.

8. See Domhoff's (2005) discussion of the influence of business and corporate leaders through the mechanism of "interlocking directorates."

9. Useem, Christman, and Boyd 2006.

10. See Boyd and Christman 2003; Gold et al. 2005.

11. As a budget-balancing strategy, Vallas moved district operations from an antiquated but imposing building located near downtown amenities to a modern but less centrally located office building.

12. In 2004 eighteen of the twenty Center City schools made Adequate Yearly Progress under the federal government's No Child Left Behind Act.

13. For example, in the 2005–6 school year, Benjamin Franklin High School was 68% African American and 21% Latino. The overwhelming majority of its students were classified as low-income. (Data from National Center for Education Statistics, Institute for Educational Sciences, U.S. Department of Education. http://nces.ed.gov/ccd/.)

14. See chapter 3 for more information on the transfer process in Philadelphia prior to the CCSI.

15. The delay between the time this new policy was first announced (November 2004) and its implementation (spring 2006) is explored in chapter 7.

16. The success of the fair is described in the CCD's 2006 report, *The State of Center City.*

17. Significant improvements to the schools' exteriors did not take place, but other renovations did occur.

18. This was not the case with Grant, where the secretaries were generally friendly.

19. The list is less impressive for the schools within the region that were not considered viable options for middle-class families. See chapter 7. The CCSI website is www.centercityschools.com.

20. As of 2011, all district schools have professionally and uniformly designed websites. The websites of the schools targeted by the CCSI, however, are still linked to the Center City Schools homepage and are still visually distinct from the websites of other district schools.

21. Greenberg 2000, 228.

22. Ibid.

23. CCD 2004.

24. Pennsylvania Department of Education Contract #618/FOS. The money for this grant came from a fund known as "Walking Around Money" (WAM). Formally titled "legislative initiative grants," WAMs are state-level versions of earmarks. Each caucus in the Pennsylvania House and Senate has a certain amount of WAM money, which members give to projects of their choosing. Because there is no transparency with respect to these grants, it is difficult to get information about how they are allocated and how the grantees account for the funds they receive. WAMs are controversial for these very reasons, with the media and various good-government groups periodically calling for them to be abolished. My efforts to track down a final report for this grant met with little success. Finally, a contact at the state Department of Education took pity on me and explained that there was no final report because the grant was a WAM and normal rules did not apply.

25. Quoted from the application's cover letter, from Paul Levy to the president of the William Penn Foundation, dated May 24, 2005.

26. This parent was paid approximately $25,000.

27. Greg Thornton, Chief Academic Officer, School District of Philadelphia, letter to Center City stakeholders, April 12, 2005.

28. Subhead quotation is from an interview with a city official. The complete comment reads: "You really do want those folks [the middle and upper-middle class] to want to go to those schools. But should they get preferential treatment in getting into those schools? That's—I don't know. I don't know."

29. Reynolds-Brown 2006.

30. *Philadelphia Daily News*, March 22, 2006.

31. Media reference suppressed to protect confidentiality.

32. Polaneczky 2006.

33. CCD 2002.

34. Beauregard 2003.

35. Wilson 1987.

36. Orwell 1946.

Chapter Five

1. All media citations related to Grant have been suppressed to protect confidentiality.

2. See Ball 2003; Campbell, Proctor, and Sherington 2009; Reay and Ball 1998.

3. Philadelphia City Planning Commission 2005; Pew Charitable Trusts 2010. In 2011, after the national financial crisis, this number dropped to just under $700,000 (*Philadelphia Inquirer*, October 16, 2011).

4. Between 2003 and 2010, this number ranged from 471 to 498.

5. These numbers remained relatively constant throughout the 2004–5 and 2005–6 school years.

6. U.S. Census data. In the eight other tracts also served by Grant, the percentages of students in private school ranged from the single digits in an adjoining immigrant neighborhood, to about 40% in the slightly less affluent neighborhoods to the north and west of Cobble Square, to 76% in a tract with few children just east of the school.

7. In 2003 358 students applied through EH-36 transfer to Grant from other schools.

8. School District of Philadelphia data.

9. One problem (discussed later in this chapter) was that neither parents nor teachers were happy with Ms. Ashton, the principal in 2003–4 and 2004–5. Perhaps because of this low morale—or perhaps because, as many parents and teachers claimed, Grant received a large number of students from other "failing" schools who transferred under No Child Left Behind—the school's academic trajectory seemed a bit unstable.

10. See appendix C for a list of Grant parents interviewed. I interviewed all parents who were active in the PTO except for the parent I call Janice, with whom I was not able to arrange an interview because of scheduling conflicts. I also interviewed a number of parents who were not active in the PTO but were involved in the school in other ways.

11. Though referred to as the library, this space did not actually function as such at this time: there was no librarian and the materials were outdated and unorganized. Rather, the room was used as a venue for meetings, fundraisers, and other events.

12. See Lareau 2000 for a discussion of the gendered nature of parental involvement in school.

13. Parents generally discussed race and class more explicitly in interviews and private conversations.

14. My efforts to interview parents from that area yielded two interviews. One provided important insights, which are included in this chapter. The other, with a mother who had recently emigrated from China, was largely unsuccessful because so many of the issues my research addressed were unfamiliar to her.

15. Lee 1996.

16. This quotation in the heading above is from an interview with a Grant teacher. The full comment reads: "When you're dealing with an affluent neighborhood, you're dealing with parents of interest. They care! As opposed to other areas. It sounds horrible, I know it does. But that's it. Realistic. I mean, that's the way it is."

17. See, for example, Horvat, Weininger, and Lareau 2003; Lew 2007; Ream and Palardy 2008.

18. Grant 2009; Kahlenberg 2001.

19. Lipman 2008, 126. Lipman's critique is discussed in chapter 1.

20. See Butler and Robson 2003.

21. Grant was one of only a few schools to get a new playground during this period.

22. Anderson 1990, 37.

23. District data show that experienced and effective teachers tend to cluster in schools that serve more advantaged populations, suggesting one way schools with significant middle-class populations are advantaged (Socolar 2009).

24. Their hesitance may also reflect an unwillingness to discuss such sensitive issues with a white researcher.

25. School District of Philadelphia data. Due to limitations in the data, I do not know the racial breakdown of the students who transferred from within the Center City Academic Region.

26. For a discussion of a similar phenomenon with respect to school integration, see Well and Crain 1999, especially pp. 167–73.

27. Henig 1996; Holme 2002. Saporito and Lareau (1999) found that white families avoid schools with large numbers of African American students, even if that means choosing schools with inferior academic performance.

28. This is consistent with the description in Edelberg and Kurland (2009) of their work in marketing Nettelhorst Elementary to affluent families in Chicago.

29. See Holme 2002.

30. See Lee 1996.

31. While I did not explore this issue in my research, I suspect that one reason white, middle-class parents felt comfortable sending their children to Grant, where the number of white students was quite small, was because the "minority" population at the school was heavily Asian American, rather than African American. Parents rarely spoke of the presence of large numbers of African American students as one of the school's "selling points." This contrasts with studies showing that some white parents seek out diverse environments to expose their children to

people of varied race and class backgrounds (Cucchiara and Horvat 2009; Reay et al. 2007).

32. Danns 2008; Hennessey 1977.

33. Epstein 1992; Henderson and Mapp 2002; Hoover-Dempsey and Sandler 1995; Stevenson and Baker 1987.

34. See, e.g., Bryk and Schneider (2002).

35. Goldring et al. 2006; see also Warren 2005.

36. Danns 2008, 69. See also Hennessey 1977; Orfield and Yun 1999.

37. Several parents speculated to me about this, but it was not confirmed.

38. I received conflicting information from parents and district administrators regarding this requirement. Ms. Ashton's policy was not one in place across the district. Middle-class parents I spoke with who had transferred their children into other high-performing schools were not required to reapply for first grade.

39. In a phone call months after our interview, Kim relayed a conversation she had with another parent, a middle-class white man who lived just outside the catchment area. He told her that to enroll his child in Grant, he simply talked to Ms. Carelli (the principal who preceded Ms. Ashton), and she said, "No problem." Kim continued, "I spent a full year fighting to get my kids into Grant. I remember meeting Ms. Carelli, and her saying we don't let people in from outside of the catchment area." This comment—and anecdotal evidence from other schools about principals prioritizing middle-class students from outside of the catchment area—reveals another layer of the shadow system of school admissions.

40. An emphasis on behavioral rather than structural causes of poverty has long shaped academic scholarship and popular culture. In its recent formulations, the discourse draws from research in the 1960s and '70s on "cultural deficits" and the "culture of poverty," and from popular portrayals of dysfunctional inner-city neighborhoods and schools (Kontos and Murphy 1967; Lewis 1966; Riessman 1962).

41. See chapter 1.

Chapter Six

1. Grant 2009; Kahlenberg 2002; Rumberger and Palardy 2005.

2. Edelberg and Kurland 2009; Graham 2010; Siefer 2010.

3. In chapter 5, I often referred to the middle- and upper-middle-class families living in the neighborhood around Grant as the "neighborhood" or "Cobble Square" families. Similarly, I referred to the largely poor and working-class families who lived outside of Center City as "transfers." I did this because the labels "transfer" and "neighborhood" were integral to the marketing of Grant. In this chapter, because I am in conversation with the literature on class differences in parental involvement in school, I use terms that index class status rather than residence, distinguishing between working-class and middle-/upper-middle-class

families. Since there was near complete overlap between the two sets of terms—the majority of "neighborhood" families were middle or upper-middle class, and the majority of "transfer" families were working-class or poor—I believe I can make this shift without compromising my analysis.

4. Paul Levy, CCD president, quoted in Snyder 2005b.

5. Hirschman 1970, 76.

6. Ibid., 21.

7. This typology is based on Ryan et al. 1997. See appendix B for the complete table.

8. My data do not allow me to draw firm conclusions about the extent to which active middle- and upper-middle-class parents channeled district resources disproportionately to their children's schools. Given the intricacies of school district budgets and decisionmaking, this process would be a difficult one to track. However, the potential for middle- and upper-middle-class families to use district resources to improve individual schools while creating greater stratification within the system as a whole is certainly a topic that merits greater exploration.

9. Butler and Robson 2003, 73, 72.

10. See chapter 5 for a discussion of dynamics within Grant around these students.

11. As discussed in chapter 5, most of the white and middle-class students at Grant were in the younger grades; after fourth grade, the classes became increasingly African American, Asian American, and poor and working-class.

12. Siefer 2010; Edelberg and Kurland 2009.

13. Lareau and Munoz 2012 is an exception. See Horvat, Weininger, and Lareau 2003; Lareau 2000, 2011; Lareau and Horvat 1999; Lew 2007; Ream and Palardy 2008; Useem 1992.

14. Bourdieu and Wacquant 1992.

15. Wells and Serna 1996.

16. Holme 2002.

17. Because my research focused on parents, I could say little about how this construction actually affected the students in question, other than raising concerns about the potential for this discourse to shape both educators' behaviors and students' own understandings of their position within the school.

18. Lipman 2004.

19. As I explain in appendix A, my original research plan was to examine the collective efforts of Grant parents to improve the school. The CCSI and the effort to market Grant emerged as such important issues that I shifted the focus of my research.

20. Students could transfer into a school under NCLB only if that school had openings. Principals had some (unofficial) discretion over how many such openings they reported having to the district.

21. See Rothstein 2004.

Chapter Seven

1. O'Riain 2000.

2. The state takeover of Philadelphia's schools and resulting changes in governance are discussed in chapter 3. Sandra Dungee Glenn was the SRC member concerned about equity issues. Her efforts to resolve them are discussed later in this chapter.

3. The full text of this quote (which appeared in a *Philadelphia Daily News* column) reads: "It sounds high-rent, and it does have some of the district's highest-performing elementary schools. But its boundaries stretch into poor neighborhoods of North and South Philly" (Polaneczky 2006)

4. As discussed in chapter 2, the CCD officially serves only a part of Center City, namely those blocks where businesses are concentrated, but its services actually benefit all of the downtown.

5. Thornton, letter to Center City stakeholders.

6. A preliminary version of the "Secondary Regional Catchment Area Admission/Transfer Policy," circulated by the school district in early 2006, explained that children applying using the EH-36 process would be admitted in this order: "a. Transfers consistent with the current Desegregation Policy; b. Children who reside in the Region; c. Children who reside outside the Region." This version clearly gave priority to students within the region, the exact specification the CCD had sought. The final version of the policy outlined admissions for transfer students grades K-8 in the following order: "a. Children who apply using an EH-35C [the NCLB-derived transfer procedure] will be admitted in accordance with the current NCLB Regulations. b. Children who apply using an EH 36 within the region will be admitted in a manner which fosters and promotes physical integration and racial and educational equity. c. Children who apply using an EH 36 from outside the region will be admitted in a manner which fosters and promotes [etc.]."

7. This did not occur, however, because when district leadership changed in 2008, this and other Vallas initiatives were lost in the transition.

8. Snyder 2006.

9. Cucchiara, Gold, and Simon 2011.

10. E.g., Simmons 2005.

11. These children would have been five to ten years old in 2005. See appendix A for details. The demographic calculations in this chapter focus only on whites and African Americans. I did this to make the presentation clearer and because those were the two groups most affected by the CCSI. It is important to note that Philadelphia had large (and growing) Asian and Latino communities during this period.

12. American Community Survey data, 2005–9.

13. For an overview of Center City's population growth between 2000 and 2010, see CCD 2011. For an example of how these developments have been treated in the

media, see Pompilio 2011 and http://www.philly.com/philly/multimedia/Changes_ in_number_of_children_by_neighborhood.html?view=graphic.

14. According to school district data, 44% of students in Center City elementary schools were transfers in 2005–6.

15. The rest of the regions were fairly evenly represented, but fewer than 1% of the transfer students came from the northeast, where the population was more heavily white and working or middle class.

16. By 2008 the CCD included Bache-Martin, an elementary school in the gentrifying Fairmount neighborhood just north of the downtown, among its targeted schools. There, as at the "Big Three," it helped sponsor "socials" for newly enrolled kindergartners and gave gifts, including crayons, pencils and a "Class of 2021" t-shirt, to families (CCD 2008).

17. http://www.centercityschools.com. (School name suppressed.)

18. Paul Vallas, speech to Building Industry Association, September 20, 2005, in author's fieldnotes.

19. For a discussion of the lack of community resources in many Philadelphia neighborhoods, see Furstenberg, Cook, Eccles, and Elder 1999.

20. Levy 2008.

21. CCD 2008, 4

22. This form of displacement resembles what gentrification scholar Peter Marcuse termed "exclusionary displacement." According to Marcuse (1986), exclusionary displacement occurs when low-income residents who might have moved into a particular neighborhood are prevented from doing so by rising real estate costs associated with gentrification. Though they are not forced out of their homes because of gentrification (another kind of displacement), they do lose an option that would have been available to them before the neighborhood gentrified. I am grateful to Linn Posey-Maddox for this connection.

23. The percentage of Asian students also increased at Grant during this period but remained steady at the other two schools. I do not include information about the percentage of students eligible for free and reduced-priced lunch because school district data do not permit accuracy in tracking changes over time (see appendix A).

24. Kimelberg and Billingham 2010; Posey 2012; Siefer 2010.

25. For a discussion of these patterns, see Anyon 1997; Kozol 1991, 2005; Neckerman 2010; and Payne 2008.

26. Babitch, Barth, Jung, and MacDonald 2006; Birch 2006; Buschmann and Coletta 2009.

27. Henry 2008; Karpewicz 2010.

28. In 2003–4, Grant's kindergarten was 15% white, 44% Asian, and 33% black. By 2009–10, it was 30% white, 50% Asian, and 15% black.

29. Gold et al 2010.

30. Snyder 2010.

31. Ibid.

32. Pattillo 2007, 106

Chapter Eight

1. In 2010 Y/BPS was incorporated into the Boston Public Schools' "Team BPS" program.

2. See Brookings Institution 2003. The cities also differed with respect to desegregation. Unlike Philadelphia, Boston's schools were desegregated abruptly and with great contention. In the 1970s court-ordered busing provoked violent opposition and drew national attention (Lukas 1985). In 1990, when the Boston Schools Committee was charged with responsibility for overseeing desegregation, a complex plan, featuring zones with similar racial and ethnic compositions and a system of "controlled choice," was initiated (and remains in place).

3. According to the U.S. Department of Education, in the 2008–9 school year, 38% of the students in Boston were black, 38% were Latino, 14% were white, and 9% were Asian. Seventy-four percent of the students qualified for free or reduced lunch. (Philadelphia's statistics for that year were 61% black, 17% Latino, 13% white and 6% Asian. Seventy-three percent of Philadelphia's students qualified for free or reduced lunch.) There were 137 schools in Boston's public system, compared to 274 in Philadelphia's (data from National Center for Education Statistics, Institute for Educational Sciences, U.S. Department of Education. http://nces.ed.gov/ccd/).

4. Herszenhorn 2006.

5. Sherman and Freeman 2004.

6. See, e.g., Blanding 2007. This assumption was also apparent in my interviews with people associated with Y/BPS.

7. Unlike in Philadelphia, schoolchildren in Boston do not have a "right" to attend their neighborhood schools. A small group of schools generally viewed as good options by middle-class parents tend to be "oversubscribed" (meaning that they attract more applicants than they can enroll), while other schools do not fill. This has led to a strategy by which some middle- and upper-middle-class parents use their social networks to identify an undersubscribed school with "potential." The parents then list the school as their first choice and, as a group, enroll their children there.

8. For a discussion of these patterns in Boston, see Kimelberg and Billingham 2010. The pool of middle-class families willing to use public schools may be larger in Boston than in Philadelphia, because Boston schools, with their history of improvement, are seen as more viable options.

9. A Y/BPS coordinator described tensions at one school between low-income and minority parents who had been there and an incoming group of white and

middle-class parents who referred to their plan to transform the school as a "take-over." This coordinator intervened, talking with the middle-class parents "about going into the school and how to include everyone and how to be considerate of people who have worked hard for four or five years in that school and have really kept it going." She saw this as a part of her job, noting that she "was on top of it" whenever similar issues arose at other schools.

10. On other cities, see Kahlenberg 2007; Rimer 2003. On Wake County, see Bazelon 2008; Finder 2005; Grant 2009; Kahlenberg 2007.

11. LaCrosse, WI, Cambridge, MA, and San Francisco, CA have also experimented with creating economically integrated schools (Kahlenberg 2007).

12. http://www.wcpss.net/demographics.

13. Kahlenberg 2007; Grant 2009.

14. See, for example, Bazelon 2008; Finder 2005; Grant 2009; Silberman 2002.

15. Bazelon 2008.

16. Brown 2010; Winerip 2011.

17. Finder 2005.

18. Park 1967, 3; Harvey 2008, 23.

19. On discussions of urban change ignoring education see, e.g., Logan and Molotch 1987; Sugrue 1996; Zukin 2011. On urban schools as casualty, see, e.g., Bissinger 1997; Wilson 1987.

20. For important exceptions, see Joseph and Feldman 2009; Turnham and Khadduri 2004; Warren 2005.

21. For discussions of historical understandings of the purpose of education, see Reese 2000; Labaree 1997; Katz 1987. New ways of thinking about schooling do not simply replace earlier ones. However, in the past several decades an individualistic orientation—evident in the popular discourse on schools and in the prominence of reform strategies like vouchers, charter schools, and private educational management companies—has increasingly prevailed over other, more collective purposes.

22. Brown-Saracino 2010. Butler and Robson 2003 and Kimelberg and Billingham 2010 are exceptions.

23. E.g., Smith 1992.

24. Anderson 1990; Levy and Cybriwsky 2010; Pattillo 2007.

25. Freeman 2010.

26. See Dreier, Mollenkopf, and Swanstrom 2004 for examples.

27. Grant makes a similar point with respect to the contrast between Wake County and Syracuse, New York, which maintains a separate school system from those in the outlying suburbs: "No candidate for major political office has dared to mention merging school districts on a metropolitan basis" (2009, p. 180).

28. Cucchiara, Gold, and Simon 2011; Gold et al. 2007.

29. Many scholars have proposed policy solutions to these broader problems. See, for example, Wilson 1997 and Darling-Hammond 2010. For a similar argu-

ment about the need to seek structural reforms to address urban poverty rather than simply "shuffling households in the hopes that they will get along and be pulled along," see Pattillo 2007, 110.

30. CCD 2011, 6.

31. In the summer of 2011, after months of conflict about the budget, staffing, and other controversies, Dr. Arlene Ackerman was "bought out" by the district for nearly $1 million.

32. See chapter 1 for a discussion of contemporary challenges to traditional notions of citizenship.

33. Hirschman 1970.

Appendix A

1. I was particularly inspired by Annette Lareau's (2000, 2011) work on class and schools.

2. Yin 2002.

3. In some ways, my dilemmas during this tense time were not dissimilar to those Jay MacLeod (1995) experienced in his fieldwork with two rival groups of young men in the "Clarendon Heights" housing project.

4. See Whyte 1993 on the value of being the secretary at one's research site.

5. Maxwell 2005.

6. My reasons for distinguishing between middle- and upper-middle class are discussed in chapters 1 and 2. I call a parent "working class" if neither the parent nor his/her partner has a college degree.

7. Kimelberg and Billingham 2010. For a discussion of FRPL in Philadelphia, see The Reinvestment Fund 2007.

8. I am grateful to Michelle Schmitt and David Ford, of (respectively) Temple University's Metropolitan Philadelphia Indicators Project and Temple's Social Science Data Laboratory for their assistance with this work.

9. To do this, I used maps to identify all the census tracts that fell within the Center City Region. This is not a perfect strategy, as census tracts and school attendance zones are not perfectly aligned (although because the Center City Academic Region was comprised of a set of contiguous school catchment zones, and Philadelphia's catchment zones tend to fall along or close to tract lines, it was not as problematic as it could have been). For researchers interested in conducting similar analyses in the future, the SABINS data system, which links 2010 U.S. Census data to school attendance boundaries (making the sort of estimating I did unnecessary), is an invaluable tool. See http://www.sabinsdata.org/home. I am grateful to David Van Riper and his staff at the University of Minnesota Population Center for their assistance with this portion of the census data analysis.

10. Maxwell 1996.

11. Glaser and Strauss 1967.

12. Maxwell 1996.

13. Hammersley and Atkinson 1986.

14. Maxwell 1996, 95.

15. For examples, see Brantlinger 2003; Demerath 2009; Gaztambide-Fernandez 2009; Lareau 2000, 2011; Lynd and Lynd 1959.

16. Duneier 1999, 384.

References

Abowitz, K. K. 2005. "On the Public and Civic Purposes of Education." *Educational Theory* 58 (3): 357–76.

Adams, C. A. 1997. "The Philadelphia Experience." *Annals of the American Academy of Political and Social Science* 551:222–34.

Adams, C. A., D. Bartelt, D. Elesh, and I. Goldstein. 2008. *Restructuring the Philadelphia Region: Metropolitan Divisions and Inequality*. Philadelphia, PA: Temple University Press.

Adams, C. A., D. Bartelt, D. Elesh, I. Goldstein, N. Kleniewski, and W. Yancy. 1991. *Philadelphia: Neighborhoods, Division, and Conflict in a Postindustrial City*. Philadelphia, PA: Temple University Press.

Anderson, E. 1990. *Streetwise: Race, Class, and Change in an Urban Community*. Chicago: University of Chicago Press.

Allen, M. 2010. "President Obama, Vice President Biden Unveil Middle-Class Agenda." *Politico*, January 25.

Anyon, J. 1980. "Social Class and the Hidden Curriculum of Work." *Journal of Education* 162 (1): 67–93.

———. 1997. *Ghetto Schooling: A Political Economy of Urban School Reform*. New York: Teachers College Press.

Apple, M. 2001. *Educating the "Right" Way: Markets, Standards, God, and Inequality*. New York: RoutledgeFalmer.

Babitch, S., C. Barth, H. Jung, and R. MacDonald. 2006. *Kids in Cities*. Chicago: IIT Institute of Design.

Ball, S. J. 2003. *Class Strategies and the Educational Marketplace: The Middle Classes and Social Advantage*. London: RoutledgeFalmer.

Bartlett, L., M. Frederick, T. Gulbrandsen, and E. Murillo. 2002. "The Marketization of Education: Public Schools for Private Ends." *Anthropology and Education Quarterly* 33 (1): 5–29.

Bazelon, E. 2008. "The Next Kind of Integration." *New York Times*, July 20.

Beauregard, R. A. 2003. *Voices of Decline: The Postwar Fate of U.S. Cities*. Cambridge, MA: Blackwell Publishers.

Birch, E. L. 2005. *Who Lives Downtown*. Living Cities Census Series. Washington, DC: Brookings.

———. 2006. "Changing Place in the New Downtown." In *New Downtowns: The Future of Urban Centers*, ed. J. Oakman, 53–82. Princeton, NJ: Woodrow Wilson School of Public and International Affairs.

Bissinger, B. 1997. *A Prayer for the City*. New York: Random House.

Blanding, M. 2007. "The Departing." *Boston Globe*, August 30.

Booza, J. C., J. Cutsinger, and G. Galster. 2006. *Where Did They Go?: The Decline of Middle-Income Neighborhoods in Metropolitan America*. Washington, DC: Brookings Institution.

Boschken, H. 2003. "Global Cities, Systemic Power, and Upper-Middle-Class Influence." *Urban Affairs Review* 38 (6): 808–30.

Bourdieu, P. 1984. *Distinction: A Social Critique of the Judgement of Taste*. London: Routledge and Kegan Paul.

———. 1985. "The Forms of Capital." In *Handbook of Theory and Research for the Sociology of Education*, ed. J. G. Richardson, 241–58. New York: Greenwood.

———. 1990. *The Logic of Practice*. Stanford, CA: Stanford University Press.

Bourdieu, P., and J.-C. Passeron. 1990. *Reproduction in Education, Society, and Culture*. Thousand Oaks, CA: Sage.

Bourdieu, P., and L. Wacquant. 1992. *An Invitation to Reflexive Sociology*. Chicago: University of Chicago Press.

Bowie, L. 2004. "State Board Lifts Limit on Charter Schools." *Baltimore Sun*, October 13.

Boyd, W. L., and J. B. Christman. 2003. "A Tall Order for Philadelphia's New Approach to School Governance: Heal the Political Rifts, Close the Budget Gaps, *and* Improve the Schools." In *Powerful Reforms with Shallow Roots*, ed. L. Cuban and M. Usdan, 96–124. New York: Teachers College Press.

Boyer, M. C. 1992. "Cities for Sale: Merchandising History at South Street Seaport." In *Variations on a Theme Park: The New American City and the End of Public Space*, ed. M. Sorkin, 181–204. New York: Hill and Wang.

Brantlinger, E. 2003. *Dividing Classes: How the Middle Class Negotiates and Rationalizes School Advantage*. New York: RoutledgeFalmer.

Brint, S. 1991. "Upper Professionals: A High Command of Commerce, Culture, and Civic Regulation." In *Dual City: Restructuring New York*, ed. John H. Mollenkopf and Manuel Castells, 155–76. New York: Russell Sage Foundation.

———. 2003. *Philadelphia in Focus: A Profile from Census 2003*. Washington, DC: Brookings Institution, Center on Urban and Metropolitan Policy.

———. 2010. *The State of Metropolitan America*. Washington, DC: Brookings Institution, Metropolitan Policy Program.

Brown, R. 2010. "School District in North Carolina Considers Ending Busing for Economic Diversity." *New York Times*, February 28.

Brown-Saracino, J., ed. 2010. *The Gentrification Debates*. London: Routledge.

Bryk, A., and B. Schneider. 2002. *Trust in Schools: A Core Resource for School Improvement*. New York: Russell Sage Foundation.

Buschmann, K., and C. Coletta. 2009. "The Call of the City: Using Design Methods to Attract Families." *Journal of Business Strategies* 30 (2/3): 21–27.

Butler, T., and G. Robson. 2003. *London Calling: The Middle Classes and the Remaking of Inner London*. Oxford: Berg Publishers.

Butler, T. and M. Savage. 1995. *Social Change and the Middle Classes*. London: Routledge.

Campbell, L. K. 2008. "Planning to Leave Town Because of the Schools? This Parent Didn't, and Couldn't Be Happier." *San Francisco Chronicle*. http://www.sfgate.com/cgi-bin/article.cgi?file=/g/a/2008/09/05/lessonplan.DTL (accessed February 16, 2011).

Campbell, C., H. Proctor, and G. Sherington. 2009. *School Choice: How Parents Negotiate the New School Market in Australia*. Crows Nest, NSW: Allen and Unwin.

Carr, N. 2006. "Courting the Middle Class: What Can Schools Do to Keep Parents from Going Private or Moving to the Suburbs?" *American School Board Journal* 193 (12): 46–49.

Cassel, A. 2003. "Downtown White-Collar Jobs Key to Entire City's Vitality." *Philadelphia Inquirer*, July 28.

CCD (Center City District). 2002. *The Success of Downtown Living: Expanding the Boundaries of Center City*. Philadelphia, PA: Center City District/Central Philadelphia Development Corporation.

———. 2004. *Growing Smarter: The Role of Center City's Public Schools in Enhancing Philadelphia's Competitiveness*. Philadelphia, PA: Center City District/Central Philadelphia Development Corporation.

———. 2005. *Plan and Budget for the Center City District*. Philadelphia, PA: Center City District/Central Philadelphia Development Corporation.

———. 2006. *State of Center City 2006*. Philadelphia, PA: Center City District/Central Philadelphia Development Corporation.

———. 2008. *Center City Digest*. Philadelphia, PA: Center City District/Central Philadelphia Development Corporation.

———. 2010a. *Philadelphia's Major Employment Nodes: Where City Residents Work*. Philadelphia, PA: Center City District/Central Philadelphia Development Corporation.

———. 2010b. *The State of Center City*. Philadelphia, PA: Center City District/Central Philadelphia Development Corporation.

———. 2011. *Leading the Way: Population Growth Downtown*. Philadelphia, PA: Center City District/Central Philadelphia Development Corporation.

Central Philadelphia Development Corporation. 2006. *Central Philadelphia Development Corporation: Celebrating Fifty Years*. Philadelphia, PA: Central Philadelphia Development Corporation.

CEOs for Cities. 2005. *The Young and Restless in a Knowledge Economy*. Chicago: CEOs for Cities.

———. n.d. *City Talent: Keeping Young Professionals (and Their Kids) in Cities*. Chicago: CEOs.

Chin, T., and M. Phillips. 2004. "Social Reproduction and Child-Rearing Practices: Social Class, Children's Agency, and the Summer Activity Gap." *Sociology of Education* 77 (3): 185–210.

Chubb, J. and T. Moe. 1990. *Politics, Markets, and America's Schools*. Washington, DC: Brookings.

Clark, T. N., R. Lloyd, K. Wong, and P. Jain. 2002. "Amenities Drive Urban Growth." *Journal of Urban Affairs* 24 (5): 493–515.

Coleman, J. 1988. "Social Capital in the Creation of Human Capital." *American Journal of Sociology* 94:S95–S120.

Coleman, J., E. Campbell, C. Hobson, J. McPartland, A. Mood, F. Weinfield, and R. York. 1966. *Equality of Educational Opportunity.* Washington, DC: U.S. Department of Health, Education, and Welfare.

Counts, S. R., and B. Lavergneau. 1992. "Choice as a Vehicle for Urban Educational Change in the 1990s." *Clearing House* 66 (2): 79–80.

Covaleskie, J. F. 2007. "What Public, Whose Schools?" *Educational Studies* 42 (1): 28–43.

Crosnoe, R. 2009. "Low-Income Students and the Socioeconomic Status of High Schools." *American Sociological Review* 74 (5): 709–30.

Crozier, G., D. Reay, D. James, F. Jamieson, P. Beedell, S. Hollingsworth, and K. Williams. 2008. "White Middle-Class Parents, Identities, Educational Choice and the Urban Comprehensive School: Dilemmas, Ambivalence and Moral Ambiguity." *British Journal of Sociology of Education* 29 (3): 261–72.

Cucchiara, M., E. Gold, and E. Simon. 2011. "Contracts, Choice, and Customer Service: Marketization and Public Engagement in Education." *Teachers College Record* 113 (11): 2460–2502.

Cucchiara, M., and E. Horvat. 2009. "Perils and Promises: Middle-Class Parental Involvement in Urban Schools." *American Educational Research Journal* 46 (4): 974–1004.

Curry, G. E. 1990. "Failed Deal Worsens Philadelphia Crisis." *Chicago Tribune,* September 13.

Danns, D. 2008. "Racial Ideology and the Sanctity of the Neighborhood School in Chicago." *Urban Review* 40:64–75.

Danziger, S., and P. Gottschalk. 1995. *America Unequal.* New York: Russell Sage Foundation.

Darling-Hammond, L. 2010. *The Flat World and Education: How America's Commitment to Equity Will Determine Our Future.* New York: Teachers College Press.

Davis, A., and M. Haller, eds. 1998. *The Peoples of Philadelphia: A History of Ethnic Groups and Lower-Class Life, 1790–1940.* Philadelphia: University of Pennsylvania Press.

DeLuca, S., and E. Dayton. 2009. "Switching Social Contexts: The Effects of Housing Mobility and School Choice Programs on Youth Outcomes." *Annual Review of Sociology* 35:457–91.

Demerath, P. 2009. *Producing Success: The Culture of Personal Advancement in an American High School.* Chicago: University of Chicago Press.

Diamond, J. B., and K. Gomez. 2004. "African American Parents' Educational Orientations: The Importance of Social Class and Parents' Perceptions of Schools." *Education and Urban Society* 36 (4): 383–427.

Diaz, M. 1999. "Parents' Concerns about Schools Are Driving Suburban Flight; Many Say That the Quality of Public Schools Outside the City Is Better. Those Who Can Afford It Make the Big Move." *Philadelphia Inquirer,* August 8.

DiGaetano, A., and P. Lawless. 1999. "Urban Governance and Industrial Decline: Governing Structures and Policy Agendas in Birmingham and Sheffield, England, and Detroit, Michigan, 1980–1997." *Urban Affairs Review* 34 (4): 546–77.

Domhoff, G. W. 2005. *Who Rules America? Power, Politics, and Social Change.* Boston: McGraw-Hill.

Dornbusch, S., and K. Wood. 1989. "Family Processes and Educational Achievement." In *Education and the American Family*, ed. W. J. Weston, 66–95. New York: New York University Press.

Dreier, P., J. Mollenkopf, and T. Swanstrom. 2004. *Place Matters: Metropolitics for the 21st Century.* Lawrence: University Press of Kansas.

Duneier, M. 1999. *Sidewalk.* New York: Farrar, Straus, and Giroux.

Edelberg, J., and S. Kurland. 2009. *How to Walk to School: Blueprint for a Neighborhood School Renaissance.* New York: Rowman and Littlefield.

Egan, T. 2007. "Vibrant Cities Find One Thing Missing: Children." *New York Times*, March 24.

El Nasser, H. 2008. "Cities Ramp Up Their Kid-Friendly Hospitality." *USA Today*, January 17.

Emeno, A., and A. J. Heavens. 2006. "Area Real Estate Market: Steady Is New Word." *Philadelphia Inquirer*, June 25.

Epstein, J. L. 1992. "School and Family Partnerships." In *Encyclopedia of Educational Research*, 6th ed., ed. M. C. Alkin, 1130–51. New York: Macmillan.

Fainstein, S. 2010. *The Just City.* Ithaca, NY: Cornell University Press.

Finder, A. 2005. "As Test Scores Jump, Raleigh Credits Integration by Income." *New York Times*, September 25.

Florida, R. 2002. *The Rise of the Creative Class: And How It's Transforming Work, Leisure, Community, and Everyday Life.* New York: Basic Books.

Frankenberg, E., and G. Siegel-Hawley. 2008. *The Forgotten Choice? Rethinking Magnet Schools in a Changing Landscape.* Los Angeles: The Civil Rights Project, University of California, Los Angeles.

Fraser, J. C., and E. L. Kick. 2007. "The Role of Public, Private, Non-Profit and Community Sectors in Shaping Mixed-Income Housing Outcomes in the U.S." *Urban Studies* 44 (12): 2357–77.

Freeman, L. 2010. "Neighborhood Effects in a Changing 'Hood." In *The Gentrification Debates*, ed. Brown-Saracino, 319–30.

Frey, W. H. 1979. "The Changing Impact of White Migration on the Population Compositions of Origin and Destination Metropolitan Areas." *Demography* 16 (2): 219–37.

Frey, W. H., and E. L. Fielding. 1995. "Changing Urban Populations: Regional Restructuring, Racial Polarization, and Poverty Concentration." *Cityscape* 1 (2): 1–66.

Frieden, B. J., and L. B. Sagalyn. 1989. *Downtown Inc.: How America Rebuilds Cities.* Cambridge, MA: MIT Press.

Furdell, K., H. Wolman, and E. Hill. 2005. "Did Central Cities Come Back? Which Ones, How Far, and Why?" *Journal of Urban Affairs* 27 (3): 283–305.

Furstenberg, F., T. Cook, J. Eccles, and G. Elder. 1999. *Managing to Make It: Urban Families and Adolescent Success.* Chicago: University of Chicago Press.

Gaztambide-Fernandez, R. A. 2009. *The Best of the Best: Becoming Elite at an American Boarding School.* Cambridge: Harvard University Press.

Gill, B., R. Zimmer, J. Christman, and S. Blanc. 2007. "State Takeover, School

Restructuring, Private Management, and Student Achievement in Philadelphia." RAND Education and Research for Action, Philadelphia.

Glaser, B. and A. Strauss. 1967. *The Discovery of Grounded Theory: Strategies for Qualitative Research*. Chicago: Aldine.

Gold, E., J. Christman, and B. Herold. 2007. "Blurring the Boundaries: A Case Study of Private Sector Involvement in Philadelphia Public Schools." *American Journal of Education* 113 (2): 181–212.

Gold, E., M. Cucchiara, E. Simon, and M. Riffer. 2005. *Time to Engage? Civic Participation in Philadelphia's School Reform*. Philadelphia: Research for Action.

Gold, E., S. A. Evans, C. Haxton, H. P. Maluk, C. A. Mitchell, E. Simon, and D. Good. 2010. *Context, Conditions, and Consequences: Freshman Year Transition in Philadelphia*. Philadelphia: Research for Action.

Gold, E., E. Simon, and C. Brown. 2002. "Strong Neighborhoods, Strong Schools: Successful Community Organizing for School Reform." Cross City Campaign for Urban School Reform, Chicago.

Gold, E., E. Simon, M. Cucchiara, M. Riffer, and C. Mitchell. 2007. *A Philadelphia Story: Building Civic Capacity for School Reform in a Privatizing System*. Philadelphia: Research for Action.

Goldring, E., L. Cohen-Vogel, C. Smrekar, and C. Taylor. 2006. "Schooling Closer to Home: Desegregation Policy and Neighborhood Contexts." *American Journal of Education* 112:335–62.

Gorenstein, N. 2001a. "In Oak Lane, an Effort Is Launched to Stop Middle-Class Flight." *Philadelphia Inquirer*, February 22.

———. 2001b. "Street Has Two New Ways to Keep Residents." *Philadelphia Inquirer*, February 27.

Gottlieb, P. D., and M. Fogarty. 2003. "Educational Attainment and Metropolitan Growth." *Economic Development Quarterly* 17 (4): 325–36.

Gragg, R. 2005. "U.S. Cities Lack Families, but Vancouver Gets It Right." *The Oregonian*, July 7.

Graham, K. A. 2010. "Parents Work to Rejuvenate a Public School." *Philadelphia Inquirer*, April 14.

Grant, G. 2009. *Hope and Despair in an American City: Why There Are No Bad Schools in Raleigh*. Cambridge: Harvard University Press.

Grazian, D. 2003. *Blue Chicago: The Search for Authenticity in Urban Blues Clubs*. Chicago: University of Chicago Press.

———. 2007. *On the Make: The Hustle of Urban Nightlife*. Chicago: University of Chicago Press.

Greenberg, M. 2000. "Branding Cities: The Social History of the Urban Lifestyle Magazine." *Urban Affairs Review* 36 (2): 228–63.

Grim, R. 2006. "A Line in the Sandbox." *Washington City Paper*. http://www.washingtoncitypaper.com/cover/2006/cover0616.html (accessed February 16, 2011).

Grossman, F. D., and R. Kamani. 2011. "Working for Change and Replicating Marginalization: Unpacking the Tensions in and Benefits of Parent-Educator Collaboration." Paper presented at the annual meeting of the American Educational Research Association, New Orleans.

Hall, J. C., S. R. Staley, M. S. Hisrich, and A. L. Barry. 2003. *Education Empower-*

ment Zones: Revitalizing Ohio's Cities Through School Choice. Columbus, OH: The Buckeye Institute.

Hammersley, M., and P. Atkinson. 1986. *Ethnography: Principles in Practice.* London: Routledge.

Hankins, K. B. 2007. "The Final Frontier: Charter Schools as New Community Institutions of Gentrification." *Urban Geography* 28 (2): 113–28.

Hart, B., and T. R. Risley. 1995. *Meaningful Differences in the Everyday Experiences of Young American Children.* Baltimore, MD: Paul H. Brookes.

Harvey, D. 2008. "The Right to the City." *New Left Review* 53 (September/October): 23–40.

Henderson, A., and K. Mapp. 2002. *A New Wave of Evidence: The Impact of School, Family, and Community Connections on Student Achievement.* Austin, TX: Southwest Educational Development Laboratory.

Hendrie, C. 2004. "City Mayors Turn to Charter Schools." *Education Week* 24 (9): 1.

Henig, J. R. 1996. "The Local Dynamics of School Choice: Ethnic Preferences and Institutional Responses." In *Who Chooses, Who Loses? Culture, Institutions, and the Unequal Effects of School Choice,* ed. B. Fuller and R. F. Elmore (with G. Orfield), 95–117. New York: Teachers College Press.

Hennessey, G. 1977. "The Neighborhood School Concept as a Deterrent to Desegregation in the 1960s and 1970s." Retrieved from EBSCO*host* (ERIC Document 134661).

Henry, K. 2008. "Do Cities Need Families?" *The Urbanite,* June.

Herszenhorn, D. 2006. "'06 Broad Prize Recognizes Gains in Boston Public Schools." *New York Times,* September 20.

Hinds, M. 1990. "Philadelphia Journal; City Waits for Rescue amid Cries of Chaos." *New York Times,* November 3.

Hirschman, A. O. 1970. *Exit, Voice, and Loyalty: Responses to Declines in Firms, Organizations, and States.* Cambridge: Harvard University Press.

Hochschild, J. 1996. *Facing Up to the American Dream.* Princeton, NJ: Princeton University Press.

Holcomb, H. 2005. "How to Maintain the Momentum: Looks and Service Must Improve." *Philadelphia Inquirer,* December 28.

Holme, J. J. 2002. "Buying Homes, Buying Schools: School Choice and the Social Construction of School Quality." *Harvard Educational Review* 72 (2): 177–205.

Hoover-Dempsey, K., and H. Sandler. 1995. "Parental Involvement in Children's Education: Why Does It Make a Difference." *Teachers College Record* 97 (2): 310–31

Horvat, E., and M. Cucchiara. N.d. "Complicating School Choice for Middle Class Parents: Identity, Ideology, Anxiety and the Search for a 'Good School.'" Manuscript in progress.

Horvat, E., E. Weininger, and A. Lareau. 2003. "From Social Ties to Social Capital: Class Differences in the Relations between Schools and Parents' Networks." *American Educational Research Journal* 40 (2): 319–51.

Hoyt, L. M. 2005. "Do Business Improvement District Organizations Make a Difference? Crime in and around Commercial Areas in Philadelphia." *Journal of Planning, Education and Research* 25:185–99.

Imbroscio, D. 2008. "'United and Actuated by Some Common Impulse of Passion':
Challenging the Dispersal Consensus in American Housing Policy Research."
Journal of Urban Affairs 30 (2): 111–30.

Inman, R. P. 1992. "Can Philadelphia Escape Its Fiscal Crisis with Another Tax
Increase?" *Business Review* (Federal Reserve Bank of Philadelphia), September/October.

Institute for the Study of Civic Values. 2006. *Safe and Supportive Communities.*
Philadelphia: Institute for the Study of Civic Values.

Jackson, K. T. 1985. *Crabgrass Frontier: The Suburbanization of the United States.*
New York: Oxford University Press.

Jacobsen, J. 2010. "Magnet Schools: A Unique Partnership Seeks to Draw Kids
Back Into Baltimore's Neighborhood Schools—and Boost Communities at the
Same Time." *Urbanite*, June 1.

James, D., D. Reay, G. Crozier, P. Beedell, S. Hollingworth, F. Jamieson, and
K. Williams. 2010. "Neoliberal Policy and the Meaning of Counterintuitive
Middle-Class School Choices." *Current Sociology* 58 (4): 623–41.

Jan, T. 2006. "School Makeovers, Fueled by the Middle Class: As Parents Raise Funds,
Standards, Some Fear Impact on Diversity." *Boston Globe*, November 26.

Jennings, J. 2004. Preface. *Annals of the American Academy of Political and Social
Science* 594:6–11.

Joseph, M. L., R. J. Chaskin, and H. S. Webber. 2007. "The Theoretical Basis for
Addressing Poverty through Mixed-Income Development." *Urban Affairs Review* 42 (3): 369–409.

Joseph, M. L., and R. Feldman. 2009. "Creating and Sustaining Successful Mixed-
Income Communities: Conceptualizing the Role of Schools." *Education and
Urban Society* 41:623–52.

Judd, D. R., and T. Swanstrom. 1994. *City Politics: Private Power and Public Policy.*
New York: HarperCollins College Publishers.

Kahlenberg, R. D. 2001. *All Together Now: Creating Middle-Class Schools through
Public School Choice.* Washington, DC: Brookings.

———. 2002. "Economic School Integration: An Update." The Century Foundation: Issue Brief Series. New York: The Century Foundation.

———. 2007. *Rescuing Brown v. Board of Education: Profiles of Twelve School
Districts Pursuing Socioeconomic School Integration.* New York: The Century
Foundation.

Kantor, H., and B. Breznel. 1992. "Urban Education and the 'Truly Disadvantaged': The Historical Roots of the Contemporary Crisis, 1945–1990." *Teachers
College Record* 94 (2): 278–314.

Karpewicz, E. 2010. "DBFA Board Members Travel to Philadelphia." Downtown
Baltimore Family Alliance, May 17. http://www.dbfam.org/tabid/236/vw/1
/ItemID/10/Default.aspx (accessed June 28, 2010).

Katz, M. 1987. *Reconstructing American Education.* Cambridge: Harvard University Press.

———. 2001. *The Price of Citizenship: Redefining the American Welfare State.* New
York: Metropolitan Books.

Kennedy, M., R. K. Jung, and M. E. Orland. 1986. *Poverty, Achievement and the*

Distribution of Compensatory Education Services. Washington, DC: Department of Education.

Kimelberg, S. M., and C. M. Billingham. 2010. "Urban Living, Urban Schooling: Class and Race in the Urban Public School." Paper presented at the Annual Meeting of the Society for the Study of Social Problems, Atlanta, GA.

Kontos, P., and J. Murphy. 1967. *Teaching Urban Youth: A Source Book for Urban Educators.* New York: John Wiley and Sons.

Kotkin, J. 2007. "The Rise of Family Friendly Cities." *Wall Street Journal,* November 27.

Kozol, J. 1991. *Savage Inequalities: Children in America's Schools.* New York: HarperCollins.

———. 2005. *The Shame of the Nation: The Restoration of Apartheid Schooling in America.* New York: Random House.

Kruse, K. 2005. *White Flight: Atlanta and the Making of Modern Conservatism.* Princeton, NJ: Princeton University Press.

Kwong, J. 2000. "Introduction: Marketization and Privatization in Education." *International Journal of Educational Development* 20:87–92.

Labaree, D. F. 1997. "Public Goods, Private Goods: The American Struggle over Educational Goals." *American Educational Research Journal* 34 (1): 39–81.

Lareau, A. 2000. *Home Advantage: Social Class and Parental Intervention in Elementary Education.* Lanham, MD: Rowman and Littlefield.

———. 2011. *Unequal Childhoods: Class, Race, and Family Life.* 2nd ed. Berkeley: University of California Press.

Lareau, A., and E. Horvat. 1999. "Moments of Social Inclusion and Exclusion: Race, Class and Cultural Capital in Family-School Relationships." *Sociology of Education* 72 (January): 37–53.

Lareau, A., and V. L. Munoz. 2012. "You're Not Going to Call the Shots: Structural Conflict between the Principal and the PTO in a Suburban Public Elementary School." *Sociology of Education* 85 (3): 201–18.

Lee, S. 1996. *Unraveling the "Model Minority" Stereotype: Listening to Asian American Youth.* New York: Teachers College Press.

Levy, D. K., Z. McDade, and K. Dumlao. 2010. *Effects from Living in Mixed-Income Communities for Low-Income Families: A Review of the Literature.* Washington, DC: The Urban Institute.

Levy, P. 2001a. "Making Downtowns Competitive." *Planning* 67 (4): 16–19.

———. 2001b. "Paying for the Public Life." *Economic Development Quarterly* 15 (2): 124–31.

———. 2003a. "Maintaining Momentum in a New Year." *Center City Digest* (Winter): 1–3.

———. 2003b. "When It Comes to Judging a City's Economic Success, Size Doesn't Matter." *Philadelphia Inquirer,* November 30.

———. 2005. "Sustaining the 24-Hour Downtown: A Focus on Public Schools." Presentation for CEOS for Cities, Center City District, Philadelphia, PA, December 2.

———. 2008. "Keeping Kids Downtown: A Philadelphia Approach." *Newgeography,* September 6.

Levy, P., and R. Cybriwsky. 2010. "The Hidden Dimensions of Culture and Class: Philadelphia." In *The Gentrification Debates*, ed. Brown-Saracino, 285–94.

Lew, J. 2007. "A Structural Analysis of Success and Failure of Asian Americans: A Case Study of Korean Americans in Urban Schools." *Teachers College Record* 109 (2): 369–90.

Lewis, N. 2010. "Grappling with Governance: The Emergence of Business Improvement Districts in a National Capital." *Urban Affairs Review* 46 (2): 180–217.

Lewis, O. 1966. "The Culture of Poverty." *Scientific American* 215:19–25

Lin, J. 2006. "Philadelphia Residents See Hope, but Also Holes." *Philadelphia Inquirer*, September 5.

Lin, N. 2001. *Social Capital: A Theory of Social Structure and Action*. Cambridge: Cambridge University Press.

Lipman, P. 1998. *Race, Class and Power in School Restructuring*. Albany: SUNY Press.

———. 2002. "Making the Global City, Making Inequality: Political Economy and Cultural Politics of Chicago's School Policy." *American Educational Research Journal* 39 (2): 379–419.

———. 2004. *High Stakes Education: Inequality, Globalization, and Urban School Reform*. New York: RoutledgeFalmer.

———. 2008. "Mixed-Income Schools and Housing: Advancing the Neoliberal Urban Agenda." *Journal of Education Policy* 23 (2): 119–34.

Logan, J., and M. Molotch. 1987. *Urban Fortunes: The Political Economy of Place*. Berkeley: University of California Press.

Lohman, J. 1967. *Cultural Patterns in Urban Schools: A Manual for Teachers, Counselors, and Administrators*. Berkeley: University of California Press.

Lukas, J. A. 1985. *Common Ground: A Turbulent Decade in the Lives of Three American Families*. New York: Random House.

Lynd, R. S., and H. M. Lynd. 1959. *Middletown: A Study in Modern American Culture*. Orlando, FL: Harcourt, Brace.

MacDonald, H. 1996a. "BIDs Really Work." *City Journal* (Spring). http://www.city-journal.org/html/6_2_a3.html (accessed August 5, 2012).

———. 1996b. "Why Business Improvement Districts Work." *Civic Bulletin* (4).

MacLeod, J. 1995. *Ain't No Makin' It: Aspirations and Attainment in a Low-Income Neighborhood*. Boulder, CO: Westview Press.

Madden, J. F., and W. J. Stull. 1991. *Work, Wages and Poverty: Income Distribution in Postindustrial Philadelphia*. Philadelphia: University of Pennsylvania Press.

Marcuse, P., J. Connolly, J. Novy, I. Olivo, C. Potter, and J. Steil. 2009. *Searching for the Just City: Debates in Urban Theory and Practice*. New York: Routledge.

Maroukian, F. 2003. "The Philadelphia Experiment." *Travel and Leisure*, September.

Marshall, T. H. 1964. *Class, Citizenship, and Social Development: Essays*. Westport, CT: Greenwood Press.

Massey, D., and N. Denton. 1993. *American Apartheid: Segregation and the Making of the Underclass*. Cambridge: Harvard University Press.

Maxwell, J. A. 1995. *Qualitative Research Design: An Interactive Approach*. 2nd ed. Thousand Oaks, CA: Sage Publications.

McGovern, S. J. 2009. "Mobilization on the Waterfront: The Ideological/Cultural Roots of Potential Regime Change in Philadelphia." *Urban Affairs Review* 44:663–94.

McGrath, D., and P. Kuriloff. 1999. "They're Going to Tear the Doors Off This Place: Upper-Middle Class Parents' School Involvement and the Educational Opportunities of Other People's Children." *Educational Policy* 13 (5): 603–29.

McPherson, E. 2011. "Moving from Separate, to Equal, to Equitable Schooling: Revisiting School Desegregation Policies." *Urban Education* 46 (3): 465–83.

Meier, D. 2003. *In Schools We Trust: Creating Communities of Learning in an Era of Testing and Standardization*. Boston: Beacon Press.

Metropolis. 2010. "Arlene Ackerman's Smile." September 15. http://www.phlmetro polis.com/2010/09/arlene-ackermans-smile.php.

Mezzacappa, D. 2009. "Is the Desegregation Case Over, or Has the Hard Part Just Begun?" *Philadelphia Public School Notebook*, July 8. http://www.thenote book.org/blog/091534/desegregation-case-over-or-has-hard-part-just-begun.

———. 2010. "Ackerman—No Changes Coming to Selective Admissions." *Philadelphia Public School Notebook*, March 18. http://www.thenotebook.org /blog/102327/ackerman-no-changes-coming-selective-admissions.

Mieszkowski, K. 2010. "Private School Refugees: The Recession-Driven Exodus of Students from Private to Public School." *Slate XX*, February 2. http://www .slate.com/id/2246417/.

Mitchell, J. 1999. "Business Improvement Districts and Innovative Service Delivery." *PricewaterhouseCoopers Endowment for the Business of Government*. http://www.jj0955.com/PdfFiles/MitchellBusinessImprovementDistricts.pdf (accessed June 11, 2012).

———. 2001. "Business Improvement Districts and the 'New' Revitalization of Downtown." *Economic Development Quarterly* 15 (2): 115–23.

Mollenkopf, J. H. 1983. *The Contested City*. Princeton, NJ: Princeton University Press.

Mollenkopf, J. H., and M. Castells. 1991. *Dual City: Restructuring New York*. New York: Russell Sage Foundation.

Moran, R., and S. Snyder. 2000. "City School-Safety Overhaul Urged." *Philadelphia Inquirer*, August 22.

Morrison, M. 2004. "An Examination of Philadelphia's School Desegregation Litigation." *Penn GSE Perspectives on Urban Education* 3 (1). http://www.urbaned journal.org/archive/vol3issue1/commentaries/comment0008.html.

Muller, C. 1993. "Parent Involvement and Academic Achievement: An Analysis of Family Resources Available to the Child." In *Parents, Their Children, and Schools*, ed. B. Schneider and J. Coleman, 77–112. Boulder, CO: Westview Press.

National Center for Education Statistics. 2010. *Trends in the Use of School Choice, 1993–2007*. Washington, DC: Institute of Education Sciences.

Neckerman, K. 2010. *Schools Betrayed: Roots of Failure in Inner-City Education*. Chicago: University of Chicago Press.

Neild, R. 2005. "Parent Management of School Choice in a Large Urban District." *Urban Education* 40 (3): 270–97.

Nelson, A. 2005. "Next Great City: Philly, Really." *National Geographic* 22 (7): 48–56.

Nevels, J. 2005. "Reading, Writing, ROI." *Forbes*, March 14.

Newman, K. 2004. "Newark, Decline and Avoidance, Renaissance and Desire: From Disinvestment to Reinvestment." *Annals of the American Academy of Political and Social Science* 594:34–48.

Orfield, G., E. Arenson, T. Kalejs, C. Bohrer, and G. Gavin. 1998. "Summary of 'City-Suburban Desegregation: Parent and Student Perspectives in Metropolitan Boston.'" *Equity and Excellence in Education* 31 (3): 6–12.

Orfield, G., and E. DeBray, eds. 2003. *Hard Work for Good Schools: Facts not Fads in Title I Reform.* Cambridge: Harvard Civil Rights Project.

Orfield, G., and J. Yun. 1999. "Resegregation in American Schools." Boston: The Civil Rights Project, Harvard University. http://www.law.harvard.edu/civil-rights/publications/resegregation99/resegregati on99.html (accessed July 22, 2010).

Orfield, M. 1997. *Metropolitics: A Regional Agenda for Community and Stability.* Washington, DC: Brookings.

———. 2009. "A Comprehensive Strategy to Integrate Twin Cities Schools and Neighborhoods." University of Minnesota Law School, Institute on Race and Poverty, Minneapolis.

O'Riain, S. 2000. "States and Markets in an Era of Globalization." *Annual Review of Sociology* 26:187–213.

Orwell, G. 1946. *Animal Farm.* New York: Harcourt Brace.

Park, R. 1967. *On Social Control and Collective Behavior.* Chicago: University of Chicago Press.

Pattillo, M. 2007. *Black on the Block: The Politics of Race and Class in the City.* Chicago: University of Chicago Press.

Payne, C. 2008. *So Much Reform, So Little Change: The Persistence of Failure in Urban Schools.* Cambridge: Harvard Education Press.

Perl, L. 2010. "Village Parents Aim to Burnish Public Schools' Image." *Baltimore Messenger*, March 2.

Pew Charitable Trusts. 2010. *Philadelphia 2010: The State of the City.* Philadelphia, PA: Pew Charitable Trusts.

Philadelphia City Planning Commission. 2005. *City Stats: General Demographic and Economic Data.* Philadelphia.

Philadelphia Daily News. 2006. "What Choice Does the District Have? Effort to Attract White and Affluent Students Is Necessary." March 22.

Philadelphia Inquirer. 2005 "Report Card on the Schools." March 6.

Philadelphia Public School Notebook. 2005. *Focus on Segregation and Equity.* Special Issue.

Philadelphia Workforce Investment Board. 2007. *A Tale of Two Cities.* Philadelphia: Workforce Investment Board.

Pittsburgh Post-Gazette. 1991. "Plight of Phila. Grows Gloomier in Many Aspects." July 10.

Polaneczky, R. 2006. "Find the Right Mix for Better Schools, Better Outcomes." *Philadelphia Daily News*, February 16.

Pompilio, N. 2011. "Center City Philly: Call It Kid Row." *Philadelphia Daily News*, July 12.

Portes, A. 1998. "Social Capital: Its Origins and Applications in Modern Sociology." *Annual Review of Sociology* 24:1–24.

Posey, L. 2012. "Middle- and Upper Middle-Class Parent Action for Urban Public Schools: Promise or Paradox?" *Teachers College Record* 114 (1).

Pressler, J. 2005. "Philadelphia Story: The Next Borough." *New York Times*, August 14.

Quinn, A. Z. 2008. "Back to School . . . In the Suburbs." *Philadelphia City Paper*, September 3.

Raveaud, M. and A. van Zanten. 2007. "Choosing the Local School: Middle-Class Parents' Values and Social and Ethnic Mix in London and Paris." *Journal of Education Policy* 22 (1): 107–24.

Ravitch, D. 2010. *The Death and Life of the Great American School System: How Testing and Choice Are Undermining Education.* New York: Basic Books.

Ream, R. K., and G. J. Palardy. 2008. "Re-examining Class Differences in the Availability and the Educational Utility of Parental Social Capital." *American Educational Research Journal* 45 (2): 238–73.

Reay, D., and S. J. Ball. 1998. "'Making Their Minds Up': Family Dynamics of School Choice." *British Educational Research Journal* 24 (4): 431–48.

Reay, D., S. Hollingworth, K. Williams, G. Crozier, F. Jamieson, D. James, and P. Beedell. 2007. "'A Darker Shade of Pale?' Whiteness, the Middle Classes and Multi-Ethnic Inner-City Schooling." *Sociology* 41:1041–60.

Reese, W. J. 2000. "Public Schools and the Elusive Search for the Common Good." In *Reconstructing the Common Good in Education: Coping with Intractable American Dilemmas*, ed. L. Cuban and D. Shipps, 13–31. Stanford, CA: Stanford University Press.

Rendell, E. 1994. "America's Cities: Can We Save Them?" *City Journal*, Winter.

Reinvestment Fund, The. 2007. "Estimating the Percentage of Students Income-Eligible for Free and Reduced-Price Lunch." The Reinvestment Fund, Philadelphia.

Reynolds-Brown, B. 2006. "New Admissions Policy Threatens Equal Enrollment Opportunities." Letter to the editor, *Philadelphia Public School Notebook*.

Riessman, F. 1962. *The Culturally Deprived Child.* New York: Harper and Row.

Rimer, S. 2003. "Schools Try Integration by Income, Not Race." *New York Times*, May 8.

Rogers, T. K. 2009. "The Sudden Charm of Public School." *New York Times*, April 5. http://www.nytimes.com/2009/04/05/realestate/05Cov.html (accessed April 6, 2009).

Rossell, C. 2003. "The Desegregation Efficiency of Magnet Schools." *Urban Affairs Review* 28 (5): 697–725.

Rothstein, R. 2004. *Class and Schools: Using Social, Economic, and Educational Reform to Close the Black-White Achievement Gap.* New York: Teachers College Press.

Rumberger, R., and G. Palardy. 2005. "Does Segregation Still Matter? The Impact of Student Composition on Academic Achievement in High School." *Teachers College Record* 107 (9): 1999–20415.

Ryan, S., Bryk, A., Lopez, G., Williams, K., Hall, K., Luppescu, S. 1997. "Charting Reform: LSCs—Local Leadership at Work." Chicago: Consortium on Chicago School Research.

Saltman, K. 2000. *Collateral Damage.* New York: Rowman and Littlefield.

———. 2005. *The Edison Schools: Corporate Schooling and the Assault on Public Education.* New York: Routledge.

Sampson, Zinie Chen. 2009. "Urban Schools Use Marketing to Woo Residents Back." *USA Today,* August 22.

Santos, F. 2011. "Success Charter Is Planning a School for Cobble Hill, Brooklyn." *New York Times,* October 6.

Saporito, S., and A. Lareau. 1999. "School Selection as a Process: The Multiple Dimensions of Race in Framing Educational Choice." *Social Problems* 46 (3): 418–39.

Schaller, S., and G. Modan. 2005. "Contesting Public Space and Citizenship: Implications for Neighborhood Business Improvement Districts." *Journal of Planning Education and Research* 24 (4): 394–407.

Shea, S. 2006. "Philadelphia Award Honors Levy as a Visionary." *Philadelphia Daily News,* May 16.

Sherman, L. P., and J. Freeman. 2004. "Promoting the Public Schools: A Review of Current Efforts and Research." Unpublished manuscript.

Shipps, D., J. Kahne, and M. A. Smylie. 1999. "The Politics of Urban School Reform: Legitimacy, City Growth, and School Improvement in Chicago." *Educational Policy* 13 (4): 518–45.

Shirley, D. 1997. *Community Organizing for Urban School Reform.* Austin: University of Texas Press.

Sieber, R. T. 1982. "The Politics of Middle-Class Success in an Inner-City Public School." *Journal of Education* 164:30–47.

Siefer, T. 2010. "'The Year the White Kids Came': Diversity Grows at JP School." Boston: WBUR. July 19. http://www.wbur.org/2010/07/19/jp-school-2 (accessed August 5, 2012).

Silberman, T. 2002. "Wake County Schools: A Question of Balance." In *Divided We Fail: Coming Together Through Public School Choice,* ed. Century Foundation, 141–63. New York: Century Foundation.

Silvestri, M. 2008. "Middle-Class Families Fight for Charter School Slots in Baltimore City." *Washington Examiner,* September 9.

Simmons, S. 2005. "Center City Residents to Get First Dibs on Transfers." *Philadelphia Public School Notebook,* Summer.

Slobodzian, J. A. 2005a. "Center City Renaissance." *Philadelphia Inquirer,* December 27.

———. 2005b. "Home to Young, Educated, Richest—and the Poorest." *Philadelphia Inquirer,* December 27.

———. 2005c. "Rising Prices Threaten Neighborhood Character." *Philadelphia Inquirer,* December 27.

———. 2007. "A Growing Trend: Center City Families." *Philadelphia Inquirer,* January 22.

Smith, J. L., and R. Lupton. 2008. "Mixed Communities: Challenges for Urban Education Policy." *Journal of Education Policy* 23 (2): 99–103.

Smith, J. L., and D. Stovall. 2008. "'Coming Home' to New Homes and New Schools: Critical Race Theory and the New Politics of Containment." *Journal of Education Policy* 23 (2): 135–52.

Smith, N. 1979. "Gentrification and Capital: Practice and Ideology in Society Hill. *Antipode* 11 (3): 24–35.

———. 1992. "New City, New Frontier: The Lower East Side as Wild, Wild West." In *Variations on a Theme Park: The New American City and the End of Public Space*, ed. M. Sorkin, 61–93. New York: Hill and Wang.

Smith, R. S. 2009. "Affluent Parents Return to Inner-City Schools for Educational Opportunities." *Edutopia*, August 26.

Smith, S. S., K. M. Kedrowski, J. M. Ellis, and J. Longshaw. 2008. "'Your Father Works for My Father': Race, Class and the Politics of Voluntarily Mandated Desegregation." *Teachers College Record* 110 (5): 986–1032.

Snyder, S. 2003. "Schools Face More Hurdles; New Leader Has Instilled Hope, But It's Only a Start." *Philadelphia Inquirer*, June 15.

———. 2004. "Teacher Assault Reports Rise: The Phila. School District Chief Said Stricter Behavior Policy Caused More Conflicts Between Students and Adults." *Philadelphia Inquirer*, July 15.

———. 2005a. "Growing Opportunities for City's Gifted Students." *Philadelphia Inquirer*, March 10.

———. 2005b. "Selling Schools—To Families." *Philadelphia Inquirer*, August 22.

———. 2006. "Neighbors Get an Edge in Getting Into Center City Schools." *Philadelphia Inquirer*, February 16

———. 2010. "Top City Schools' Criteria in Flux?" *Philadelphia Inquirer*, March 18.

Socolar, P. 2009. "New Data, Same Staffing Patterns at High-Poverty Schools." *Philadelphia Public School Notebook*, Summer.

Solnit, R. 2000. *Hollow City: The Siege of San Francisco and the Crisis of American Urbanism*. London: Verso.

Somers, M. 2008. *The Genealogies of Citizenship: Markets, Statelessness, and the Right to Have Rights*. New York: Cambridge University Press.

Steel, M., and M. Symes. 2005. "The Privatization of Public Space? The American Experience of Business Improvement Districts and Their Relationship to Local Governance." *Local Government Studies* 31 (3): 321–34.

Steinke, P. 2006. "The Pros and Cons of Philadelphia's Business Improvement Districts." *The Next American City* (Summer).

Stevenson, D. L., and D. P. Baker. 1987. "The Family-School Relation and Children's School Performance." *Child Development* 58:1348–57.

Stillman, J. B. 2012. *Gentrification and Schools: The Process of Integration When Whites Reverse Flight*. New York: Palgrave Macmillan.

Stone, C. N. 1989. *Regime Politics: Governing Atlanta, 1946–1988*. Lawrence: University Press of Kansas

———. 2005. "Rethinking the Policy-Politics Connection." *Policy Studies* 26 (3–4): 241–60.

Stone, C. N., J. R. Henig, B. D. Jones, and C. Pierannunzi. 2001. *Building Civic Capacity: The Politics of Reforming Urban Schools*. Lawrence: University Press of Kansas.

Sugrue, T. 1996. *The Origins of the Urban Crisis: Race and Inequality in Postwar Detroit*. Princeton, NJ: Princeton University Press.

Swartz, D. 1998. *Culture and Power: The Sociology of Pierre Bourdieu*. Chicago: University of Chicago Press.

Tach, L. M. 2009. "More than Bricks and Mortar: Neighborhood Frames, Social Processes, and the Mixed-Income Redevelopment of a Public Housing Project." *City and Community* 8 (3): 269–98.

Tanaka, W., and J. Von Bergen. 2005. "Retail Resurgence." *Philadelphia Inquirer*, December 28.

Taylor, P., R. Kochhar, R. Fry, G. Velasco, and S. Motel. 2011. "Twenty-To-One: Wealth Gaps Rise to Record Heights Between Whites, Blacks, and Hispanics." Washington, DC: Pew Social and Demographic Trends.

Thompson, I. 2011. "The King of Center City." *Philadelphia City Paper*, October 6.

Travers, E. 2003. "Philadelphia School Reform: Historical Roots and Reflections on the 2002–2003 School Year under State Takeover." *Penn GSE Perspectives on Urban Education* 2 (2).

Turnham, J., and J. Khadduri. 2004. "Integrating School Reform and Neighborhood Revitalization: Opportunities and Challenges." Abt Associates, Cambridge, MA.

Useem, E. 1992. "Middle Schools and Math Groups: Parents' Involvement in Children's Placement." *Sociology of Education* 65 (4): 263–79.

———. 2005. *Learning from Philadelphia's School Reform. What Do the Research Findings Show So Far?* Philadelphia: Research for Action.

Useem, E., J. Christman, and W. Boyd. 2006. *The Role of District Leadership in Radical Reform: Philadelphia's Experience under the State Takeover 2001–2006*. Philadelphia: Research for Action.

Varady, D. P., and J. A. Raffel. 1995. *Selling Cities: Attracting Homebuyers through Schools and Housing Programs*. Albany: State University of New York Press.

Venkatesh, S. A., and W. J. Wilson. 2002. *American Project: The Rise and Fall of a Modern Ghetto*. Cambridge: Harvard University Press.

Warren, M. R. 2005. "Communities and Schools: A New View of Urban Education Reform." *Harvard Educational Review* 75 (2): 133–73.

———. 2011. "Building a Political Constituency for Urban School Reform." *Urban Education* 46 (3): 484–512.

Weininger, E. and A. Lareau. 2003. "Cultural Capital in Educational Research: A Critical Assessment." *Theory and Society* 32 (5/6): 567–606.

Weissbourd, R., and C. Berry. 2003. *The Changing Dynamics of Urban America*. Chicago: CEOs for Cities.

Wells, A. S., and R. Crain. 1999. *Stepping Over the Color Line: African American Students in White Suburban Schools*. New Haven, CT: Yale University Press.

Wells, A. S., and L. Serna. 1996. "The Politics of Culture: Understanding Local Political Resistance to Detracking in Racially Mixed Schools." *Harvard Educational Review* 66:93–118.

Whitty, G., and S. Power. 2000. "Marketization and Privatization in Mass Education Systems." *International Journal of Economic Development* 20 (2): 93–107.

Whyte, W. F. 1993. *Street Corner Society: The Social Structure of an Italian Slum.* Chicago: University of Chicago Press.

Wilson, W. J. 1987. *The Truly Disadvantaged: The City, the Underclass, and Public Policy.* Chicago: University of Chicago Press.

———. 1997. *When Work Disappears: The World of the New Urban Poor.* New York: Random House.

Winerip, M. 2011. "Seeking Integration, Whatever the Path." *New York Times,* February 28.

Witte, J. 2001. *The Market Approach to Education. An Analysis of America's First Voucher Program.* Princeton, NJ: Princeton University Press.

Wright, E. O. 1989. "A General Framework for the Analysis of Class Structure." In *The Debate on Classes,* ed. E. O Wright, 3–48. New York: Verso.

Yin, R. 2002. *Case Study Research: Design and Methods.* Thousand Oaks, CA: Sage Publications.

Zukin, S. 1995. *The Cultures of Cities.* Cambridge, MA: Blackwell.

———. 2011. *Naked City: The Death and Life of Authentic Urban Places.* New York: Oxford University Press.

Index

Page numbers in italics refer to figures and tables.